DATE DUE

DEMCO 38-296

Passional Culture

Passional Culture

Emotion, Religion, and Society in Southern Spain

TIMOTHY MITCHELL

upp

University of Pennsylvania Press / PHILADELPHIA

Between Spain's Ministry of Culture and
provided financial support toward the publication

Library of Congress Cataloging-in-Publication Data

Mitchell, Timothy.
  Passional culture: emotion, religion, and society in Southern
Spain / Timothy Mitchell.
    p. cm.
  ISBN 0-8122-8202-7
    1. Andalusia (Spain)—Social life and customs. 2. Andalusia
(Spain)—Religious life and customs. 3. Holy Week—Spain—
Andalusia. 4. Emotions—Religious aspects—Catholic Church.
I. Title.
DP302.A467M58 1990
946'.8—dc20   89-40398
                                        CIP

To my mother and father

Contents

Preface   ix

Introduction   1

1   Emotion Magic
     Passionate Fatalism   8
     Autonomy, Death, and the Devil   19
     Superstition: Theory and Praxis   28

2   The Uses of Pain
     Penitential Culture   40
     Miguel Mañara   53
     The Symbiosis of Rich and Poor   66
     Penitentiary Culture   72

3   Social Psychology of the *Cofradía*
     A Question of Identity   83
     Warring Brotherhoods   92
     Holy Week Players   103
     A Family Affair   113

4   The Passion Retold
     Romance Catholicism   128
     The Passion According to Andalusia   137
     Mater Dolorosa   164

Glossary   181

Bibliography   185

Index   195

Preface

Two competing and potentially contradictory aspirations guided me during the writing of this book. The first was the desire to present a realistic and undistorted picture of "Passional culture" in and around Andalusia: this entailed the introduction of many Spanish words that have no exact English equivalents. The second was to make my study as user-friendly as possible, including those users with no knowledge of Spanish: this militated against an excessive introduction of new terms. But the world's growing familiarity with Spanish, as well as this tongue's numerous lexical similarities with English, convinced me that a workable compromise could be reached. Therefore, for all Spanish words used in the text I will either let the context be the guide or supply an explicit definition upon initial use. In addition, all Spanish terms employed more than once are listed and defined in a special glossary. A handful of Latin or German terms I recurred to have also been glossed.

The twin concerns mentioned above can also be discerned in my constant use of the *copla*, the *saeta*, the *romance litúrgico,* and other musical or dramatic genres. To my knowledge, this volume includes the largest number of such works ever presented in a bilingual format. Every Spanish verse is accompanied by an English translation; my translations are in prose, however, and that leads to an immediate and irreparable loss in sonority, rhythm, rhyme, and sometimes reason. I felt it better to publish these anonymous poems with an inadequate translation than to omit them, however. As priceless documents of Andalusian feelings and beliefs, it was essential to make them as accessible as possible, even in the knowledge that no translation could truly convey everything. The works have been drawn from a large number of edited collections, each with its own quaint idea of how the Andalusian dialect should look in print. Rather than inventing my own quaint style, I have let theirs stand. In any case, the original folk compositions have enough nonstandard words and structures to confuse even Spanish-speakers; there is hardly a line of verse that should not have a "[sic]" somewhere in it. But to read "[sic]" over and over again would surely try the patience of all, so here too I have followed a laissez-faire policy. I have not reproduced the original Spanish when translating quotations from scholarly studies or other works of prose.

Introduction

No drama has ever weighed so heavily upon Western consciousness as that of the arrest, torture, and execution of Christ. In every century and in every land, the episodes of the Passion have been recreated in every available medium. This book is based on the premise that what people make of or read into the universal drama is often determined by their own historical circumstances and mind-set. In the case of the people of southern Spain, this premise is borne out to a phenomenal degree. Caught up in social rigidity and anachronistic folkways, they have fashioned a most powerful and heterodox retelling of Christ's ordeal.

For centuries, non-Catholics from northern Europe have been stricken with awe during their Lenten sojourns in the south of Spain. Even travelers from the Hispanic world who are familiar with Catholic street liturgy typically cite Andalusia's *Semana Santa* as the most moving and dramatic one they know of. This is no accident. Andalusians literally go for baroque during Holy Week, purposefully setting out to make sure their processions eclipse all others in splendor and pathos.

Striking as they are, however, the rituals of *Semana Santa* are only the highly visible tip of a cultural iceberg. Few suspect the depth and extent of Andalusia's cult of the Passion. Casual visitors cannot guess how Holy Week weighs upon the other fifty-one weeks of the year, how it shapes daily behavior and thought patterns. "The Passion according to Andalusia," as it has been called, is closely linked with

(1) a penitential ideology that still governs how many Andalusians feel about life, death, wealth, and poverty;
(2) a complicated and highly influential system of lay religious societies known as *cofradías;*
(3) the predominance of the Sorrowful Mother (*Mater Dolorosa*) over all other facets of the Virgin Mary;
(4) the infusion of a guilt and suffering complex upon both male and female roles and relations between the sexes;

(5) the growth of an idiosyncratic taste for spectacles of strong emotion with victimization as a central motif;

(6) the appearance of a unique folkloric genre, the *saeta;* and

(7) the reinforcement of a double-sided, gender-related fatalism that has served to buffer and rationalize the socioeconomic inequities of life in southern Spain.

These are but a few of the important phenomena that can be traced to or associated with the Passion as it is understood in southern Spain. I cite them now to give the reader an idea of the size of the "iceberg" that constitutes the subject matter of my study. In effect, this book represents the first full-length, in-depth exploration of the great cultural complex that lies beneath the surface of the Andalusian Holy Week.

"Passional" is a particularly apt word for the complex culture in question. I employ the term in order to keep a number of crucial elements in view. The first is of course the Passion and Death of Christ—the historical, metaphorical, and ritual frame of reference for everything else. In southern Spain, the so-called Passion of Mary is also an integral part of this frame of reference. Passion in this case refers to suffering, but the word's other senses are relevant to Passional culture as well. Passion can refer to fervor and enthusiasm; it can refer to libidinal drives; it can imply the preponderance of external forces over personal freedom; it is synonymous with strong emotion of all kinds. As we will see, none of these senses should be omitted. Passional culture is truly passionate culture.

The highly emotional nature of the Andalusian Holy Week has not been lost on learned natives. Their reactions to the same fall into three main categories—celebration, embarrassment, or condemnation. The first of these is far and away the most common attitude taken by authors, and combines art criticism, piety, and more than a little boosterism. Reason often becomes the accomplice of an unreasoning, highly sentimental approach to the tradition (which is nothing if not sentiment itself). By contrast, Andalusian scholars of an agnostic or rationalistic frame of mind seem distinctly uncomfortable with the excesses of their fellow citizens; emotion is downplayed in their writings in order to emphasize the social functionality of ritual, its connection to agrotown politics, and other practical themes. Ironically, such works can often be quite *passionate* in describing how Holy Week buttresses the unjust socioeconomic status quo that holds sway in the south. There are, finally, a small number of Catholic sociologists and reform-minded theologians who confront Holy Week emotionality head on and find it to be paganistic, immature, or both. (The Church hierarchy itself prefers to look the other way, chastened by years of battles lost to its impassioned flock.)

There is something of value and significance in each of these three general perspectives, and throughout my study I make use of works written from each. What all three have in common, of course, is their failure to approach the passionate nature of Andalusia's Passion with genuine, unprejudiced inquisitiveness. To glorify, shrug off, or condemn is not to explore. I do not mean that value judgments should not be made, but that they must be preceded by understanding. By taking this stance, I immediately place myself at odds with the many authors who claim that since Holy Week is emotion, only those who get emotional about it can properly understand it: an understanding that goes beyond words, naturally, an enigma and a mystery not susceptible to reductive analysis. But as soon as one capitulates to this non-rational approach, truth values might as well be thrown to the winds. One ends up countenancing all the things people say when driven by passion—for example, my Christ is better than yours and my Virgin is prettier, Seville's Holy Week is incomparable, Granada's has moments like no other, God loves a cheerful sufferer, or the right-wing bourgeoisie is bent on kidnapping the "real" proletarian meaning of Holy Week. Approximately ninety percent of all books and articles dealing with Holy Week in southern Spain are written from the perspective of faith, nostalgia, *cofradía*-glorification, class vindication, or some other patently emotional viewpoint. How, then, can we achieve an accurate view of Andalusia's Passional culture without prior immunization against its thoroughly contagious emotionality?

The role of culture in shaping emotion has been of major concern for many during the decade of the 1980s. Scholars from a number of different disciplines have offered new ideas and fresh perspectives (cf. the anthologies of Levy and Rosaldo 1983; Harré 1986; Scruton 1986; Scherer *et al.* 1986). Although a few might think that good disciplinary fences make good neighbors, most would tend to accept Izard's emphasis on scholarly collaboration (1983). In fact, the enormity and complexity of the issues involved seem to cry out for an interdisciplinary perspective. All approaches ought to have their day in court, including those that invert the terms of the proposition and investigate the role of emotion in shaping culture.

The later strategy is adopted by David Gilmore in a recent study (1987), and our understanding of Andalusian culture has been much enhanced as a result. Briefly, Gilmore shows how such an allegedly destructive thing as aggression plays a salutary role in constructing customs and social controls in southern Spain. Though Andalusians are normally quite nonviolent, Gilmore describes how certain folk rituals and "gossip genres" allow them to give vent to their most unspeakable emotions and stabilize their communities all at once. Such cathartic processes are not unique to the south: they can be found at work all over Spain and all through Spanish history, forging both the form and the content of countless legends, rites, fiestas, and folk dramas (Mitchell 1988).

By all means, a broad interdisciplinary approach is essential if we are to understand Andalusian emotionality in general and Passional culture in particular. As I see it, the inquiry would have to move forward on a number of fronts and wrestle with a variety of questions. Just what is it about Andalusian society that favors or foments the display of strong emotion? What are its causes and current modes of reinforcement? How are we to account for each of the apparent traits of emotionality in the south of Spain? In other words, why does it seem fatalistic, magical, anxiety-ridden, tribalistic, and sadomasochistic? And finally, what is it about the Passion of Jesus and Mary that makes it the preferred vehicle for the expression of all these traits?

It is not my goal to describe every facet and every manifestation of Andalusian emotionality, still less to write a treatise on human emotion. While this book can certainly be read with modern research on emotion in mind, digressive references to the same will be minimized to better describe how emotion remakes religion in the south of Spain and to better explore the heady emotions of *Semana Santa*. Despite an ongoing interest in popular religiosity among scholars, we have nothing that tells us how passion relates to the Passion in any particular culture. To my mind, this constitutes an enormous gap in our understanding; one book cannot fill this gap, but it might serve to bridge it. The different perspectives I adopt (psychological, folkloristic, historical, sociological, narratological) are subordinated to this broadly anthropological end.

One of the goals of my study is to show how the particular kind of emotionality that Andalusian society breeds is intense enough to constitute a belief system, one that inexorably twists religion into—putting it mildly—unorthodox directions. In order to do this, however, I must first show how emotion can take so-called secular culture and twist it into a patently religious direction, infusing everything it touches with an uncanny faith in fate. A recent article by Ronald Grambo has incisively laid bare the failings of prior approaches to fatalism, which have often treated the subject "in a socio-economic vacuum" (1988:16). Ecological, historical, social, and many other factors determine the exact nature of the fatalistic beliefs that a given people develop. Interestingly, Grambo cites "the emotional attitude" as a major factor, characterized as it may be by "anxiety, expectations, resignation, rage, powerless frustration, depression, stoical frame of mind, etc." (16). Grambo's tentative blueprint for further research can be improved upon if we separate causal factors from mediating ones. In my view, emotion is what mediates between objective material reality and belief systems. In other words, fatalistic beliefs should not be seen as the *direct* result of harsh or unjust social conditions, but as one possible product of a group's reaction to those conditions. The harsher the conditions, the more irrational the response *may* be, and subsequently the more elaborate or far-reaching the espousal of fatalism. This qualification is important if we are to avoid treating human groups as if they were automata, blindly adopting belief X in response to condition Y. A further qualification to Grambo's schema is that the stoical frame of mind cannot be classified as an emotional attitude. It is quite the opposite.

Paradoxical as it may sound, the term *passionate fatalism* accurately sums up the nature of Andalusian emotionality. It is the predominant Andalusian way of designing world, that is, of constructing or rehabilitating cultural forms in accordance with a specific mode of consciousness (cf. Binswanger 1958:195–201; Spiegelberg 1972:193–232). In Chapter One, I discuss a number of folkloric forms that are elemental and elementary enough to give us a relatively unobstructed view of passionate fatalism. I compare this world-design with the one it negates: traditional Spanish stoicism. I show how it relates to autonomy-stifling, dependency-fostering Andalusian society. I show how it fills the power vacuum left by the Catholic Church. I disclose its connection to death rites and sex roles. Then, once the basic "designing principles" of passionate fatalism have been clarified, I go on to study their effects at the levels of ideology (Chapter Two), family and community (Chapter Three), and street liturgy (Chapter Four).

Although my study deals primarily with groups, there is one individual to whom I devote considerable attention: Miguel Mañara. It may at first seem strange that a seventeenth-century Sevillian noble and reputed model for Don Juan could tell us anything about the mentality of contemporary Andalusians. Yet in southern Spain, bygone days have not really gone by in the same way as they have in the United States. Mañara was no misfit, but the true "neurotic personality" of his time and place; to study him is to grasp essential aspects of the patriarchal/penitential ethos that still governs Holy Week in southern Spain. The dramatic sufferings of Jesus and Mary have never lost their magnetic appeal for Andalusians, practitioners *avant la lettre* of "no pain, no gain."

To be sure, one of Andalusia's leading anthropologists would like us to believe that "penitential sadomasochism" is not particularly worthy of attention (Moreno 1982 : 62–67). Reason: too many of today's penitents belong to the wrong social class, the bourgeoisie (128–130). The only suffering that matters is that of the oppressed and impoverished *pueblo* (231–232). Not even that matters so much any more: for Moreno, the Andalusian Holy Week is essentially the same as Christmas or Saint John's Eve or any other popular, exhilarating *fiesta total* (222–235). People participate for fun, out of habit, to show off—belief has nothing to do with it. Only the Church, the bourgeoisie, and cynical right-wing politicians will tell you otherwise.

If it is a mistake to dismiss the penitential spirit from consideration, it is a bigger mistake to take sides with one part of society and take aim at another. Passional culture has arisen in a strictly bipolar society; to adequately interpret it, *both* poles must be kept in view and given their due. To dismiss one or the other will doom one's hermeneutics from the start. "Interpretive kidnappings," to use Moreno's felicitous phrase (1982 : 17), have been forthcoming from both the right and the left. The Church exemplifies the former, and Moreno himself the latter. It is only with difficulty that he contains his scorn for the allegedly omnipotent, castrating, oppressor class of Seville. In so doing, he projects a passionate and very Andalusian obsession with autonomy onto the yearly replication of Christ's ordeal.

As we will see, thousands of other Andalusians have done the same thing. The victimized *pueblo* has quite consciously identified with the victimized Christ for several centuries—with the active encouragement of their social betters. The result has been a cultural "reading" of the Passion that is powerful, elemental, riddled with doctrinal errors, and bursting with social truth. Holy Week in southern Spain represents the canny symbiosis of rich and poor, oppressors and oppressed. Is it not revealing that tunic-clad bluebloods carry their icons to the prison so that wretched inmates can sing *saetas* to them? This ritual (discussed in Chapter Two) is only one of many that facilitate emotional highs inside the year-round, continuous emotional predisposition typified by the brotherliness of brotherhoods, the devotion to Paternal and Maternal protectors, the heated affirmation of group belonging, works of charity, and so forth. In other words, what holds the bipolar society together in the first place is an emotional consensus.

Emotion is purposive. The Andalusian way of being-in-the-world has reshaped whole regions of religious and secular culture in accordance with its needs. Passionate fatalism has designed a peculiarly intense and constricted world wherein anything that happens is taken personally. It is a world where suffering is a cultural ideal of the first magnitude. If you resist your fate, you can suffer gloriously, like a hero; if you accept it, you can also suffer gloriously, like a martyr.

What, the reader may ask, can people find so rewarding in this torment? What makes these "people of the Passion" tick? Why have they steadfastly sanctified misery and celebrated death? Why have they done battle with the Church itself for proprietorship of the Passion? Why have they hyperbolized the sufferings of Jesus and Mary almost beyond recognition? And, most intriguing of all, why have they set their faces against the very dogma of the Resurrection? These are some of the outstanding questions that I seek to answer.

Chapter 1

Emotion Magic

Passionate Fatalism

> Perhaps it is not at all difficult to envision a society in which
> *only* emotional behavior would appear rational—where
> only short-term emotional responses had any meaning at all.
> [Solomon 1984 : 321]

An initial understanding of the Andalusian penchant for passion can be obtained by reference to what it is not. Without leaving the Iberian Peninsula we can identify a temperament that is its polar opposite: traditional Spanish stoicism. The comparison I am about to draw will be based on each temperament's principal folk genre.

The most characteristic formulations of Spain's stoic tradition can be found in its *refranero* (proverb corpus). This is not to say that the *refranero* is genetically derived from a school of Greek philosophy, for proverbs were in existence long before Zeno founded the Stoa in third-century Athens. "Stoic" is the right adjective for Spain's proverbs, nevertheless, in that they are distanced, unsentimental, pragmatic, fate-accepting, and serene; they are as epigrammatic as Epictetus and as satirical as Seneca. Spain boasts one of the world's great proverb traditions and one of the world's most famous (albeit fictional) proverb users, Sancho Panza. Cervantes put more than 500 different *refranes* into Sancho's mouth in order to amuse, rile, and educate his emotionally voluble companion, Don Quixote. The total number of Spanish proverbs in circulation at one time or another approaches 100,000. There are 18,000 that deal with maritime themes alone. The bibliography is immense and includes almost 500 separate anthologies (Gómez-Tabanera 1968b : 402–403).

Needless to say, the opposite temperament has had its traditional folkloric forms as well. Chief among them are *coplas*, anonymous lyric poems of three, four, or five verses sung in a great variety of rhythms and melodies. The *copla* has been the superb expressive vehicle for passions of all kinds, just as the *refrán* has specialized in stoical dispassion. Nowadays the Spanish *copla* is almost always identified with Andalusia's *copla flamenca*, a telling indication of the excess supply of emotionality in the south. Where the stoical *refrán* avoids strong emotion like the plague, seeking to distance itself from ecstasy and misery alike, the *copla* embraces unruly passion and suffers the consequences. Here are two *coplas* that typify the general pattern:

Cuando pasas por mi vera	When you pass by my side
y no me dices adiós,	and you don't say hello,
ni las ánimas benditas	not even souls in purgatory
pasan más penas que yo.	feel as much pain as I do.
[Fernández and Pérez 1986 : 121]	
Nadie diga qu'estoy loco	Nobody should say I'm crazy
porque he tiraíyo piedras,	because I've thrown rocks,
que se ponga en mi lugá	let him put himself in my place
aquer que quiere de beras.	he who really loves.
[Ropero 1984 : 173]	

Naturally there have been mutual contacts and crossovers between these two folk genres, the *copla* and the *refrán*. And it would be folly to suggest that Andalusians know no proverbs or that no Andalusian can view life in a distanced or caustic way. Nevertheless, the geographic strongholds of the *refrán* lie in the northern half of Spain and those of the *copla* lie in the south (Manfredi 1963 : 57–90). Is this a mere coincidence? Or could it be that social and historical factors have predisposed Andalusians to a greater susceptibility to emotionality and emotional instruments like the *copla*? One thing is certain: the happy-go-lucky image of tourist-oriented flamenco is belied by the pathos and rage of genuine folk lyrics:

Que se pique a cangrena	May gangrene infect
La boca con que me riñas	the mouth you scold me with
La mano con que me pegas.	the hand you strike me with.
Tu cuerpo tenga mar fin.	May your body meet an evil end.
Los cordeles er berdugo	May the hangman's rope
Te sirban e corbatín.	Serve you for a necktie.
Te den una puñalá	May they give you a knife wound
Que er Pare Santo e Roma	That even the Holy Father in Rome
No te la puea curá.	Cannot cure.
[Machado y Alvarez 1975 (1881): 65, 70, 77]	

In the Pandora's box of passion that the *copla* opens up, love is typically associated with anguish and insanity; it provokes violent jealousy; it slides easily into hate. Metaphors of pain alternate with maledictions of all kinds. And all of these heady emotions are accompanied by concepts of causality and fate that are quite unlike those of traditional Spanish stoicism.

Confusion has arisen precisely on this point, for some equate stoicism with fatalism, recall having heard that Andalusians are fatalistic, and erroneously conclude that therefore they are stoical. Fatalism as a feature of the stoic attitude and the emotion-based fatalism that holds sway in the south of Spain are two very different species, however. It would be preferable, in fact, to reserve the term "fatalism" for the latter and call the first "determinism." As it happens, philosophical discourse on determinism began with the early Stoics, who were deeply interested in the predictive and predicative truth-value of signs and omens. Pure logic led them "quite naturally to the view that no man's actions are ever free or that nothing any man ever does was ever avoidable, it having always been true that he was going to do whatever he eventually did" (Taylor 1967 : 360). As Joseph Campbell reminds us, philosophers' discussions of fate as "an abstract word game played according to classical rules" may have little to do with a given people's *lived* sense of inevitability or subjective approach to cause and effect (1968 : 138–139). Yet the lack of capacity for or interest in abstract word games does not automatically mean that certain popular ideas of fate will not converge with an eminently "philosophical" attitude. This is just what we find in the Spanish *refranero* or proverb corpus, which adopts a resigned, pragmatic, naturalistic, nonsuperstitious, and even satirical stance with regard to destiny. To illustrate:

> *La suerte no es para quien la busca.*
> (Luck is not for the one who seeks it.)

> *A cerdo que es para boca de lobo, no hay San Antón que lo guarde.*
> (Not even St. Anthony can save a hog meant for the wolf's jaws.)

> *Quien nace para burro muere rebuznando.*
> (He who is born to be a donkey dies braying.)

These examples could be multiplied ad infinitum. For Spanish proverb-users, it is pointless to struggle against destiny or pine for good fortune. What is preordained will not be changed; and when something is going to happen, all antecedent events point toward it. But let it not be thought that this thoroughly deterministic view leads to a "why bother?" attitude among *refrán*-users. On the contrary, time not wasted worrying about the future should be employed in useful and productive pursuits. Spanish proverb-users always censure idleness and indolence and praise stick-to-itiveness and hard work.

As might be expected, the hard work praised is often of an agricultural nature. The traditionally rural character of the *refrán* occasions yet another coincidence with classical Stoicism. For like the early philosophers, Iberian peasants are highly observant of the ways in which Nature foreshadows inevitable future events with signs and portents. Gómez-Tabanera roundly affirms that there is no Spanish *agricultor* who does not know at least 100 proverbs devoted to weather prediction. Many reckon time by the Church-year calendar:

> *Por San Blas la cigüeña verás, y si no la vieres, año de nieves.*
> (If you don't see the stork by San Blas, it'll be a snow-year.)

> *De los vientos de junio, los de San Antonio o ninguno.*
> (No June winds are stronger than those near San Antonio's day.)

> *Por San Miguel, gran calor será de mucho valor.*
> (Great heat will be of much value near the feast of San Miguel.)

> *Cielo de panza de burra, agua segura.*
> (When the sky looks like the belly of a she-ass, it's sure to rain.)

As Gómez-Tabanera observes, many of these proverbs are veritable hieroglyphics for those of us who do not live in constant contact with nature (1968b : 414–417)—or in constant conformity with nature, it should be added. This is one of the great tenets retrievable in equal measure from the *refranero* and the extant writings of the great Stoic thinkers (Epictetus 1985; Seneca 1946). Mental serenity is to be found in adapting oneself to the rhythms of the natural world. Any farmer who does not, of course, will soon be out of a job.

What a contrast here with the world of the *copla*, where references to nature are very rare and the only awesome forces that enter into account are arbitrary, unpredictable, unstable human emotions. As Zambrano notes, the early Stoics of Hispania did not feel threatened by the movements of the cosmos or the periodic alterations of nature; they were preoccupied with rising above the painful and upsetting passions inside themselves (1984:55). In Greek religion, notes Nilsson, it was precisely the attempt to account for the unruly realm of the passions that gave rise to the concept of *moira* (fate), since the anthropomorphized and rationalized Homeric gods "could not be made responsible for the irrational in life"—just where the power of the supernatural seemed to be most in evidence (1964:167). That we are not dealing with logical or deterministic concepts of fate is demonstrated by the fact that the *Moerae* or Fates were worshipped in many parts of rural Greece (Tripp 1970:246–247). In other words, popular piety was convinced that the Fates could be persuaded to *alter* one's destiny.

Fatalism, therefore, arises in connection with the passions in three ways: as a way of acknowledging other-directedness, avoiding personal responsibility for one's actions, or influencing the future. Additional insight into fatalism is provided by La Barre as part of his discussion of mana and charisma (1972:357–385). Rather than "tough-minded respect for that which is," fatalism depends on "contingent benevolence," "nurturantly-biased happenstance," "Lady Luck," and a "tailored-to-self infantile gambler's universe" (367–368). La Barre traces it all to neoteny:

> In several senses, a lucky fate is, literally, kind parents, just as "Lady Luck" is a gentle mother, tendentiously concerned for her favored child. To put it biologically, lizards can have no idea of "luck" because they never experience it: they *lack mammalian nurture*. The notion of one's own "luck" would hardly arise except in an animal that at some time had *experienced* being favored by parental grace, an arbitrarily kindly moderation of the rules, an intentionally protective editing of the environment by another organism, and an effectively "omnipotent" one in the situation. [1972:369; emphasis in original]

The relevance of such considerations becomes clear when we examine the vocabulary of the *copla*. For one thing, the word *mare* (from *madre*, or mother) is one of the most frequently occurring terms in the entire corpus, according to Ropero's statistical analysis (1984:151). (Only a handful of Spanish proverbs mention mothers.) We find, simultaneously, a great variety of terms that refer to every conceivable nuance or disposition of fate: *ángel, estrella, fario, malage, sino, sombra,* and so forth. Almost everything becomes a matter of luck, and in keeping with the intense degrees of love and hate noted earlier, the luck is frequently bad. Fate does not maintain a neutral indifference in Andalusia; it seems to have an abiding personal interest in martyrizing people. Self-pitying flamenco lyrics express an infinite regret that childhood is past and life is no longer edited in a nurturantly biased way:

Qué desgraciadito soy,	What a wretched little one am I,
mala estrella a mí me guía	an evil star guides me
por dondequiera que voy.	wherever I go.
El hombre va por la vía	Man goes through life
como la piedra en el aire	like a stone in the air,
esperando la caía.	waiting to fall.
Qué bonito está el camino	How pretty the road is
de olivos y de palmeras	with olive and palm trees
pero que triste es mi sino	but how sad is my fate
sembrao de sudó y pena.	sown with sweat and pain.

[Fernández and Pérez 1986 : 86, 73, 152]

The Andalusian concept of fate is perhaps best summarized by the word *sino*. The Romantic-era cliché had it that *sino* was the result of centuries of Moorish domination and could be derived from the Koranic submission to an utterly powerful God—expressed in the very word *Islam*.[1] González Climent has affirmed, however, that *sino* differs from the Semitic concepts of fate that existed at one time in southern Spain, because

> it is not inexorably punitive, blind, disintegrating, or exclusive. Personal *sino* exists, even of a favorable type; *buen ángel* and *buena sombra* exist. An infinite play of light and shadows becomes possible. *Sino* situates itself in a maximum range of possibilities. Above all, it encarnates itself personally and uniquely. It is up to each individual to come to an understanding with his own *sino*. [1964 : 197]

This view largely coincides with that of the great nineteenth-century folklorist, Antonio Machado y Alvarez (1975 [1881] : 288−290). Unlike the Islamic notion of destiny, destiny in southern Spain is of the "soft" variety—personalistic, charged with affect, even narcissistic. Even a man with *mala sombra* (evil shadow) might feel a certain perverse satisfaction in noting how the universe goes out of its way just to ruin his life. In the meantime, the fellow who believes he possesses *buena sombra* or any of its equivalents (*sal, salero, gracia, buen ángel, duende*) can feel himself to be fate's fair-haired boy. It would seem evident, however, that in neither case

1. For an overview of Islamic fatalism, see Ringgren 1967.

could a man claim responsibility for or personal control over his life. Thus, González Climent goes seriously astray when he attempts to equate *sino* with "the integral freedom of man that God disposes for His own infinite legitimation" and "the degree of absolute freedom that makes all chance relative" (1964:382–384). In my view, no amount of Jesuitical double-talk should be allowed to obscure the manifest message of the *copla:* a person's life and luck are shaped by outside forces—even when the outside forces are felt as an inner psychic presence—and not by individual volition. This attitude contrasts sharply with the one voiced by the stoical *refranero,* which manages to win a space for personal initiative by keeping the universe impersonal, by imposing distance, by steadfastly preventing passion from gaining the upper hand. For me, therefore, the question is not how to trace *sino* or passionate fatalism to God but how to clarify its connection to the Andalusian way of being-in-the-world.

The *coplas* cited above reveal a particular way of perceiving the universe (or *Umwelt*); but if fatalism is a world-design, we should also find it informing the way people perceive their social relations (*Mitwelt*)—and we do. All over Andalusia, affirms Brandes,

> power relationships are uppermost in people's minds, and provide one of the most pervasive themes of interaction. No matter what a person's status, the tendency is to feel dominated and controlled by those of the opposing group. In everyone, from all segments of society, there is a perpetual yearning for personal autonomy, which is perceived as being somehow seriously limited or threatened. The hatred and fear of allegedly powerful elements in society can only be described as immediate and pressing. [1980:25]

The fear of outside domination that Brandes studies is redoubled by the rigid standards of morality that hold sway in small towns throughout the south. The way in which the moral code maintains itself through the punitive power of public mockery has been described in detail by Gilmore (1987:29–52). The "iron fist," as he calls it, powers local gossip mills and these in turn are responsible for hounding nonconformists, breaking up engagements, ruining reputations, and making everyone paranoid to various degrees. I have found numerous *coplas* that testify to the all-pervasive power of *malas lenguas* (evil tongues) and to the fear and loathing they engender:

Más mata una mala lengua	An evil tongue kills more than
que las manos der berdugo,	the hands of the executioner,
que er berdugo mata a un hombre	the executioner kills one man
y una mala lengua a muchos.	but an evil tongue kills many.
[Machado y Alvarez 1975 (1881): 102]	

A un torito en plaza	A little bull in the plaza
no le temo tanto,	I do not fear as much
como le temo a una malina lengua	as I fear an evil tongue
y un testigo falso.	and a false witness.
[Fernández and Pérez 1986 : 114]	

Si yo supiera la lengua	If I knew whose tongue
que de mí murmura	is whispering about me
yo la cortara por en medio	I would cut it in half
y la ejara múa.	and leave it dumb.
[Molina and Mairena 1979 : 109]	

Gilmore's invisible fist is connected to the long arm of popular morality and reflects a number of old but still relevant concepts of honor and shame. Behind these can be found the legacy of caste society, patriarchy, lingering myths of blood purity, a decadent *latifundista* economy, the lack of a strong middle class, and other factors that contribute to Andalusia's social inertia. Altogether, they provide a most fertile terrain for feelings of other-directedness. If people in the south tend to be fatalistic, it is not because they are in the grip of delusion. No one could ever accuse their society of being upwardly mobile. Socioeconomic conditions *are* stifling, personal initiative *is* frequently blocked. Andalusians are human beings, of course, not animals, and are therefore capable of transcending the givens of their environment. This is easier said than done, unfortunately: in general, such transcendence has not been forthcoming. If it is incorrect to speak of a direct environmental determination of world-design, then what needs to be clarified is the intervening mode of consciousness that takes us from point X (stagnant society) to point Z (fatalism).

It might be helpful in this regard to recall Sartre's seminal definition of emotion as a "magical" transformation of a no-win world:

When the paths before us become too difficult, or when we cannot see our way, we can no longer put up with such an exacting and difficult world. All ways are barred and nevertheless we must act. So then we try to change the world; that is, to live it as though the relations between things and their potentialities were not governed by deterministic processes but by magic. . . . Emotional behavior seeks by itself, and without modifying the structure of the object, to confer another quality upon it, a lesser existence or lesser presence (or a greater existence, etc.). In a word, during emotion it is the body which, directed by the consciousness, changes its relationship with the world so that the world should change its qualities. [1962 : 63–65]

For Sartre, the numerous forms of sadness or melancholy that psychologists have described inevitably involve "a magical exaggeration of the difficulty of the world" and a concomitant "magical play-acting of impotence" (68–70). Even joy is a magical conduct that seeks "to realize the possession of the desired object as an instantaneous totality" (72). In all cases, consciousness debases itself when it leaps into emotion's magic world (78–79). One correlative of Sartre's theory merits special attention: the way in which consciousness perpetuates itself in this degraded state. This happens because, to begin with, true emotion is inseparable from true belief; consciousness *believes* in the magical plane it has fled to because it *lives* it. As a result,

consciousness is caught in its own snare. Precisely because it is living in the new aspect of the world by believing in it, the consciousness is captured by its own belief, exactly as it is in dreams and hysteria. . . . Thus, when consciousness is living the magical world into which it has precipitated itself, it tends to perpetuate that world, by which it is captivated: the emotion tends to perpetuate itself. . . . Liberation can come only from a purifying reflection or from the total disappearance of the emotional situation. [80–81][2]

One of our best modern thinkers on emotion views it as a kind of "hasty judgment"—rational and purposive in the short run but potentially destructive in the long run. Emotions, says Robert Solomon, "are always urgent, even desperate, responses to situations in which one finds oneself unprepared, helpless, frustrated, impotent, 'caught.' It is the situation, not the emotion, which is disruptive and 'irrational'" (1984 : 320).

Let it not be thought that the ideas of Sartre and Solomon are so many exercises in unprovable hypotheses; in fact, they are indirectly supported by the classic experiments on "level of aspiration" and "achievement motivation" carried out in this century by Hoppe, Sears, McClelland, Atkinson, and others (cf. Biehler 1978 : 520–521). In such experiments, youngsters exposed to the systematic frustrations of a controlled "failure condition" took refuge in desperate, short-term strategies. Some chose

2. For appraisals of Sartre's views on emotion, see Fell 1965 and Strasser 1977 : 65–86.

the security of absurdly easy tasks that they were sure to succeed at. Others set goals so far out of reach that they were comforted by the removal of personal responsibility for their failure, since they could not possibly be blamed for not doing the impossible (521).

Although Sartre and Solomon are chiefly concerned with emotion in the sense of transient emotional states, it is not hard to see how the susceptibility to such states could orient an entire way of being-in-the-world. Subjected to a more or less permanent "failure condition," consciousness would tend to seek refuge in emotion, cling to ego-assuaging illusion, value safety and continuity, and design a world accordingly. It would seem reasonable to assume that for this option to be adopted by large numbers of people, there would have to be both a general frustrating situation in existence and some escapist social mechanism in place. In other words, the autonomy-limiting factors of society (the failure condition) would have to be matched by dependency-rewarding factors in the same society.

We have already discussed certain aspects of the Andalusian failure condition. Now it is time to point out that emotional flight or denial has led many an Andalusian to treasure the consolations of dependency—familial dependency, above all, in both the material and psychological spheres. As many have observed, Andalusians are not inclined to a hasty cutting of the umbilical cord (in a figurative sense). Family is everything, and the potential disruption of family continuity arouses great anxiety. This does not rule out the possibility of ambivalent feelings regarding dependency. It simply ensures that the feelings will be unusually intense and contradictory. Intra-familial conflicts will tend to be extreme; by the same token, affection and self-sacrifice will often know no limits. In any clime, the family is an institution based not on reason but on something as utterly pre-rational as blood ties. In an advanced technological society, rationality relentlessly encroaches on blood ties; in southern Spain, blood ties have relentlessly encroached on rationality and have often shaped society in their own image.

The emotional mode of being-in-Andalusia tends to project a family pattern onto both the cosmos and the social environment. In the *Umwelt*, as we have already seen, a gender-conscious fatalism alternates between a nurturant and all-protective *buena estrella* on the one hand and an implacable *mal fario* on the other. In the *Mitwelt*, similarly, grossly inequitable relations of production or arbitrary cruelties of government have been paternalized, so to speak, while societal agents that seek to soften such injustices are maternalized (when they are not already mothers). In either case, people carry out an ultimately comforting personalization of phenomena.

Andalusian fatalism, then, is a selective reading of the environment; it is a "world" designed by an emotional mode of consciousness that is purposive and intentional in the phenomenological sense, magical in the Sartrian sense, and hastily judgmental in Solomon's sense. What I have been describing somewhat abstractly as Andalusian fatalism ought to be understood as the sum total of the fatalistic world-designs of individuals and small groups in and around Andalusia. Perhaps no two world-designs would possess the same mixture of ideas about *sino, sombra, ángel,* and *estrella.* Fatalism might vary in accordance with the exact nature of the failure condition that a person is saddled with, his or her early childhood experiences, and other biographical factors. The same would hold true for the life history of groups: it might be possible to identify distinct varieties of passionate fatalism among beggars, miners, prostitutes, *bandidos,* Gypsies, prisoners, soldiers, or any other group of men and women whose lives have not been in their own control to one extent or another.

One does not have to be at the bottom of society to feel other-directed, however. For centuries, upper-class Andalusians have internalized Spanish caste society and its rigid concepts of honor and shame. The personal and cultural consequences of this internalization can be seen with particular clarity in the career of Miguel Mañara, a man whose immense power and wealth did nothing to liberate his thoughts. In other words, certain types of freedom-quashing pressures can actually increase as one climbs the social ladder. The *latifundista* system creates another kind of psychological constriction. According to Brandes, the landholding elite of Monteros "feel far from omnipotent" and "desperately fear" the potential violence of the daily wage workers (1980:26).

We are now in a better position to appraise the significance of the *copla.* It can hardly be an accident that this expressive vehicle has reached its maximum degree of development in the south of Spain. A recent study views it as the quintessence of the lyric attitude, inasmuch as it seeks to erase the real relationship between the ego and the external object and restructure reality in accordance with the "suggestive contagion" of sentiment (Fernández and Pérez 1983:22–23). This definition of the *copla* might almost have been written by Sartre. Moreover, just as the *copla* is the poetic and musical form most suited to Andalusian emotion magic, fatalism is the *copla*'s most appropriate content. It is steeped in *sino* and obsessed with good and bad *estrella*, malevolent *fario*, lurking *sombras*, mischievous *duendes*, and similar personalized destinies. In the Andalusian *copla* we find a hyperbolic exaggeration of the world's difficulty alternating with fantasies of uncanny luck—just the contradictory attitudes we might have anticipated for people subjected to a long-standing socioeconomic failure condition. We find curious individual *coplas* that simultaneously voice a desire for and fear of autonomy:

Si hubiera alguno en el mundo
que la libertad me diera,
me echara un hierro a la cara
y esclavito suyo fuera.
   [Fernández and Pérez 1986:156]

If there were somebody in the world
who could give me freedom,
I would brand my own face
and be his little slave.

For over 150 years, passionately fatalistic Andalusians have spoken their minds in flamenco song. Revealing as it is, however, it is not the only cultural vehicle that gives expression to the Andalusian way of being-in-the-world; nor is it the oldest. Socioeconomic decadence was already well underway at the beginning of the seventeenth century; the Counter-Reformation had reached full virulence much earlier. For many centuries now, Andalusian culture has consistently favored spectacles of strong emotion of a magical or thaumaturgic variety; it has fostered a wide range of magical beliefs in general, consistently concerned with some kind of autonomy conflict; it has succumbed to the greatest degrees of magic emotionality in just that aspect of life that most threatens human autonomy: death.

Autonomy, Death, and the Devil

If the classic writings of the Stoic philosophers of Iberia and elsewhere have an overriding theme, it is that death is a trivial matter, far too trivial to be allowed to interfere with the dignity and serenity of a virtuous man. Stoicism, as described by Zambrano, is the

> morality of the pilgrim who knows he has nothing of his own. Who knows that he has not been especially created, but is only a collection of elements that, when their fragile unity (reinforced by virtue) is broken, will go to be reinte-

grated. It is the greatest conformity with death that has ever existed; its most complete acceptance, its most total justification. [1984:58]

Numerous attempts have been made over the centuries to assimilate Stoicism into Christianity, to save Seneca's soul, as it were, by portraying him as a resigned but hopeful Christian *avant la lettre* (cf. Rodríguez Navarro 1969:168–207). But we must not allow ourselves to be led astray. Stoic resignation expects nothing from the universe; Christian resignation expects everything. The latter is a tactical serenity that I adopt because I know I will still get my heart's desire—salvation and eternal life. It is not really resignation at all, only time-biding patience. Seneca may have pondered the nature of a natural God in some of his later writings but his meditations can in no way be confused with the eager and emotional faith of the Christian. The Cordoban sage thundered against all myths and illusions, without exception, while the fledgling Church cherished an unquenchable hope in a better world to come (while simultaneously nurturing the fear of a world of awful punishment that could also come). The Spanish Inquisition understood this well: as soon as a certain sect of Spanish Catholicism drew too close to true stoic resignation (*molinismo*), the Holy Office stepped in and clamped down (Caro Baroja 1985:498–502).

The Christian attitude toward death has always been inseparable from Christian ideas regarding the extent of man's autonomy vis-à-vis the Godhead. A fifth-century neo-Stoic named Pelagius tried to promote the idea of a benign, rational God who was willing to grant humans a fair measure of freedom and dignity; his teachings were eventually declared heretical through the efforts of Augustine (Caro Baroja 1985:239–240). Augustine's God was a God of wrath and passion, no serene philosopher, and the recommended posture for wretched humans was abject servility. This notion was slowly eroded over the centuries by Scholastic doctrines and especially by the proliferation of cults of saintly advocates like María or the *ánimas benditas*. But then came the "return to Augustine," protagonized by Martin Luther and others in the sixteenth century, which rapidly led some to envision a God who was not merely wrathful but frankly ferocious, for there was *nothing* a worm-like man could do to change His mind once it was made up. In general the Church managed to steer clear of the harsh concepts of predestination adopted by certain Protestant sects, but there was still plenty of theological elbow-room within Catholicism for disagreements and violent debates:

Once the doctrine of predestination was formulated more or less radically, it first separated Catholics from Protestants, then Catholics from Jansenists, and then went on to separate Dominicans and Augustinians from Jesuits, *rigoristas* from *laxistas,* and inside Catholicism a series of strange or subtle accusations began to be made, such as "Semi-Pelagian" (directed against those who emphasized free will) or "Semi-Calvinist" (against those who emphasized predestination). [Caro Baroja 1985 : 240]

In-fighting aside, Catholicism has never abandoned the belief that even the most wretched sinner can move God to forgive him through sincere repentance. This idea lies at the heart of the Passional/penitential tradition as I will discuss it in Chapter Two. At this point we are poised to approach this tradition in the light of death, autonomy conflicts, and emotion magic. Problem one: How much penitence is enough? Logically, the more I trust in God's ultimate benignity, the more inclined I will be to adopt an attitude of serene resignation à la Pelagius. Conversely, the more I fear God's omnipotent wrath, the more compulsed I will feel to curry His pardon with penitential acts of all kinds. Enter Mañara.

Here, as in so much else, the Big Brother of the *Santa Caridad* exemplifies (in extreme fashion) the general cultural trend of his native Andalusia. There were scarcely any limits to his appetite for self-recrimination and self-humiliation. No amount of penitence seemed sufficient to appease his Augustinian, Rigorist, and thoroughly fatalistic notion of divinity. This leads to problem two: Why? We can understand why a beggar or a *pícaro* might feel other-directed, but how could a man of Mañara's wealth and power come to hold such an oppressed view of humanity in general and of his own worth in particular? This is not the place for a major disquisition on his personality, but, assuming that his was the neurotic one of his time, we might briefly conjecture that Don Miguel had carried out a massive introjection of Spanish caste society and its rigid value system—wherein people could be scorned because their great-great-grandfathers had been processed by the Inquisition and wherein even those with the cleanest blood could not move a muscle without weighing the consequences for their reputations. In Golden Age and post–Golden Age society, certain forms of autonomy-limiting social pressure *intensified* in proportion to social prestige.

The particularly patriarchal and arteriosclerotic society of decadent Andalusia was little predisposed to foment a relaxed approach to life.

One day when he was in his youth Mañara stopped to chat with some women on a street in Seville. We do not know what kind of women they were, but Miguel's honor-obsessed father chanced to pass by in that moment and find something highly offensive in his son's conduct. Punishment was swift and public: the surprised lad received a stunning slap on the face. Young Miguel dropped to his knees immediately to beg his father's forgiveness (Granero 1981 : 62–63). Perhaps such disciplinary actions caused Mañara to interiorize authoritarianism and affective ambivalence in equal amounts. Perhaps his later saintly career, in which he stood the honor code on its head, reflected a secret urge to "top" his overbearing human father while simultaneously embracing fantastic degrees of mortification at the behest of his divine Father. Conjecture aside, it is clear that Mañara's perceived lack of autonomy was replicated in his obsession with death. We find little evidence of Christian resignation in Don Miguel, and none whatsoever of stoic resignation. There is another revealing anecdote. In the Royal Jail of Seville, sometime between the years 1665 and 1669, a condemned prisoner was awaiting his execution with aplomb, quaffing wine and cracking jokes with his cellmates. Somehow Mañara received word of this foolhardy (and utterly Socratic) behavior; rushing to the jail, he broke up the party, expelled the other delinquents, and "remained alone with the wretched one in order to reduce him. It was not an easy thing to reach his heart, but at long last grace triumphed" (Granero 1981 : 184).

Mañara was able to reach many more hearts (and defuse creeping stoicism) with his best-selling *Discurso de la Verdad*. In direct contrast to earlier death-preparation manuals, the *Discurso* was an impassioned, fearmongering tract. Mañara portrays the men and women of his age as depraved creatures paving their way to hell with vice and hypocrisy; he reserves his most biting sarcasm for those *filósofos mesurados* (moderate philosophers) who were busy finding ways to overlook or condone lust, gluttony, homicide, and—worst of all—stinginess. Literary critics consider Mañara's writing to be a model of baroque rhetorical style. A small sample:

> Oh damned ones, sons of Baal! You are not Israelites of straightforward and simple heart, but sons of the demon, ministers of Babylonia, doctrinaires of Beelzebub, and perverters of the teachings of Jesus Christ! [from Martín 1981 : 172]

Manichaean as all this may seem, however, Mañara never went over the deep end of predestination; he remained the neurotic personality of his time and place. His method of alerting people to the vanity of the world and the proximity of death was always tempered by a belief in the efficacy of penitence. Penitence could conquer death; penitential charity could transform death from a punishment into a source of eternal life; and the memory of Christ's own efficacious and Father-pleasing death could serve as an example for everyone. During the century following Mañara's own demise, mortal agony underwent an increasing degree of ritualization designed to maximize its thaumaturgic effects. The "how to" books published during the period were relentlessly monothematic: *how to die.* This was the great concern of the people and they went about it with an eager, almost impetuous attitude, entirely devoid of the squeamishness about death that had begun to take hold in other climes. Rivas even speaks of the spirit of "recreation" with which both the dying person and his spectators awaited the inevitable (1986 : 114). And once death arrived, there was no trace of the hurried movement to occult the cadaver, which was common north of the Pyrenees. To the contrary, close public inspection of a corpse was the one way to determine if its owner had received some special supernatural dispensation or grace at the last moment. The body of Sister Teresa de Jesús remained on view for several days in 1712 to allow all Sevillians to confirm the miracle, for it had remained soft and manageable despite the nun's advanced age at the time of death (115–116). Two years later the demise of a ruggedly handsome Franciscan friar drove his many "spiritual daughters" into a state of superstitious hysteria: rivaling each other for relics, they threw themselves on the body and made off with almost every shred of his tunic and hair on his head. "One notes a tactile relationship with the lifeless body of uncommon intensity," Rivas observes dryly (116).

Yet we do not have to rely on such colorful episodes to document the Andalusian attitude toward death. The testaments of hundreds of ordinary citizens prove that a baroque love of theatre was alive and well in eighteenth-century Seville. They often include detailed dispositions regarding where the body was to be displayed, how it was to be dressed, and how many candles were to be lit, rosaries said, tapestries hung, and refreshments served at the wake. Here we find the first of many "Franciscan connections," for the robes normally worn in life by the humble friars were in great demand as graveclothes, saturated as they were with indulgence power (112–131). The funeral procession was the fitting climax to these assorted prolegomena.

> The transfer of the cadaver must not always have taken place within the boundaries of gravity and restraint. The immense crowds at certain funerals, the distribution of alms to the poor along the way, the rivalry between *cofradías,* the attendance of professional mourners, and the cries of the widow did not allow, on occasions, for the recommended seriousness to be maintained. . . . Music was also present in some cases, and to it must be added the discordant weeping that accompanied the funeral march. [143]

Let us return to the truly decisive scenario of the deathbed, for here is where a moribund sinner had his or her last great chance to avoid damnation. Officially, of course, the Church saw greater merit in a good life than in a beautiful death; yet it was the sacrament of Extreme Unction itself that formed the nucleus around which all of the other agonic rituals converged. Moreover, the example of Christ's own thaumaturgic agony was there for all to ponder in the ubiquitous crucifix. A typical eighteenth-century guide to a good death outlines the ten parts of a proper leave-taking: (1) You confess your sins and the priest absolves them through the sacrament of penance. (2) In the meantime, the viaticum has arrived (the sacrament of the Eucharist in a traveling form). The priest sprinkles you with holy water while you make the sign of the cross on your forehead, and (3) he quizzes you on the principal doctrines of the faith. (4) You kiss the crucifix, (5) declare your belief in the sacraments, and (6) pardon all of those who have offended you in life while asking them to do the same. (7) You recite the *Confiteor* (Latin version of the Creed), (8) receive the viaticum, and, if you are near death, (9) you are anointed with the holy oils of extreme unction. (10) Finally, if you have any strength left, you recite a long litany requesting the intercession of the main heavenly advocates and any other private ones that have been useful to you in the past (cit. by Rivas 1986:107–108). The viaticum could not be administered to drunks or deaf-mutes, given their inability to engage in the above rituals. The priest was authorized to use a long instrument for feeding the host to those dying of contagious diseases (108).

One will search in vain for some hint of stoicism in all this, and any resignation present will be of the tactical kind mentioned earlier. I have no doubt that many Andalusians arrived at the moment of death with a resigned outlook, and a few may even have been stoical about it. Yet social and cultural patterns militated against this. True stoicism is anti-heroic, detached, nonsuperstitious, and occasionally flippant: *El muerto al hoyo y el vivo al bollo,* as the saying has it (The dead man to his hole and the living man to his bread). While there may have been isolated proverb-users in southern Spain who practiced what they preached, the *general cultural trend*—just as in declining and falling Rome, another age of chronic crisis—was in the direction of emotion magic, passionate fatalism, sacrificial cult, fear, rigidity, and ritualism. The stoic stance, with its naturalistic determinism, acceptance of the Reality Principle, serenity, dignity, and psychological autonomy, has been accessible to a minority. It requires considerable emotional maturity and self-possession, just what the growth-stunting socioeconomic conditions of Andalusia militated against. These conditions constitute the material matrix of emotion-centered culture in general and Passional culture in particular.

Doctors of the Church prefer to picture penitence as a natural result of God-given free will. It does seem highly unlikely, however, that anyone would "freely" choose the opposite course in order to spend all eternity sweating and freezing, hearing horrible screams, smelling vile odors, and suffering all of the other revolting torments that imaginative preachers have described. Nevertheless, Catholicism does not seem particularly rigorous (or Rigorist) on the surface of it, since it spells out very simple, clear-cut, easy-to-follow rules for the avoidance of hell. All may apply, and no one is "condemned for lack of confidence," to paraphrase the title of Tirso's play. All we need do is trust in the Holy Mother Church and follow her directives, especially at the hour of death. This would be in consonance with genuine, optimistic Christian resignation. Yet people in southern Spain *did* worry, especially at the hour of death. For as it happens, there was a spoiler in their world, an all-powerful fly in the ointment of extreme unction. This winged creature and his cohorts were perennially poised to tempt, deceive, and pervert. If we are to understand fully the fatalistically emotional attitudes toward both life and death that have predominated in Andalusia, we must necessarily speak of the devil.

If ever there was a "magical exaggeration of the world's difficulties," to use the Sartrian phrase, it was the devil lore that filled the heads of both upper- and lower-class Spaniards for centuries. One scholar even speaks of the devil as one of the more important figures in the history of Spain (Flores 1985:33). In this area, as in so many others, the south is distinguished not so much by the content of its devil lore as by its intensity and longevity. Toward the end of the nineteenth century there were still large numbers of Andalusians who routinely made the sign of the cross over their mouths when yawning to keep the devil out, who avoided looking into the mirror at night, or who believed that strong winds meant that demons were running loose (Guichot 1986:103–105). The occasional hurricanes that visited destruction upon lower Andalusia seemed to confirm this latter belief. One such hurricane in March of 1608 struck terror into the hearts of the *Dominicas Descalzas* of Seville. Sister Francisca Dorotea, the mother superior, heard voices in the wind howling "We have come to destroy this house, we will not stop until it has collapsed!" While the other nuns lay prostrate on the floor, praying desperately with eyes tightly closed, their valiant leader frightened the demons off by using her scapular as a whip and sprinkling holy water on the walls of the besieged convent (Abascal 1984:265–267). In 1842 the clergy of Seville unanimously blamed another terrible hurricane on the *Demonio*, with the sins of the city's residents as an adjunct cause. Such incidents confirm that, first, the ecclesiastical mind was hardly less prone to superstition than the popular one, and second, the devil could be every bit as wrathful and passionate as God Himself was held to be.

There were as many reasons for people to feel threatened as there were devils—exactly 7,405,926, according to one authority cited by Flores (1985:43). Devils could disguise themselves in a thousand ways; they had been located in amulets, furniture, animals, voices, and even heads of lettuce (30). They could employ a thousand insidious stratagems to make humans fall, cannily allying themselves with repressed desires. The more saintly the human—that is, the more repressed the desire—the more vicious a devil's tactics. It will come as no shock to the reader to learn that Miguel Mañara and the devil were no strangers to one another. In his mansion in Seville, demons appeared to Don Miguel in the guise of repulsive animals. They tried to drown him in his sleep on more than one occasion. When he made inspection tours of the *Iglesia de la Caridad* during its construction, Satan sometimes tried to throw him off the scaffolding. One day the *Hermano Mayor* actually fell from a considerable height; brothers and bricklayers rushed to his side, fearing the worst. But Don

Miguel got to his feet, dusted himself off with a grim smile, and said, "Dog, your tricks will be of no avail!" (Martín 1981:183).

Naturally Catholics had allies in their struggles with the devil. Not God, to be sure, the very one who permitted the devils to do their worst while He sat in judgment. God the Father could only be reached by powerful advocates—the saints, the souls of ex-inmates of purgatory, His Son, and above all María. It seems certain that in every age Marianism has been inseparable from fear of the devil; of the Virgin's many functions, one of the principal ones was to crush the serpent's head underfoot and protect frail humans from stratagems like the ones Eve had succumbed to at the beginning of time (Caro Baroja 1985:88–89; Flores 1985:26–27).

María was the prime antidote for evil and slowly but surely her cult became habit-forming. Like all forms of dependency, it did nothing to fortify its dependents' anemic sense of personal autonomy. One's soul was simply the object of a tug-of-war between the Virgin and the devil; at the crucial hour of death, one's sphere of action was limited to a kind of ritual rooting for the first, in the form of rosaries, litanies, and ejaculations. One Sevillian testatrix cited by Rivas had three poor men brought to her deathbed to recite the rosary in unison until the moment she expired (1986:111)—the spiritual efficacy of the Mother of God being thus redoubled by the indulgence power of poverty.

I hope that by now the reader is persuaded that Andalusian fatalism does not imply stoic resignation. If it is bound up with the magic emotionality with which people respond to failure conditions of one kind or another, then it signifies precisely the opposite. Insofar as it represents a magical exaggeration of the world's difficulties, fear of the devil can be seen as part and parcel of the passionate worldview. Andalusian fatalism does not even imply Christian resignation; it cannot achieve serenity, and it certainly has no patience with passivity.

Political, socioeconomic, or psychological repression can put an end to autonomy but it cannot put an end to wish, only intensify it and force it to resort to some sort of subterfuge. In the hair-raising world that Andalusia has designed, practical endeavors to control current events have always taken a back seat to fantasy techniques of controlling the future (death magic, superstitious praxis, augury). This would not have happened, in my view, if Andalusian society had been in a position to reward practicality and enterprise on a large scale. It never was. The psycho-cultural consequences of this have been formidable. Rather than the synthetic view of time and empirical certainty that characterizes upwardly mobile societies, many men and women of the south have been saddled with a "blocked future" and oppressed by a "static feeling of evil" (cf. Minkowski 1958 : 132–138). Moreover, it is curious to note that the beliefs and practices that have arisen out of this dark obsession with impending destruction reinforce the very social inertia that spawned the obsession. In the last analysis, to cultivate fantasy techniques of destiny control is to relinquish a hands-on control of one's own becoming in the present.

Superstition: Theory and Praxis

Whether or not Andalusian emotionality is magical in a phenomenological sense, it has clearly been caught up with magic in the ethnographic sense. In southern Spain, superstition blends imperceptibly into mainstream religion. It employs the *copla* and other traditional genres (minus the *refrán*) to further itself. It is inseparably linked to the fear of domination by the cosmos or by people, and consequently it is obsessed with manipulating them both in a kind of "preventive retaliation." The roots of Andalusian superstition go deep and reflect centuries of occupation by omen-conscious Romans and Arabic astrologers. There are also a great many pre-Roman superstitions or belief fragments of ancient Mediterranean religions that have managed to survive at marginal levels of folk expression (Blázquez 1975 : 11–22). Andalusia has traditionally been a net exporter of superstitions to other parts of the Iberian Peninsula (Alonso del Real 1971 : 56).

The limited social base of official religion is one reason why superstition remains widespread in today's Andalusia. Unlike the Catholic Church in Latin America, with its liberation theology and its espousal of the poor, the Church in Andalusia tends to draw its strength from the middle and upper classes. As one moves from higher to lower on the social scale, factors like Sunday Mass attendance and knowledge of dogma drop proportionately (Castón 1985 : 108–109). It is interesting to note, however, that regardless of social class, the dioceses of Andalusia have one of the lowest rates of Mass attendance in all of Spain. There are fewer parishes in the south, and relatively fewer priests. In northern Spain

(Castilla-León), there is one priest for every 851 inhabitants; in Seville there is one priest for every 3,345 inhabitants, and in Cádiz the ratio rises to one for every 4,430 (1985:116). Furthermore, the greater rapport or identification of the Church with the upper classes does not mean that the latter are free of superstition. Alonso del Real has affirmed that superstition is "vertical" in the south, present in all social classes; Andalusia is even the natural habitat for an intelligent, cultured, and "sincerely superstitious" bourgeoisie that is unique in Spain (1971:126). The wave of Spiritism that spread through Europe and North America during the late nineteenth century was enthusiastically embraced by the cultivated classes of southern Spain; Spiritist meetings with mediums and magnetizations were common in Seville through the 1920s (Abascal 1984:210–214).

Superstition, thus, like so many other aspects of popular culture in the south of Spain, cannot be confined to one social class. When it portrays itself as piety, its ability to agitate all social classes is remarkable. To illustrate, one summer in 1872 a long-bearded beggar showed up at the Sevillian mansion of the Oliva family, known for its generosity to the poor. The maid who opened the door and handed him a small kettle of food was struck by the beggar's resemblance to Saint Joseph (as depicted in the murals of a local church). When he had finished eating, he handed the kettle back to the maid and said, "Tell your mistress that as a reward for the act of charity that she has made by giving food to the hungry, any medicine that is placed in this little kettle will cure the sick to whom it is given in the name of the glorious Patriarch San José." The maid did as she was told but when she returned for a clarification of the instructions, the old man had vanished into thin air. Miracles were not long in coming, the most spectacular one being wrought in the person of Doña Juana Cañaveral. Three swallows of water that had been placed in the diminutive kettle were enough to send her, an incurable paralytic, running out of the house in ecstasy. Rich and poor Sevillians alike were electrified. Miracles continued in the following years and the magic kettle became the center of a passionate journalistic-ecclesiastical debate. The Cardinal Archbishop of Seville finally stepped in and stamped out in 1880 (Abascal 1984:229–231). Two centuries after the death of Miguel Mañara, his native city remained convinced of the spiritual efficacy of charity to the poor. The mysterious beggar had only given a superstitious twist to a very old and very Andalusian tradition.

An entire order of excommunicated priests and nuns is at the service of the beggars of today. The order, or sect, has its headquarters in the small town of Palmar de Troya (Seville Province) and its leader is none other than Clemente Domínguez Gómez, the blind seer and stigmata recipient who proclaimed himself Pope Gregory XVII and Universal Emperor in 1978. *El Papa Clemente,* as he is popularly known, heads an ultraconservative church that retains the Tridentine ritual (e.g., Masses in Latin only) and has canonized Christopher Columbus, José Antonio Primo de Rivera (founder of the *Falange*), and Generalísimo Franco. With the support of wealthy reactionaries in Spain and Latin America, the Andalusian pontiff and his cardinals have overseen the construction of a beautiful basilica in Palmar de Troya. Its eighty priests and nuns wear severely traditional habits as they drive around Seville in white vans and distribute food to the poor. They are forbidden to read newspapers, watch television, or listen to the radio. In compensation, they are allowed to exorcise regularly, kiss their pope's feet, and receive occasional messages from the Virgin regarding the course of future events. Clemente himself has made innumerable catastrophic prophecies. He has also excommunicated the rest of the Catholic Church. Whatever one makes of the psychological or political aspects of the affair, it somehow seems appropriate that the part of Spain most abandoned by the official Church should harbor its own pope.

A stronger Church would not necessarily have been enough to retard the growth of superstition in southern Spain. The Church has hardly been immune itself, as a cursory glance at its history confirms. For one thing, Catholicism propagated the view that the universe was full of good and evil spirits of all kinds and numbers and that these beings were prone to intervene in human affairs on a routine basis; miraculous happenings were behind the cults of patron saints, with their fetish-like relics and folk legends. Guichot cites a long list of Andalusian superstitions that attach themselves to one saint or another for instrumental purposes, including noncanonical ones like San Pascual Bailón or San Cucufate (1986 [1883] : 113–116). The Church also contributed greatly to the survival of astrology. If this pseudoscience remained influential for centuries from the top of society to the bottom, it was largely due to the many theologian-astrologers who scrutinized God's will in the stars. The great free will versus predestination debate that raged within and without Catholicism was closely tied to astrology, divination, and other techniques of foreknowledge. Significantly, one of Spain's great social historians has traced it all to unbridled emotion:

> Christianity has not been able to unseat old fatalistic concepts nor constant and vehement desires to know the future. . . . It is not a question of the history of ideas and dogmas so much as passions and desires, wishes and anxieties, collective and individual rivalries between orders, professors, etc. The great get caught up in the passions just like the small, and in this the moderns are no different from the ancients. [Caro Baroja 1985 : 255]

Finally, Catholicism is intimately connected with magic-like rituals known as sacraments—baptism, penance, extreme unction, and so on. If we are to hearken Krappe, the very success of the early Church can be attributed to its retention of the magic element (1929 : 289). Sacraments and superstitions alike grow up in the same vital fluid of anxiety-reducing rites of passage; superstition is simply the more literal-minded sibling.

Bearing all of the above in mind, it might be stated as a general rule of thumb that whenever the Church gives an inch, Andalusia will take a mile. This is especially evident in the literalistic interpretation of the sacraments to which people in the south are prone. One superstition parasitic of the sacrament of baptism, for example, has had considerable repercussions for popular speech as well as for popular concepts of causality. It is held that the more salt a priest sprinkles on a baby's forehead, the more grace he or she will have—grace not in the sense of divine favor but of human "flair." This belief is at the root of the Andalusian obsession with *sal* or *salero* (or *gracia* or *sandunga*), words that appear with "extraordinary frequence" in oral poetry and songs (Ropero 1984 : 184–186). They also abound in *piropos*, the formulaic compliments paid to women full of grace as they stroll down the street. A woman without *sal* is bound to lead a dis-graceful existence; as one popular *copla* laments,

Qué desgraciada nací,	How unfortunate I was born,
que en la pila del bautismo	for in the baptismal font
faltó la sal para mí.	there was no salt for me.
[Guichot 1986 (1883) : 140]	

Significantly, what is supposed to be a symbol of spiritual efficacy available to all becomes a matter of fickle fate in Andalusian folklore. And there is a structural, if not chronological, link to pre-Christian fatalistic beliefs: Tripp tells us that the alternative name for the Fates in Mediterranean mythology was *Parcae,* meaning Bringers Forth (1970:246); your destiny was inseparable from the gifts given you at the very beginning of your life. No Andalusian mother worth her salt could be expected to stand idly by and let the Fates have their way, however, especially when a Gypsy could be hired to stamp her feet thrice during a child's baptism and recite magic prayers of the kind collected by Machado (1986 [1882]:171–175).

The pattern that can be abstracted from the *sal* superstition shows up again in many other beliefs. First, a sacrament or some other religious ritual or concept is given a fatalistic twist, then a mode of superstitious praxis evolves to manipulate fate in accordance with wish. This magic wish-fulfillment often seeks to siphon off some of the power tapped by a sacrament during a "liminal" moment. Hence, in Andalusia it is thought that the interval between the consecration of the bread and the consecration of the wine during Mass is a particularly apt time to wrench some favor from divinity—even when the favor is of the kind sung of in the following *copla flamenca:*

Entre la hostia y el cáliz	Between the host and the chalice
a mi Dios se lo pedí	I asked my God for it;
que t'ajoguen las duquelas	that miseries suffocate you
como m'ajogan a mí.	like they suffocate me.
[Molina and Mairena 1979:116]	

To return to birth-day fatalism: being born with *gracia* was no easier than being born with clean, Old Christian blood (another thoroughly fatalistic concept supported by the Church in Spain). All over the peninsula, folk medicine has traditionally been practiced by men and women with an inborn God-given *gracia* to do so. This is the case of the Manchegan *curanderos* studied by Ramírez Rodrigo, who despite their rusticity possess "a high degree of intelligence and a marked power of persuasion" and are often female epileptics (1985:356–358). In earlier centuries a class of people known as *saludadores* or *ensalmadores* rivaled the priests themselves in their powers. They were normally men born on Good Friday, the most thaumaturgic day of the year, who made their living by casting out devils, curing rabies, and chasing plagues away (Flores 1985:188–189). These men aspired to the posts of *saludador del pueblo* (town healer) that existed in many localities of the south well into the eighteenth century. But they had to pass a unique examination. In

1696, for instance, a man named Fulgencio Sevilla appeared in Murcia, announced that God had given him a special *gracia,* and declared his readiness to undergo the prescribed tests. In a special session of the city assembly, Fulgencio walked barefoot on a red hot iron bar (test one), grabbed it with his bare hands (test two), and licked it (test three). Having passed all three trials, he was appointed official *saludador* and began to collect his salary like any other municipal employee (189).

Special qualities derived from the circumstances of birth were also necessary to be a *sabia.* According to Abascal, this is the profession that most differentiates Andalusian ritual magic from that of the rest of Spain. For unlike the Galician *meiga* or the Basque *xorguiña,* the Andalusian *sabia* was not feared as a wicked witch but revered as a wise woman.

> The Andalusian people never had an exaggerated fear of witches, but rather the opposite since its witches practiced not evil but good, although logically there were exceptions inside the social context in which they operated. Proof of the aforesaid is that the Andalusian people, then and now, continue to designate some of its witches with the honorary and extremely respectful title of "*sabias.*" And thus in our investigations, whenever we have asked for the local witch we have been contemplated with perplexity and even with hostility; but not when we have inquired about the local *sabia.* Today's Andalusian *sabia* is a worthy descendant of her predecessors. [1984 : 167]

The powers of a *sabia* are derived from God, not from a pact with the devil; she attends no Black Sabbaths and afflicts no children or cattle with evil eye. Evil eye is something she cures, just like the epileptic *curanderas* of Ciudad Real.

During the nineteenth and early twentieth centuries, the *sabias* came to be rivaled in popular appeal by women known as *endemoniadas.* Contrary to what the name might suggest, the *endemoniadas* were not bedeviled or possessed by demons; they were extremely religious women who in certain contexts had the power to work miracles. Unlike the solitary *sabia,* the *endemoniadas* always performed together as a group, publically assembled on the occasion of some religious feast day or *romería* (a pilgrimage-like procession). Gathered together near a church or shrine, the *endemoniadas* would employ rosaries and endless liturgical chants to work themselves into a swooning trance:

> This was their big moment; in this situation people would draw near to have them touch the clothes of the sick, objects that they wanted to acquire magical powers, or small children; they would even inquire about future events. The

endemoniada, with great hemming and hawing and amidst moans, fainting spells, and extravagance, would sometimes respond and sometimes not; when she did it was in a rather sibylline way which could admit diverse interpretations. The people would keep silence sometimes and at other times participate in the ceremonies through the diffusion of a collective hysteria, it being frequent that even women who had no reputation as *endemoniadas* would also faint or talk incoherently. [Abascal 1984:176]

Abascal attributes the nineteenth-century flowering of the *endemoniadas* to a "fanatical public thirst for miracles" no longer checked by a moribund Inquisition, which in its glory days would never have allowed such behaviors (176–178).

Fortune-telling is yet another form of ritual magic that can be seen as the continuation of emotion magic by other means. Knowledge is power only for those who are in tune with reality; for those who have been devastated by reality, real power is represented by foreknowledge. In Andalusia, augury has been the hope of the hopeless and the fantasy of control for those who feel controlled. Superstitious methods of learning fate's designs, and profiting thereby, run very deep in Andalusia, as deep as the fatalistic world-design of which they partake. The possible involvement of the devil in foretelling the future was a point hotly debated by priests and theologians—who were themselves unwilling or unable to renounce the belief that divine will could be divined in some way (Abascal 1984:154–163; Caro Baroja 1985:255–260; Flores 1985:194–230).

Today's Andalusian fortune-tellers, and those whose fortunes they tell, are almost exclusively female. The usual method of divination is to *echar las cartas,* to "cast" the cards of the Spanish deck and decipher their messages; hence the name of *echadoras* for the women who practice this traditional craft. A recent study of *echadoras* in the province of Cádiz (Martín Díaz 1984) sheds further light on the nature of passionate fatalism in Andalusia. Martín states that the clientele of the fortune-tellers can be divided into two groups: (1) lower-class women with a combination of economic and psychological problems relating to their precarious social standing (unwed mothers, women separated from their husbands, young widows, spouses doubtful of their husbands' fidelity, and prostitutes)— all under forty years of age and all possessed of a genuine faith in the *echadora*'s abilities; and (2) women with a high school or college education who are usually no older than twenty-five, single, and fairly skeptical about the reliability of card-casting (322). The overriding concern of the first group is to know what kind of treatment is in store for them at the hands of their men. Fear and mistrust are their characteristic emotional states. Men are equally on the minds of the women of the second category, most of whom want to know what sort of husband they will have or whether they will have one at all. Interestingly, those who are already involved in a premarital relationship tend to exhibit the same insecure attitudes observed in the women of the first group (323).

Martín traces the anxieties of both groups to the fact that a woman abandoned by a man suffers severe economic hardships and to the belief that a woman who never marries will remain vitally unfulfilled. Either way, anxiety is the result of a lack of personal autonomy:

> The economic and/or psychological dependence of the woman with respect to the man makes the woman adopt a passive attitude in a relationship, which makes its survival the almost exclusive prerogative of the man. [325]

Education, the slow erosion of traditional male-female roles, and the evolution of the labor market have all contributed to a growing sense of control and independence among Andalusian women. Accordingly, the clientele of the *echadoras* is now drawn mostly from the socially conservative, unschooled lower classes (326).

The reader may be wondering why such women feel they require the services of a fortune-teller. Could they not just ask their men and receive a direct answer from the controllers of their fate? Martín wondered the same thing and subsequently discovered that some women are afraid to approach their mates on an equal footing; others are sure they will be lied to anyway; still others are terrified that such a dialogue might lead to a beating and/or their expulsion from home (323).

Equally instructive is the profile of a typical *echadora*. She is usually a spinster or a woman who became a widow at a very young age, who belongs to the bottom rung of society, and who lives in the oldest part of the city—most often a corroded *casa de vecindad* (321). The *casa de vecindad* is essentially the same as the *corral de vecinos,* that is, a variable number of humble three- or four-room dwellings grouped around a central patio. Another researcher terms them "micro-neighborhoods" and affirms that the already precarious privacy of the lower classes is reduced to a minimum in such structures, where secrets—from a love affair to a visit to the bathroom—are almost physically impossible to keep (Carloni 1984 : 260–261). *Echadoras,* then, would be the most marginal members of this marginal world. Martín reports that they feel themselves to be under the special scrutiny of their neighbors; for this reason they would not consent to *echar las cartas* for a man even if he so desired, to avoid "feeling themselves to be more observed and criticized than they feel habitually" (1984 : 321). Here again is the pervasive policing power of the evil tongues described by Gilmore.

Despite Krappe's observation that "the distinction between a witch and a fortune-teller is of the most delicate" (1929 : 292), witchcraft is the one accusation that the *echadora* will not be open to. An extremely religious woman who has nothing to do with the occult, the *echadora* believes that things happen because God wants them to; to cast the cards is to seek to know God's will, not to change it, since that is out of the question (Martín 1984 : 324). Nevertheless, forewarned is forearmed. Martín notes that fortune-telling sessions frequently include advice regarding certain steps or precautions to be taken in the future (320). This brings the attitude of the *echadora* into line with instrumental Andalusian fatalism in general.

Sabias, endemoniadas, and *echadoras*—and the esteem and popularity they have enjoyed—demonstrate fatalism's link to gender in the south of Spain. It would be hard to believe that the devout respect for God's implacable will found in fortune-tellers is not somehow related to the subjugation to patriarchal will (macho-style) found in their unfortunate clients. But fatalism is by no means confined to females in the south. The fact that men are less anxious about marital stability does not mean that they are free from autonomy-anxieties of a different order. *Machismo* itself, as a matter of fact, constitutes a prime example of how a failure condition can provoke an emotional reaction, leading in turn to a fatalistic belief system. This is, at least, what I will argue in the remainder of this chapter.

To begin with, *machismo* has its roots in the same complex of political, social, and economic factors that have crippled personal initiative in the south for centuries:

> Denied access to the means of economic production, politically impotent, the lower-class Andalusian responds to these historical deficiencies by appropriating the means of reproduction. He thereby establishes a compensatory genital hegemony. He achieves in the purely sexual sphere an aggressive mastery of his

social environment that is denied him in other areas. Thus for the Andalusian worker or peasant, a sociopolitical impotence is counterbalanced by the consolation of a purely erotic potency. The man ascribes a putative weakness to women, displacing his own feelings of inadequacy and vulnerability on her, making her a victim of sexual (but not physical) aggression. [Gilmore 1987:150]

Gilmore's description of the sociopsychological origins of Andalusian *machismo* is correct in most respects; unfortunately, his idea that a macho's aggression is sexual but not physical will have to be revised. Recent statistics suggest that the number of battered women in the south may be well above the national average (*El Correo de Andalucía,* 4 June 1988, p. 40). The normally peaceful males of the south cannot always refrain from "passing the buck" of their own victimization on to their womenfolk.

The crisis of male confidence wrought by poverty has produced a male mystique, characterized by a curious overvaluing of the genitals. Many an Andalusian man has reified and almost deified his penis, converting it into a veritable "Other" that holds sway over or at least orients his thoughts, words, and deeds. Brandes has affirmed that, for many men of the south, "the locus of power and will, of emotions and strength, lies within the male genitals. Men speak as if they were impelled to act according to opinions and desires that originate in their testicles or penis" (1980:92). "Male sexuality," writes Gilmore, "has a certain preordained autonomy. The body acts by itself, and the man follows. . . . On the other hand, a man who fails to be aroused, who phlegmatically fails to act according to his majesty the penis, is not a man" (1987:130).

I refer the reader to Gilmore for a witty analysis of the phallocentric worldview and to Brandes for a comprehensive discussion of male identity anxiety expressed in folk speech, pranks, riddles, skits, and jokes. To the extent that men really feel themselves to be subordinate to their genitals, of course, *machismo* is no laughing matter. It represents a degrading concept of self that can be traced directly to a degraded consciousness, a magical attitude that resists rationality and perpetuates itself in servitude. Testicular willpower is really no willpower at all, only another way of being dominated by the passions. The other-directed essence of *machismo* is patent: to be a man in Andalusia, at least in certain circles, one must be quick to relinquish self-control and blindly follow the dictates of a lower power. One's own body looms as an alien and omnipotent presence.

It is interesting to note that such idea-feelings parallel the beliefs about the devil that have permeated Iberian folklore for centuries. Like the Andalusian male organ, the devil represents an irrational force of great power that plays havoc with one's sense of autonomy. The sexual appetite, to be sure, was always one of the devil's favorite means for subjugating weak-kneed humans. This is why celibacy and virginity came to be so highly prized. *Machismo* maintains an equally mystified view of sex, even as it glories in subjugation to "his majesty the penis." It therefore comes as no surprise to discover that the hyperphallic fantasies of lower-class Andalusian males are a simple transmutation of the view of male sexuality held by the early Church fathers, Saint Augustine in particular. In a fascinating study, Ruether has discussed Augustine's belief that the seat of all sin

> is the male penis, whose spontaneous tumescence, in response to sensual stimuli and independent of consciousness, is the literal embodiment of "that law in the members that wars against the law of the minds." Augustine's horrified description of the male erection and its key role in his doctrine of sin and the transmission of original sin usually brings embarrassed laughter from historians of doctrine, if they have the temerity to refer to this view in explicit terms at all. It is usually supposed to reflect some personal sexual hang-up of Augustine's resulting from obsessions caused by illicit sexual experiences, and thus not to reflect on these doctrines themselves. A personal obsession it may well have been, but one that reflected a collective obsession of Augustine's religious culture. [1974:162–163]

Ruether connects the misogynistic, dualistic, and pessimistic view of sex propagated by patristic authors with their veneration of the Virgin, and traces both to the apocalyptic despair caused by *loss of political autonomy* in the Mediterranean basin (150–154). This strikes me as highly significant, and highly relevant to Andalusian *machismo*. The lower-class men of southern Spain are thoroughly "Augustinian" in their lack of political autonomy, their stress-provoked fatalism, their obsession with genitalia, their depersonalization of women, and their phenomenal devotion to the Virgin Mary.

Gilmore may well be right in associating *machismo* with fear of female dominance in a "culturally androcentric yet matriarchal society" (1987: 150–151). Men fleeing from their domineering wives and mothers resort to *machismo,* perhaps, just as women cowering from their macho husbands or lovers resort to fortune-tellers. Both sexes can be seen behaving in accordance with the same schema: AUTONOMY CRISES → EMOTION MAGIC → FATALISTIC BELIEFS → RITUALISM. The posturing folklore of *machismo,* after all, is a ritualistic drumbeating, a superstitious whistling in the dark, a behavioral complex that is as desperate and ridden with anxiety as card-casting.

One final consideration: *machismo* cannot be uncritically identified with patriarchy. In fact, it seems to be the result of a failure of patriarchal civilization as we know it. In Andalusia, patriarchy has based its success on a different sort of failure condition and a different mode of passionate fatalism. If we shift our attention away from socially marginal superstition toward mainstream popular piety, we discover that Father-fearing, Mother-revering emotionality has been propagated on a grand scale by the penitential brotherhoods.

Chapter 2

The Uses of Pain

Penitential Culture

I hold at least one truth to be self-evident: Passional culture is penitential culture. Strictly speaking, there is no such thing as a Holy Week "procession"—the term employed by the people involved is *Estación de Penitencia*. And while the ornate *pasos* orient the devotional and aesthetic fervor of the masses, the silent ranks of the repentant that escort the icons carry the indispensable moral message of the *Estación* as a whole. *Penitentes* are not the only "people of the Passion" in southern Spain, of course, but as the living bearers of an archaic but still relevant ideology, they merit special attention.

It is common nowadays to distinguish between *nazarenos* (who simply wear the penitential garb, carry large candles, and accompany the images) and *penitentes* (who often go barefoot and always carry wooden crosses of variable sizes). This distinction can be somewhat confusing in view of the fact that *Nazareno* is the name reserved for the images of Christ with His cross. In theory, to be sure, participation in an *Estación de Penitencia* automatically makes one a *penitente;* and in practice, many so-called *nazarenos* can be seen walking barefoot, counting their beads, or keeping total silence during the eight to twelve hours they spend in the street. One sure way to tell them apart is the shape of the *caperuza* or hood: that of the *nazareno* points skyward, that of the *penitente* lies on his back. It is usually some vow made or heavenly favor granted that influences the former to adopt the guise of the latter in any given year. There are also a few especially devout *cofradías* who dress their members in *túnicas de cola* that recall the robes of cloistered monks. Whatever the superficial resemblance a *nazareno* may have with a knight of the Ku Klux Klan, his motivations could not be more dissimilar; his garments are designed not for secrecy and terror but for intimacy and exemplarity. All *penitentes* conceal their identities so that their acts will remain free of human vanity—to the extent that any public display of piety can accomplish this goal.

The nature and degree of penitential actions have varied over the ages. The heroic approach to penitence favored by nobles of the sixteenth and seventeenth centuries led them not only to carry crosses but also to tie them to their naked torsos with ropes; some even had themselves carried along bound to decussate or X-shaped crosses. They were known as *empalados* and *aspados*, respectively (Palomero 1987:53). *Flagelantes*, for their part, wore short tunics of harsh purple cloth with an opening in the back that allowed them to receive the lashes of the *flagelantes* marching behind them. These men, also known as "Blood Brothers," never failed to provoke the awe of their fellow citizens and the horror of squeamish foreigners (cf. Bennassar 1985:40–41). If a flagellant happened to faint during his bloody ordeal, other brothers known as *conserveros* and *confortadores* were on hand to revive and anoint him with a concoction of spices and boiled wine. By all evidence, it was the growing tendency of the common people to emulate the violent acts of their social betters that led Carlos III to prohibit all excessive forms of mortification in 1769 (Ortega Sagrista 1984a:193; Palomero 1987:50–52). News of the prohibition did not reach every town in southern Spain, however; the famous *empalaos* of Valverde de la Vera (Cáceres) continue to commemorate the Passion by having their arms roped to a rough-hewn wooden beam slung across their shoulders. While their friends and relatives console and encourage them, the *empalaos* wander through the streets in severe pain every Good Friday (Pérez Gallego 1986:17).

In Seville, *cofrades* I spoke with agreed that the most rigorous Holy Week penitence of all is, paradoxically, to stay home during the entire week (thereby sacrificing the emotion, the fellowship, the music, the bejeweled *Dolorosas*, the haunting *pasos* of the Crucified). When one Sevillian woman learned that her husband planned to go barefoot and take up his cross a few years ago, she fashioned a small cushion and sewed it into the side of the tunic that was to bear the burden; she earned only a scolding for her compassionate ruse (Marín 1986:88). Each, it might be observed, was playing a culturally sanctioned role: woman the comforter, man the stalwart sufferer. As I will discuss in the next chapter, popular religion in Andalusia often equates the spirit of penitence with the demands of masculinity. Women must suffer too, of course, but in a way that befits their traditional sex-role expectations.

A brief acquaintance with the history and evolution of penitential brotherhoods will help in understanding the mentality they foster. There had always been *cofradías* in the sense of associations of men or women belonging to the same guild or social class who organized themselves for recreational, professional, pious, or political purposes under the advocation of a patron saint or Virgin (Sánchez 1985:10–13). But the *Cofradías de Pasión,* organized around the cult of the crucified Christ and its annual public commemoration with ranks of flagellators, began to appear only in the final years of the fifteenth century (28–33). Scholars concur in citing the zeal of the Franciscan order as the determining factor. Many years spent as guardians of the Holy Places of the Middle East— and the fact that their founder had merited the stigmata—had inspired the friars with a special devotion to Christ's anguish; the monks became missionaries to spread the devotion throughout Europe. In city after city in Spain, notes Sánchez, historical records prove that the first *Cofradía de Pasión* was almost invariably that of the *Vera Cruz* (True Cross), with its headquarters at the local Franciscan convent or monastery (32–33).

The Passional/penitential culture of southern Spain was forged in other ways as well. In the first years of the fifteenth century another religious order, the Dominicans, organized companies of *disciplinantes* throughout the peninsula in the belief that public flagellation was good for the souls of flagellators and onlookers alike (Sánchez 1985:31–32). The same historical period witnessed the creation of the West's first *Via Crucis* (Way of the Cross) in the province of Córdoba: a holy man back from Palestine discovered a place in the Sierra Morena that closely resembled the environs of Jerusalem and set to work building chapels that symbolized the Holy Places. Early in the next century, a Sevillian nobleman returned from the Middle East and recreated the complete trajectory of Christ's Passion, beginning with his own house and ending at the outskirts of Seville (Christian 1976:67–68; Sánchez 1985:33). In the centuries that followed, the *Via Crucis* became one of Andalusia's favorite Lenten rituals. The benign climate allowed the pious procession to take place as early as Ash Wednesday of each year. In Jaén, for example, the Third Order of the Franciscans officiated a Lenten Way of the Cross that lasted until the twentieth century. Friars led multitudes of black-veiled women and their children through stations marked by rough stone crosses, all uphill in lonely surroundings to a small shrine housing a venerated image of *Nuestra Señora de los Dolores.* Despite its stark simplicity— or perhaps because of it—the ritual was enormously popular (López

Pérez 1987:26–30). The Franciscans, by the way, had doubled the number of "stations" in the seventeenth century (Palomero 1987:102).

The penitential ethos was given new impetus in the latter part of the eighteenth century by fiery preachers and missionaries. In the forefront once again, the Franciscans reaped their greatest successes in the south, as it turns out, to the point that the eloquent Fray Diego de Cádiz came to be known as "the Apostle of Andalusia" (Melgar and Marín 1987:15). The friars practiced a particularly effective form of street theatre in order to drive home their message of repentance. Walking barefoot with downcast eyes, they brandished large crucifixes while one of their number sounded a bell and recited *saetas penetrantes* in a clamorous voice (13–14). These *saetas,* or arrows, were short formulas designed to strike contrition into the hearts of their hearers. Examples: .

Dios vengará sus ofensas el día que menos piensas.	God will avenge his offenses the day you least think.
El deleite pasó luego y sin fin durará el fuego.	Pleasure passed by quickly and fire will last forever.
En asco y horror acaba todo lo que el mundo alaba.	In disgust and horror ends all that the world praises.

　　[14–15]

The lugubrious epigrams of the Franciscans were influential over the practices of the *hermandades de ánimas.* The brothers of these ubiquitous associations took it upon themselves to warn *specific* sinners of their impending doom. Marching at night through deserted streets, they would pause in front of the mansion of some notorious libertine to chant their *saetas del pecado mortal:*

Hombre que estás en pecado, si esta noche murieras mira bien a donde fueras.	Man in a state of sin, if you died tonight think of where you would go.
De parte de Dios te aviso que trates de confesarte si no quieres condenarte.	On behalf of God I warn you that you try to make confession if you do not wish to be damned.

　　[16]

For one historian, Fray Diego and his contemporaries were reactionary, fear-mongering demagogues, determined to reverse even the lukewarm reforms of Carlos III and prevent a French-style corruption of Spanish life, customs, and morals; some of the preachers even flaunted skulls and paintings of hellish torments during their marathon mass meetings (Gómez Marín 1972:60–61). But why did they succeed? What was it that made Andalusians particularly receptive to firebrand missionaries like Fray Diego? Why did people in the south maintain and build onto the penitential devotions that languished in other parts of Spain? The Franciscans sang their *saetas* all over the peninsula, but only in the south were they incorporated into popular oral tradition (Gómez Pérez 1984:35–38). To this day in Andalusia, the notion that death is essentially a punishment remains deeply entrenched (García Díaz 1980:73–76). Several possible answers suggest themselves. For example, perhaps Andalusians were bigger sinners and therefore had greater need of repentance. Fanciful as the thought may seem, we do have solid evidence that men of the south excelled at the Spanish sin par excellence: pride.

In their all-consuming concern with honor, Spaniards revealed not so much an inborn personality trait as the legacy of a warlike caste that had subjugated the Moors, conquered the New World, and ruled the largest empire since Rome. Eventually Spain was to be, in Elliott's phrase, "the victim of its own history" (1972:247), as the ethos forged and reinforced by success failed to adapt to changing times. The "Calderonian" sense of honor constitutes an outstanding example of the many cultural values that remained in place and were even exacerbated during the decline and fall of the Spanish Empire. By the early seventeenth century, a permanent climate of violence had installed itself in just that region of Spain where young honor-obsessed aristocrats had always been a law unto themselves: Andalusia. The scions of the noble families of Córdoba, Jaén, Baeza, Ubeda, Andújar, and elsewhere went nowhere without a cape and dagger—literally—and a mind to spill blood at the slightest affront of a real or imaginary nature (Caro Baroja 1964:419–431; Bennassar 1985:207–208, 219).

As Caro reminds us, the barbarous dualists of decadent Spain, present in all social classes by the nineteenth century, were nevertheless *believers* (1985:443–452). The centuries-long period of violent honor squabbles was simultaneously the period that witnessed the consolidation of the *Cofradías de Pasión*. The early people of the Passion were extremely passionate people, people whose passion led them frequently into sin. When they did, deeply cathartic religious structures were in place to assuage their guilt and orient their penitence. Sometimes they even sinned *during*

The penitents of Seville's *Hermandad de Santa Genoveva* carry their crosses for twelve hours on Holy Monday.

penitence. In 1679 one Sevillian aristocrat was murdered by another as they marched through the streets with their brothers in a Holy Week *Estación de Penitencia* (Moreno 1985b : 40). Another Holy Week in Jaén a century earlier had supplied the ritual setting for even worse violence: dagger-wielding members of the *Pontificia y Real Congregación del Santísimo Cristo de la Vera Cruz* ambushed their archrivals of the *Cofradía de las Cinco Llagas* just as the latter left the temple to begin their penitential station (López Pérez 1987 : 44). A similar rivalry between two other brotherhoods led to bloodshed in 1595 in the same city (124).

Such incidents demonstrate that *Semana Santa* in the south has not always responded to "orthodox religious logic," as Moreno notes with considerable understatement (1985b : 40). Innumerable episcopal warnings provide indirect evidence that in many ways the penitential brotherhoods were a continuation of politics by other means, vehicles for violence, one-upmanship, conspicuous consumption, vanity, lasciviousness, and all of the other flaws of Golden Age society in general and Andalusian society in particular. There are historical grounds, therefore, for hypothesizing that the men of Andalusia were great sinners and therefore had greater need of penitential catharsis. It could also be argued, however, that it was the very existence of efficient means of catharsis that incited them to sin with greater enthusiasm. These two unprovable propositions can readily combine to form a vicious dialetical circle that takes us no closer to the logic of Passional penitence itself.

Ideally, penitence is preceded by repentance, sincere contrition for harm done; it would thus be a ritual means for the removal of the harm or at least of the guilt. Idealism apart, however, the bottom line of both contrition and penitence is the prospect of punishment: the sting of death is nothing compared with the potential sting that awaits me afterwards; the wounds I have symbolically inflicted on the person of Christ, heinous that they are, become all the more hideous in view of His Father's power to avenge them. This much is clear from the verses popularized by Fray Diego de Cádiz during one of his many missions to Andalusia:

Los tormentos y las penas
del Divino Redentor
son efectos del pecado
con que el hombre le ofendió.

The torments and the pains
of the Divine Redeemer
are effects of the sin
with which man offended Him.

Some men tape two or more crosses together and walk barefoot for an extra measure of penitence.

Santa Genoveva's *nazarenos* pause before the Plaza de España during their nine-kilometer procession, Seville's longest.

Si por las culpas ajenas
castiga Dios a su Hijo,
¿qué será del pecador,
su declarado enemigo?
   [Melgar and Marín 1987:15]

If for the faults of others
God punishes His Son,
what will happen to the sinner,
His declared enemy?

A number of premises can be distilled from this kind of discursive poetry. First, God can and will punish the sinner out of an unabashedly Old-Testament spirit of vengeance. Next, the Passion of Christ provides the symbolic yardstick by which both the gravity of the sins and the degree of punishment in store for the sinner are measured. Eternal damnation was one distinct possibility, and the suffering awaiting there had been described in great detail by preachers since the Middle Ages. It was typical to emphasize the sensorial side of it all: both fire *and* horrible cold were reserved for the skin; the nose would perceive an unbearable stench; for the ears, a cacaphony of shrill screams and blasphemies; for the eyes, the revolting view of Satan himself (Caro Baroja 1985:80–84; Rivas 1986:105). Yet Spaniards were Catholics, not Calvinists, and therefore clung to the notion that God could be moved to forgive, that no one was predestined from all time to be damned. This leads to the third and most clearly operative axiom: God can and will save the sinner if he repents. It is not that he or she should get off "scot-free," though, especially in view of what Christ had to go through to arrange the possibility of salvation in the first place. Some degree of purging pain is therefore appropriate in the world beyond the grave.

When it came to describing purgatory, unfortunately, all of the imagination and eloquence that the preachers had exercised to describe hellish torments turned into opacity and ambiguity. This only increased the anxiety of the faithful. Saint Thomas of Aquinas had surmised that, whatever the degree of the pain, it would surely be *worse* than Christ's Passion (cit. by Rivas 1986:102). And with regard to its duration, we can well imagine how unsettling it was when popes like Sixtus VI or Gregory XIII granted indulgences of 11,000 and 74,000 years, respectively (224). The raw supply of anxiety the Church had placed in circulation led to an intensified dependence on heavenly "lawyers"—the saints, the spirits of those who had already died and gone through purgatory (*ánimas*), and, above all, the Virgin Mary. They were empowered to plead a sinner's case before the Godhead and in many cases could win a reduction of the sentence.

The point I wish to emphasize about penitence is this: no matter how informed it is by sorrow, love of God, or other selfless motives, it will always contain an aspect of instrumentality. The model for all this is none other than Christ Himself—undergoing the punishment sent down by His Father, to paraphrase Fray Diego, in return for the possibility of universal pardon. Suffering of a divine or human nature, therefore, is never gratuitous. It is a tool with which to act upon Patriarchal Providence. So is death, for that matter, and here again Christ is the model; in the right circumstances, death is the most powerful redemptive instrument of all. The inner logic of penitence can thus be summarized as follows:

(1) The fact that Christ died not for His sins but for mine forces me to associate my own certain death with the possibility of a fate worse than death.

(2) In consequence I seek to undergo a self-inflicted suffering that will free my soul from sin just as Christ suffered on the Cross to free the world from sin.

(3) Finally, I enlist the help of supernatural advocates, the sacraments, and especially my fellow believers in reducing the time I will surely have to spend in purgatory.

With this we return to the *cofradía* network, for just as it was in place to structure the penitence of the brothers in this world, it also functioned as a kind of insurance policy for the penitence awaiting them after death.

> In all *cofradías* this end was present: to pray and offer suffrages, Masses, vigils, and other cults for the dead. What is more, many became *cofrades* in the hope that their suffrages would not be unheeded as they might be by their inheritors. We can affirm with complete certainty that it was the sense of security people felt in a particular *cofradía* that always maintained its member roster full, enriched it, and ensured its survival. [Sánchez 1985 : 18]

Sánchez goes on to cite Seville's *Cofradía de los Santos Angeles,* founded in the fifteenth century, as one that achieved enormous popularity through its special rituals *pro remedio animae*—for the souls of the deceased (19). It was not just the brotherhoods that benefitted from the other-worldly anxieties of the Sevillians: the entire religious infrastructure of churches, convents, shrines, and so on was involved. Here we come to yet another key connection between penitential and Passional culture, for the main liturgical means for the suffrage of souls was none other than the Mass, that is, the ritual remembrance of Christ's redemptive Passion. Testaments from the fifteenth century onward reveal, says Rivas, a "massive predilection" for this type of action *pro remedio animae* (1986:201). If one Mass was good medicine, then ten were better, or fifty, or one hundred, or more. Testaments show that preoccupation with the soul's fate grew in southern Spain as it diminished in the rest of Europe. By the eighteenth century, what might be called the Mass business was big business:

> If we apply the average number of Masses per testament (drawn from those that tell us of the number of suffrages desired) to the total of the testators, it can be defended that the quantity of Masses solicited in each of the three samplings must have approached 160,000 in 1702, 95,000 in 1750, and 110,000 in 1799, calculating with the utmost prudence. [227]

These statistics are for Seville alone.

Logically, all of these Masses had to be paid for. There was even a price scale. By the end of the century, Masses celebrated on the very day of your death were costlier since they were assumed to be more efficacious (175–176). In addition, High Masses (which were sung) were worth more than Low Masses (which were merely recited). Rivas provides invaluable statistics regarding who ordered how many Masses to be said or sung when and where in eighteenth century Seville. He breaks down the suffrages by the sex and profession of the testator as well as the religious centers and orders most favored by the bequests. The Franciscans, significantly, were always first in the preferences of the Sevillians, followed by the Augustinians, the Dominicans, the Carmelites, the Trinitarians, and the Jesuits (179–194).

Lest it be thought that these statistics apply only to the wealthy, Rivas underlines at the beginning of his study that the testament itself was one of the rites of salvation, an instrument of religious praxis more than a legal one (21). The 908 testaments he examines are broadly representative of society as a whole; they present us with the dying desires of artisans, tradesmen, doctors, lawyers, bureaucrats, peasants, and domestic employees, as well as members of the nobility and the clergy (46). Nor should the validity of his conclusions be confined to Seville; studies by Pascua (1984), Pulido (1983), and Reder (1983) document the same mentality during the same time period for the cities of Cádiz, Huelva, and Málaga, respectively.

The wealth of a given testator was the major factor in the *number* of Masses he could bequeath. And for the wealthiest, there existed the institution of *misas perpetuas,* whereby a certain *cofradía* or religious order was charged with the celebration of Masses for the sake of one's soul until the end of time, literally. One opulent testatrix, for example, donated a mansion to the *Hermandad del Santísimo Sacramento y Animas Benditas del Purgatorio* with the understanding that the brothers would schedule, in her own words, "a High Mass with a deacon and a subdeacon on the altar of Santa Rosa, every year, perpetually, forevermore, on the feast day of Santa Ana" (cit. by Rivas 1986:196–197). An even wealthier— or guiltier—man ordered a Mass to be sung on the first Tuesday of every month at the altar of the chapel of San Antonio with, as he put it, "candles, ministers, incense, organ, and the other solemnities," for which he bequeathed a capital of 6,000 *reales* that would yield an annual interest of 180 *reales* to pay for the Masses, *saecula saeculorum* (197). These legacies, along with others, which specify the exact time of day and the most visible altar, lead Rivas to wonder whether the testators were more interested in being remembered by society or in pleasing God (200). Some even managed to kill two birds with one stone, as it were, by using their testaments to set up a *capellanía* for the recital of fifty or one hundred Masses per year forever and simultaneously naming some needy ecclesiastical relative to be the *capellán* (201).

The *Estación de Penitencia,* the "insurance policy" of the *cofradía,* the belief in the magic efficacy of the Mass that testaments evidence, the ritual of the testament itself—these are the instruments of salvation I have dealt with so far. It is in the same context of instrumental piety that we can understand the *Hermandades de la Santa Caridad,* which reached such an unprecedented degree of development in the south. Unlike a *Cofradía de Pasión,* organized to render cult to the Crucified, or a *Cofradía de Animas* that specialized in the recovery of souls and rituals for the dead, a *Cofradía de Caridad* was designed to be of benefit to the poor— chiefly through almsgiving, the construction and maintenance of hospitals, the distribution of bread, and other charitable acts (Sánchez 1985: 19–20). This typology should not obscure the reality: no penitential brotherhood failed to be involved in charity in some way, no charitable brotherhood failed to render cult to the Passion, and neither neglected the souls of the deceased. A great many *cofradías* of different types had their own hospitals; the *Cofradía de la Vera Cruz* of Jaén, for example, had the foresight to establish one in the same year (1550) that its members were getting into knife fights (López Pérez 1984 : 105). The structural distinction introduced by Moreno is perhaps more apropos than the typological one Sánchez uses. In contrast to the majority of sixteenth- and seventeenth-century *cofradías,* which were "vertical" and included members from a variety of social classes, the *Cofradías de Caridad* were strictly "horizontal" and drew their *cofrades* from the cream of the nobility—who in addition had to prove that they were "Old Christians" completely free of Semitic blood (Moreno 1985a : 53–55). Stringent entrance requirements went hand in hand with illustrious patrons. In Córdoba, the title of "Royal" was bestowed on the *Hermandad y Cofradía del Señor de la Caridad* by two of its highly placed *cofrades,* Ferdinand and Isabella. Charles V and Philip II belonged to the same brotherhood, as well as six bishops, ten General Inquisitors, the *Gran Capitán* Gonzalo de Córdoba, and a long list of *condes, duques, marqueses,* and so on. For over 300 years this blue-blooded group sponsored the Hospital of the Holy Charity of the Lord in Córdoba (Gutiérrez 1978 : 152–153). Of the many *Cofradías de Caridad* in the south—Sánchez asserts that they were peculiar to Andalusia (1985 : 20)—the most famous was the *Hermandad de la Santa Caridad* of Seville. Its most celebrated *hermano* was undoubtedly Miguel Mañara (1627–1679), thought by some to have been the real-life replica of Don Juan himself. A brief review of his career will demonstrate that truth is stranger than fiction, and, more important, allow me to recapitulate the many aspects of penitential culture I have dealt with and to introduce several others.

Miguel Mañara

To understand Mañara is to understand the spirit of the Counter-Reformation as well as the dynamics of Spanish/Andalusian decadence. His life and works unfold themselves against a backdrop of racism, rigid concepts of honor, absurd institutional prejudices against commerce, and the resultant multiplication of socioeconomic crises of all kinds. It is during Mañara's lifetime that the great "divorce" between Spain and the rest of Europe takes place, the period that witnesses the consolidation of attitudes that will eventually deprive Spain of an industrial revolution

(Elliott 1972:246–252; Bennassar 1985:221–224; Nadal 1975:226–245). In the last analysis, to understand Mañara is to grasp the essential points of the ideology that will hold sway in the most "backward" region of Spain for centuries to come.

Mañara might not have been a recognized aristocrat at all had it not been for the diligence of his father, Tomás Mañara Leca, a native of Corsica who made a fortune in Peru and subsequently settled in Seville to put it to good use. In theory those who had engaged in "vile" commercial pursuits, to use the contemporary adjective, could not accede to titles of nobility for themselves or for their offspring; but the Spanish crown's inordinate need for new sources of revenue and Tomás Mañara's superior ability to spend eventually enabled him to place his sons in the privileged pureblood ranks of the Order of Santiago (firstborn Juan Antonio) and the Order of Calatrava (Miguel). The insignia of "the true and perfect military religion" were bestowed upon the latter when he was eight years old (Granero 1981:32–55; Martín 1981:41–45).

In the meantime his father had not neglected to cultivate the other great status symbols of the highborn—houses, carriages, art, servants, and so on. His annual income of 30,000 ducats had helped him to become a member of the *Hermandad de San Pedro Mártir,* which was closely allied with, if not identical to, the Inquisition. Thus he belonged to a select group of fifty men whose blood had been certified clean, with no trace of descendence from Jews, Moors, heretics, or converts, and he was thereby guaranteed access to every other honor or office he coveted for himself or his sons (Granero 1981:27–28). To complete the picture, both Tomás and his wife were patrons of the Franciscans, annually assigning 375,000 *maravedís* to their Saint Bonaventure School in Seville. The school chapel received the bones of Tomás when he died in 1648. His wife, Jerónima, followed him three years later, leaving a will that contained several "pious legacies" (*mandas pías*). She arranged to have no fewer than 4,000 Masses said for her soul in twelve different convents, left a fair share of money to the servants, and requested to be buried "with as much moderation, modesty, and humility as possible" (cit. by Martín 1981:38). And she took special pains to shorten her husband's pains in purgatory:

> It is my will that every year perpetually forevermore, on the 29th of April, feast of San Pedro Mártir, which is the day my husband and lord Tomás Mañara

died, the guardian father of Saint Bonaventure School give, one year, 12 woolen blankets to 12 poor women, whomsoever the aforementioned guardian father selects, and the following year 12 suits of clothing to 12 poor men, likewise whomsoever the aforementioned guardian father chooses, with each one costing as much as 10 ducats . . . , on condition that the same day they are given blankets or suits of clothing the aforementioned guardian father obliges them to hear Mass and pray for me in the aforementioned Saint Bonaventure School and for the soul of Tomás Mañara, my husband. [38]

How could Miguel Mañara's mother be certain that there would always and forevermore be twelve poor women and twelve poor men to receive her donations and be pressed to express their gratitude with prayers *pro remedio animae*? This question touches upon one of the major ideological premises of Andalusian society and is best answered in the context of the life and works of her son, who eventually proved to be charity personified.

Miguel became the heir to the family fortune upon his mother's death (his elder brother Juan Antonio had died years before, ordering 11,000 Masses to be said for his soul). As Father Martín points out, the young Mañara's position could not have been more enviable—twenty-four years old, Knight of Calatrava, married to a beautiful noblewoman, fabulously rich (1981:38–39). For the next ten years, apparently, he enjoyed himself to the hilt, living the life that his great wealth and status permitted. The sudden death of his wife in 1661 was to mark the turning point. Mañara lapsed into a state of profound melancholy, exchanged society for seclusion, and meditated obsessively on the fragility of life and the deceits of the world. A year later, wandering alone on horseback alongside the Guadalquivir River, he chanced to meet several brothers of the small but select *Hermandad de la Santa Caridad*. This *cofradía* had charged itself with the pious task of burying the nameless. In many cases they were vagabonds, cripples, and beggars who had literally dropped dead under some lonely bridge; sometimes they were thieves who had been cut down by the muskets of one of the vigilante-style brotherhoods responsible for civil defense (Mañara himself belonged to one). There was also a never-ending supply of corpses tossed into the river by relatives too poor to pay for a funeral. The brothers were in the midst of recovering one of these bodies when the young widower requested permission to become one of their number (Granero 1981:85–87, 96–98; Martín 1981:69–77).

The brothers were surprised, and some were doubtful. They remembered that as a youth Mañara had been vain, defiant, and even bellicose; his temperament and exaggerated sense of honor had led him into one skirmish after another. He had been, in Father Granero's words, "a violent gentleman" (56). That he might also have been a libertine is suggested by certain passages of his own testament:

> I served Babylon and the devil, its prince, with a thousand abominations, insolences, adulteries, oaths, scandals, and thefts; my sins and evildoings are numberless and only the great wisdom of God can number them, and His infinite patience suffer them, and His infinite mercy forgive them. [Cit. by Martín 1981:49]

Mañara's haughty reputation and heartfelt confession, along with his morbid obsession with death and corruption, formed the basis of a popular tradition that would become even more popular in the nineteenth century, thanks to the collusion of French Romantics and Spanish *costumbristas* (Bonachera and Piñero 1985:109–120; Caro Baroja 1979:122–124; Granero 1981:1–8; Martín 1981:9–15). As soon as Mañara became known as a Don Juan it was only a matter of time before he was identified as *the* Don Juan, the historical basis for Tirso de Molina's seminal seventeenth-century drama. The literal-minded scholars who made this hasty faux pas are to be trusted no further than the literary-minded scholars of today who treat Don Juan as pure fiction. The existence of a whole class of spoiled, violent, honor-obsessed Andalusian aristocrats is not open to dispute (Caro Baroja 1964:444–445; Bennassar 1985: 194–199); as I discussed earlier, feuds and bloodshed were possible even during the rituals of Holy Week. To this can be added the patriarchal identification of female honor with purity and the culturewide preoccupation with death and the afterlife. It was no accident that a country like Spain gave birth to a myth like that of Don Juan. By the same token, the bizarre reality of a Don Miguel requires no fictional embellishment.

In truth it would have been unusual if Mañara had *not* behaved with the arrogance and temerity that were the privileged trademarks of his caste. If the *cofrades* of the *Santa Caridad* had their misgivings about admitting him to their ranks, it was due to the humanitarian nature of their duties: how could a man of Mañara's temperament submit himself to the discipline and humility required for the burial of the penniless? Admit him they did, nevertheless, partly to concede him the benefit of the doubt

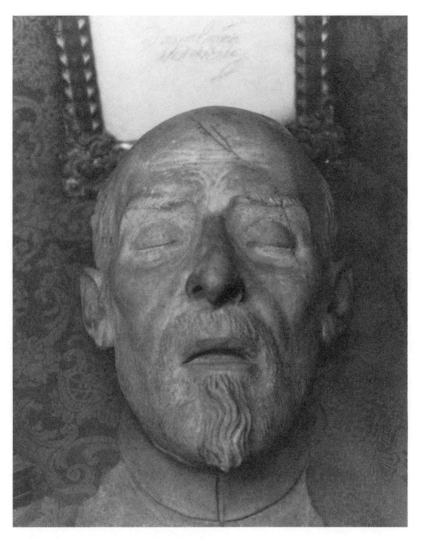
The death mask of Miguel Mañara (Church of the Santa Caridad).

Completed in 1674, five years before Mañara's death, the Church of the Santa Caridad is still headquarters to the *hermandad* of the same name.

and mostly because he fulfilled the entrance requirements. He had never exercised a vile commercial pursuit, nor had he been dishonored in any way. His blood was free from Semitic or negroid taints. He certainly possessed the riches required to maintain the quality of his person. And he was more than willing to swear fidelity to the doctrine of the Immaculate Conception, the standard oath required by *cofradías* throughout Andalusia. All of these requirements are stated in Chapter 33 of the statutes of the *Hermandad* (Granero 1981 : 100–104).

To the surprise and delight of the brothers, Mañara immediately volunteered for a task that would have gone against the grain of any Spanish aristocrat. Beginning in January of 1663, he begged for alms along the *cofradía*'s regular funeral route. The satisfaction of his fellows turned into awe and veneration over the following years as Mañara proved that his appetite for humility was second to none. He fasted and flagellated himself daily. He pleaded with his brothers to mock him with demeaning nicknames. He wore a harsh scapulary that rubbed and irritated his skin twenty-four hours a day. He engaged in penitential retreats at the Franciscan Convent of San Pablo that made him seriously ill (Martín 1981 : 75, 120, 127, 183).

Mañara's most enduring penitence, however, was not his self-mortification but his acts of charity, to the extent that he is still revered in Seville as "the father of the poor." In effect, Don Miguel did more than any other person to further a penitential concept of charity, which provided a much-needed safety net for the needy even as it served to shore up the Andalusian caste system itself.

Mañara did not invent the concept, of course; the poor had always fulfilled an important symbolic function for Christians (Caro Baroja 1985 : 461–480). What made him so influential was the clarity and vigor with which he promoted the spiritual advantages of almsgiving. In a celebrated epistle, which Father Martín dubs "the Carta Magna of Charity," Mañara marshals his arguments. God has created different social stations, he affirms, and has assigned a particular function to each. God wants to see the hermit living in solitude, the professor teaching the ignorant, and the rich man distributing alms in the hospital. Where would we be without the poor? Christ has promised His kingdom to those who help the poor. Charity is more in the almsgiver's interest than it is in the receiver's. No charitable man or woman has ever had a bad death (cit. by Martín

1981:136–139). Mañara's public relations skills, along with his willingness to put his own great fortune at the disposal of the *Hermandad,* played a large part in his election as *Hermano Mayor* less than a year after his admittance (89–93). From then until his death in 1679 he worked to involve the "best people" in his charitable projects. He was enormously successful in attracting counts, dukes, and other titled nobility from all over Andalusia into the *cofradía.* Sister brotherhoods, if I may be allowed the expression, were founded in Utrera, Cádiz, Carmona, Gibraltar, Coria del Río, Rota, Marchena, Antequera, Ayamonte, and other towns in the south (Martín 1981:135–136; Granero 1981:203–206).

Significantly, many of the new chapters doubled as *Cofradías de Pasión.* Mañara had already found Christ's sufferings to be of great use in "reducing" his brothers and instilling in them a Franciscan-like attitude of chastened humility (Martín 1981:114). The corps of "penitential brothers" that he created to serve the poor in his hospital was especially devoted to the crucified Christ. As the *Hermano Mayor,* it was his duty to read aloud from Passional texts on certain Fridays, an exercise that never failed to cause him acute emotional distress (Granero 1981:146). It was the suffering Christ, after all, as He manifested Himself in the suffering poor, that constituted the ostensible motor of Mañara's every act. The indigent sick were brought to hospital "in the name of the Lord Himself, Who suffered such utter poverty for us." When they died they were buried "in the name of our Lord Jesus Christ, poor and defunct" (cit. by Granero 1981:217).

It seems that the more wretched the condition of a given poor or sick man, the more Mañara venerated him. A witness in his beatification hearings testified that one day Don Miguel knelt down before a man under treatment for "an ulcer so disgusting that one could hardly look at it." Drawing near he kissed the sore, filling his own face with pus and provoking the admiration of onlookers (cit. by Granero 1981:136). He got down on his knees on another occasion to reverently drink the vomit of a dying beggar (Martín 1981:185). With facts like these, fiction becomes superfluous. For all of his wealth and apparent autonomy, Mañara had managed to find his way to what La Barre called "the bottom of the sadomasochistic heap" (1972:372).

To do anything for the sick poor, then, was to do it for Christ. To do it for Christ was to do it for one's own salvation, in the last analysis. Behind every charitable act, or at least inseparable from it, lay the fear of the pains of purgatory. To help the poor was to assure one "time off for good behavior" in the penal colony of the afterlife. The plaque set into the wall in the patio of the Hospital of Charity in Seville is unambiguous in this respect:

1,740 DAYS OF INDULGENCE ARE GRANTED BY SEVERAL MOST EMINENT, MOST EXCELLENT, AND MOST ILLUSTRIOUS PRELATES TO THE FAITHFUL WHO PRACTICE IN THIS HOUSE ANY OF THE FOLLOWING ACTS: FOR CONDUCTING THE SOUP KETTLE AND DISTRIBUTING BREAD TO THE POOR; FOR EACH PLATE THEY HAND OUT; FOR GIVING THANKS TO GOD AFTER THE MEAL; FOR EACH TIME THEY REPRESS ANGER, EXERCISE PATIENCE, DEDICATE THEM-SELVES TO THE IMPROVEMENT OF THE HOSPITAL, AND CONSOLE AND GIVE HOLY ADVICE TO THE POOR SICK. FOR THE LATTER AS WELL AS FOR THE FAITHFUL: FOR EACH ACT OF FAITH-HOPE-AND-CHARITY OR CONTRITION THAT THEY PROFFER; EACH MASS THEY HEAR, EACH HAIL MARY THAT THEY PRAY DURING THE HOLY ROSARY, EACH TIME THEY SAY BLESSED AND PRAISED BE THE LOVE OF GOD OR LET IT BE FOR THE LOVE OF GOD; AND FOR EACH ONE OF THE STATIONS OF THE CROSS. ESPECIALLY FOR THE POOR: FOR EACH COMMUNION THEY RECEIVE; AND FOR EACH TIME THEY STIFLE ANGER AND IMPATIENCE, OFFERING TO GOD THEIR PAINS AND THEIR HARDSHIPS.

Thus, poverty and sickness themselves were loaded with penitential power, as long as they were borne with resignation and a sense of sacrifice. Suffering is confirmed, once again, as the most effective way to gain heavenly favors or limit heavenly wrath. The value of this doctrine in the control of hungry masses can scarcely be overestimated.

The chances for winning a reduction of one's sentence in purgatory were actually limitless, as limitless as the numbers of poor people that the decadent economy of southern Spain had begun to churn out. The situation was already critical during the boyhood of Mañara: on the 13th of April 1636, Seville was host to a miserable procession of 20,000 beggars—men, women, and children. In 1648 some 6,000 hungry citizens of Granada revolted and stormed the town hall under the sacred banner of San Cecilio; a massive distribution of bread by a concerned aristocrat was crucial in mollifying the crowds (Martín 1981:29; Caro Baroja 1985: 475–476). Things were to continue along the same vein throughout the reign of the inept Philip IV. It was not always easy for the downtrodden to control their anger and impatience, even at the risk of adding to their time in purgatory.

Beggars were only the tip of the iceberg of poverty; they were the "declared" or "recognized" poor. There were also great numbers of *pobres vergonzantes,* those with too much *vergüenza* (pride/shame) to beg and who preferred to harbor their hunger in secret (Caro Baroja 1985: 471–472). The waning years of the Golden Age were not lacking in noble-born individuals who literally preferred to starve to death before begging—or working, for that matter (cf. Elliott 1972:246–247). Conditions were right for the steady growth of a vast criminal underworld and the proliferation of *pícaros* of all kinds. There was even a special subgenre of picaresque literature that narrated the stratagems of vagabonds and beggars. The "Establishment" came to wonder how many of the beggars were truly poor and how many were merely feigning poverty to get something for nothing. As Caro points out, however, it seems highly unlikely that anyone could have opted for the career of "poor man" without starting from poverty in the first place (1985:477–478).

In the meantime, the action of the law was harsh and implacable. This kept Mañara's *cofradía* busy with its other traditional activity—assistance to criminals condemned to die by hanging or strangling (*garrote vil*). They too were representatives of Jesus, argued Don Miguel, and the brothers did everything in their power to ensure that the reprobate died a proper death. They collected alms on the way to the gallows, prayed for his soul, provided for any widows or children, and gathered up the limbs of those who had been drawn and quartered (Martín 1981:130–135). Capital punishment as spectacle was not unique to Spain, but it was in Spain and especially in the south that it came to be surrounded with the baroque pomp of a religious ritual. The moment of death had already become, for all social classes, the supreme moment of life; the state of one's mind upon crossing the "great threshold" was considered crucial to the salvation of the soul. In fact, one of the great baroque formulations of the uses of death was Mañara's own *Discurso de la Verdad* (1671). A good death was already credited with the power to cancel out a bad life; the fact that a bad man's body was being given the supreme punishment did not exempt the civil-religious authorities from every attention possible to his soul. In one way or another Christ served as the model for all of the above—the original "criminal," condemned to death by the law, whose execution was/is a never-ending source of grace for humanity. To those who censured the ritual accompaniments as excessive or who dared to doubt that a hanged felon could represent Christ, Mañara replied that "there are two considerations in a man put to death: one, that of punished delinquent; the other, that of the helpless poor man. And since in the second Our Lord is represented, any demonstration that is made in this respect falls short" (cit. by Martín 1981:134).

The considerable revenues of the *Hermandad de la Santa Caridad* disappeared into the black hole of Sevillian poverty almost as soon as they were donated. How to distribute the alms with equity was a constant problem for Mañara. At one time he was so vexed over what to do with a gift of 500 *reales* that he asked God to guide the horse he was riding to the proper beneficiary. After an apparently aimless ride the horse led Mañara to a house full of naked and hungry children (Martín 1981: 145–146). Don Miguel's confidence in providence was absolute and at crucial moments it seemed to be justified. When the needy had been reduced to eating cats during the famine of 1678, one of the wealthiest men of the city, who had never been known to give a *real* to anyone, died and left his entire fortune to Mañara for the benefit of the poor. The *Hermano Mayor* was content but not surprised: he had already dreamed that a huge sum of money would be coming his way and had even drawn up plans for spending it. With these God-sent funds the *Santa Caridad* was able to distribute 20,000 loaves of bread per day for eight months (Granero 1981:172–175; Martín 1981:186–188).

Instrumental though it might have been, the kind of penitential charity promoted by Mañara was the one hope of the destitute of his age—and the ages to come, for that matter. Small wonder that his passing in 1679 provoked genuine and massive outpourings of grief. The epitaph he had ordered to be placed on his sepulcher was to be the most memorable expression of his overweening humility:

AQVI YAZEN LOS HVESSOS Y CENIZAS
DEL PEOR HOMBRE QVE A AVIDO EN EL MVNDO
RVEGVEN A DIOS POR EL.

HERE LIE THE BONES AND ASHES
OF THE WORST MAN THERE HAS BEEN IN THE WORLD
PRAY TO GOD FOR HIM.

A devil's advocate might conjecture that all of the arrogance of the Andalusian aristocrat had secretly remained intact in Mañara's desire to be first in humility. This interpretation would find little favor with his principal biographers, however, convinced as they are that Mañara's self-abnegation was genuine and wholly devoid of selfish interest. Yet many facts assembled by Father Granero and Father Martín in their exacting studies can be cited in support of an alternative viewpoint. The latter admits, for instance, that the brothers who had tried to block Mañara's entry into the *Santa Caridad* proved to be substantially correct in their suspicions. They did indeed end up under the total domination of the passionate newcomer, for once they realized that he was the instrument of God's will, none dared to contradict him (122). As if his appetite for punishment were not enough to convince them of his holiness, on at least one occasion Mañara explicitly attributed knowledge of divine intentions to himself (Granero 1981:211). Moreover, during the same period in which the obsession with subverting his own honor reached alarming proportions, he never passed up a chance to vindicate God's, sometimes vehemently (213). Mañara was no respecter of persons when going about his Father's business, as numerous nobles and even the King himself found out (133–135).

A devil's advocate with a rudimentary knowledge of psychoanalysis might even introduce the word "paranoia" into his arguments. One day, during a discussion of the sorry state of the nation, Mañara dumbfounded a friar by telling him that he alone (Mañara) was to blame for the great calamities of Spain's decadence, that he ought to have a millstone hung around his neck and be tossed into the Guadalquivir (142–143). Like Freud's Rat Man, the great man inside of Mañara was bent on vanquishing the equally great criminal sharing the same body (cf. Siebers 1983:121). Like La Barre's vatic, Don Miguel seemed to vacillate "between two poles, whether to be or to bow down to omnipotence" (1972: 372). As he struggled to make his life one long act of self-sacrifice, Mañara never lost sight of the supreme model of the same—Christ. All of his acts of servility and discipline were nothing compared to what the Savior had gone through. In a revealing fantasy, Mañara confided to a brother that it would have been a "great consolation" to find himself seated on a donkey and being whipped like a common thief through the streets of Seville (cit. by Granero 1981:219).

In effect, few mortals could have topped Don Miguel down there at the bottom. It was never difficult for Mañara to have his confessor "order" him to do what he wanted to do anyway—and always on a Friday. Praying for several hours at a time, kissing the feet of the lowborn, begging his fellow *cofrades* to repute him as a scoundrel, flinging himself on the floor to be symbolically stepped on by them all—these were some of the ways by which God wanted Mañara to learn humility (Granero 1981:146–148). He was happy to let himself be physically or verbally abused by the many ragged beggars who were unable to accept their lot with resignation (176–178). What might be called the practical benefits of penitential self-mortification were demonstrated in 1672 with the "voluntary" baptism of a large group of captured Moors. Mañara had called the brothers into a brain-storming session and had urged each to think of some appropriate sacrifice that could be offered up to win over the heathens. Not surprisingly, the *Hermano Mayor* outthought them all: for every Moor that opted to be born again, he promised to kiss the "putrid sore" of a sick man. He was able to keep his promise exactly forty-three times by his own count (Granero 1981:189–190; Martín 1981:141).

If the first part of his life was reminiscent of the intemperance of Don Juan, the second part recalls the penitential excesses recounted in other Spanish legends. One thinks of Don Rodrigo climbing into his own tomb with a venomous serpent, or Don Teodosio wandering through hill and valley in chains and sackcloth. The pious legends of Spain tend to prolong the familiar medieval pattern, wherein episodes of horrible sin (usually of an Oedipal nature) are followed by periods of inhuman mortification and heavenly pardon (Mitchell 1988:75–92). But again, who needs fiction? In Spain there was no lack of real flesh-and-blood men who went from violence to sanctity over the course of their lives—Don Tiburcio de Redin, Miguel de Castro, Don Juan Diego, the Duke of Estrada, and others (Caro Baroja 1985:455–456). In Spanish history, as well as folklore and literature, passion and penitence go together.

In the last analysis, not even the most diabolical advocate could write Mañara off as a quixotic masochist. Even if his compassion can be read as upside-down pride, or simple terror over God's punitive might, it was clearly preferable to no compassion at all. Over a half-million ducats distributed to the hungry and the naked from 1671 to 1679 speak for themselves, since "by their works you shall know them." We can no more accept Mañara's claim that he was the worst man on earth than the weeping poor he left behind him. The heroic spirituality he exemplified was one of the few counterweights available for the injustice of caste society in southern Spain.

At one time or another of his life, Mañara embodied most of the values and ideas of his society. The most critical period of Spanish decadence, the final great flowering of baroque art and literature, the culmination of the Counter-Reformation—all these were contemporaneous with his life. His personality readily lends itself to hagiographical or novelistic treatments. The bare facts are novelistic enough, however, and frequently attain the category of an *esperpento*. That Mañara was a true "neurotic personality of his time" is evidenced by the compelling influence he exercised over all sectors of society and especially the leading ones. Neither this influence nor the mentality he incarnated so perfectly went to the grave with him. As any historian can attest, the ancien régime died a very slow death in Spain and enjoyed numerous periods of partial recovery. If I have dealt with Mañara at length it is because of the invaluable light he sheds on Andalusian culture in the eighteenth, nineteenth, and twentieth centuries.

The Symbiosis of Rich and Poor

Spain was by no means impervious to the intellectual currents of the Enlightenment. Those who truly wanted to study the nature of the physical world or the new doctrines of political science were generally able to obtain books and maintain contacts (Bennassar 1985:223). The problem, it seems, is that few wanted to. There was little French-style "de-Christianization" in the Iberian Peninsula, and none whatsoever in sensitive areas like death and the afterlife. The groundbreaking studies of Andalusian testaments that I referred to earlier reveal that the preoccupation with life's final moments actually grew in the south during the same century that it was diminishing elsewhere. Penitence, charity, *cofradías*— all of these retained their relevance in consequence.

The two chief pillars of instrumental penitence after death remained in place: Masses and charitable bequests (*mandas pías*). The first, as discussed earlier, sought to reduce the pains of purgatory through the repeated ritual remembrance of Christ's Passion. Rivas underlines the role played by these suffrages in the maintenance of the religious infrastructure and its beneficiaries:

A source of income that must have meant something on the order of 40 million *reales* throughout the century just in the suffrages of those who made a will (less than 20% of the population) is no laughing matter. Now we understand better the enterprising presence of religious personnel at the bedside of the dying person, and why the discourse on death was not watered down in the 18th century. [227]

Alms, the other great antidote for the terrors of the afterlife, will become ever more identified with the aristocracy and will thus retain its status appeal for all those intent on emulating the aristocratic life-style, that is, the commercial classes. Rivas affirms that the continuing prestige of baroque death ritual in general and penitential charity in particular is what most confirms the hypothesis of "bourgeois betrayal" advanced by economic historians of the south (230). This betrayal probably secured the loyalty of the most destitute classes. While other European nations were busy "rationalizing" poverty by persecuting beggars and slapping the poor into workhouses, the Spanish needy continued to enjoy the respect and protection of the powerful. One of the most prestigious nineteenth-century travelers to Spain, the Englishman George Borrow, was amazed at the kindness with which beggars were treated throughout the peninsula; he never saw any of them being insulted, kicked, or spat upon as in certain other nations of Europe (cit. by Bennassar 1985:114–117). The reader will not be surprised to learn that one of the most forthright denunciations of the "rational" approach to poverty had already been penned by Miguel Mañara. The progressive municipal authorities of Madrid had funded a pilot program, as it were, by which the unsightly poor were to be swept from the streets and confined against their will in the "*Casa del Ave María.*" Mañara was indignant:

> These very beloved brothers that you keep secluded for political purposes, are they not the porters of the goods of the rich to heaven? Is it not by their hand that we store up our riches in heaven? Then how can you hide them from the eyes of the wealthy? The ulcerated poor man shouting on the street corner, does he not often move the hearts of the rich? Do you wish to hide the spectacle of the poor so that the little warmth of charity left in your souls is extinguished altogether? [Cit. by Granero 1981:118]

Throughout the eighteenth and nineteenth centuries, the poor of Andalusia retained a large measure of the socioreligious functionality Mañara had promoted so brilliantly. Evidence of this can be found in art.

Murillo, the painter Mañara picked to portray his ideology of charity (in paintings that decorate the *Iglesia de la Santa Caridad* of Seville), was far and away the artist most admired by the nineteenth-century *costumbristas* of the same city. They appropriated his luminous images of beggars and orphans and placed them at the disposal of a sincerely sentimental upper middle class that viewed charity as its special prerogative (Reina 1979: 70–72). One of the painters, Esquivel, produced a work that succinctly captures the pious view of almsgiving that the affluent had made their own. Titled *La Caridad,* the painting shows a well-dressed couple looking on with satisfaction as their golden-curled daughter hands out bread to a trio of beggars whose faces are illuminated with expressions of saintly gratitude. The allegory now hangs in Mañara's hospital.

The urban development of Seville provides further mute testimony of the persistence of established social and mental patterns. Throughout the nineteenth century and well into the twentieth, the traditionally aristocratic south side remained the choice area for all projects of prestige— new gardens, parks, *paseos,* the splendid Plaza de España built for the World Exposition of 1929. During the same period, the poor neighborhoods of the north side were the beneficiaries of all of the charitable construction projects: the orphan asylum, the school for deaf-mutes, the home for ex-prostitutes (*casa de arrepentidas*), and the insane asylum were built to accompany the leprosy hospital and the cemetery already in existence (García Ferrero 1984: 275–276).

Numerous studies have dealt with the uncanny survival of ancien régime customs and concepts in Spain and have associated them with its aborted industrial revolution and its peculiarly regressive bourgeoisie. To be sure, during the period of the war with Napoleon the *Cortes de Cádiz* proved that Spain's professional classes could be at least as liberal-minded as anywhere else in Europe. Yet they, like Napoleon, failed to take the measure of an extremely tradition-bound and monarchist peasantry in league with the wily Fernando VII—"cowardly, ignorant, and lazy, but cunning and vindictive as few men in high position have ever been" (Lovett 1965: I, 24). Carbine-toting monks with cartridge belts strapped to their chests and wildly valiant women with scissors struck terror into the hearts of the regicidal French Republic's soldiers (Ropp 1962: 126–127). A fiercely independent spirit bordering on xenophobia and natural toughness can be added to the list of things Napoleon should have been told and that spelled the beginning of his end. The reactionary Fernando and his cohorts managed to keep the liberals out of power for years; when the latter finally took over, the country was bankrupt and the old lifeline of taxes and commissions from the New World colonies had ended (Nadal 1975: 25–27). To build up the treasury and keep themselves in power, the liberals opted to end aristocratic/ecclesiastic entail in a way that only worsened the traditionally unjust agricultural system. Under disentailment (*desamortización*), "serfs with land became free men without it," as well as instant allies of the ultra-Catholic and monarchist Carlist movement (62–64). Unlike anywhere else in Europe, the aristocracy actually supported disentailment and joined hands with the new class of absentee landlords created thereby. What holds for Spain holds doubly in Andalusia, where the grapevine revealed itself to be the perfect pursuit for these urban, nonprogressive bourgeoisie looking for safe investment in an export industry. Significantly, the first railroad concession in all of Spain was for the sherry route of Jerez, Rota, and Sanlúcar de Barrameda (73). In the meantime, Andalusia's middle-class landowners were liquidated by the new laws, and the landless day-laborers (*jornaleros*) who were already growing in number in the eighteenth century became the most numerous class in the nineteenth (83). These unlucky masses were not to be absorbed by industry as had happened in other nations. As Nadal notes, cheap labor is a necessary but insufficient precondition for development (86). The *desamortización,* in sum, had made losers out of those who should have been winners and vice versa, and the *jornaleros* were forced into desperate pursuits like anarchism, banditry, or bullfighting. Of course there were always charitable handouts available from the respectable members of society.

History had confirmed the prescience of Miguel Mañara's mother: there was never to be a shortage of poor men and women waiting in line for clothing and blankets in Seville. History had reinforced the mentality that lay behind such testamentary dispositions, or perhaps it was the other way around. Was it the mentality itself that had shaped history in order to keep the country as medieval as possible? Such a viewpoint might take its cue from historians like Américo Castro, who came close to suggesting that Spaniards freely chose decadence and economic stagnation in order to go on with their "*vivir desviviéndose*" (1954: 589–666). This phrase is impossible to translate but can be roughly described as an amalgam of honor-obsession, metaphysical moping, and know-nothingism. Castro overstated his case in the direction of idealism; one does not have to be a historical-materialist to accept that Spanish/Andalusian decadence has genuine historical and material causes. Still, not even a vulgar Marxist could deny nowadays that beliefs and values act forcibly on historical processes.

In any case it is clear that the relationship between values and under-development is a good deal more complicated than the theorizing of certain Andalusian anthropologists might lead us to expect. This complexity increases when we consider the interclass nature of values in the south, where the wealthy have exhibited traits we might associate with poverty, such as illiteracy and superstition, and the poor are often straitlaced, touchy about honor, and generous to a fault. As Bennassar notes, the pattern of power → wealth → consumption that characterized the life-style of the upper classes had its counterpart in the work → salary → consumption ethos of the lower classes, both being opposed to the work → profit → accumulation → investment model that prevailed elsewhere (1985:141). The rich-poor symbiosis wrought by decadence was responsible for, among other things, the triumph of baroque art. As one expert on religious sculpture attests,

> The Baroque period . . . found an extraordinary reception among the proud and haughty nobles that saw in it a good way to fulfill their eagerness for ostentation. On the other hand, the *pueblo,* given to exaltation and lovers of excess, fully identified themselves with this movement as well. The importance and development of Baroque art in Spain, therefore, is founded upon the scarce presence that the bourgeoisie had in our country and the markedly Catholic nature of the same. [Aroca Lara 1987:112]

The so-called bourgeoisie of Andalusia was quick to throw in its lot with this same ethos, as I have discussed. This so-called bourgeois betrayal was to have profound cultural consequences, for it allowed the traditional rich-poor symbiosis of values to survive and prevail in the south. The treatise I embarked upon at the beginning of this chapter has now come full circle, since the key instrument of this baroque, interclass, integrative, nonrational, nonbourgeois mentality was to be the *cofradía.*

During the first part of the nineteenth century, the system of penitential brotherhoods was battered by war, political crises, disentailment, the suppression of convents, and so on. During the second half of the century it was re-established and strengthened all over the south. By 1882, Seville had fifty-six *cofradías,* more than ever in its history (Sánchez 1985 : 8). During the 1930s, the brotherhoods were caught in the middle of the knee-jerk anticlericalism of the Second Republic and the forces of re-action galvanized thereby. Franco's uprising in 1936 set off a wave of vio-lence incapable of distinguishing between popular piety and ecclesiastical prerogative. Icons of incalculable historical value went up in smoke, and *cofradía*-lore still abounds in anecdotes that narrate how beloved icons were saved from incendiary mobs by heroic *cofrades* at the risk of their lives—the *Virgen de la Esperanza (Macarena)* and the *Santísimo Cristo de la Sentencia* in Seville, Juan de Mesa's superb *Cristo de las Angustias* in Córdoba (Marín 1986 : 32, 71; Gutiérrez 1978 : 164–166).

The *cofradía* system flourished again following Franco's victory. To cite the example of just one city, Jaén, the *Cofradía de la Clemencia* was founded in 1945, that of the *Cristo de las Misericordias* in 1946, that of the *Entrada de Jesús en Jerusalén* in 1949, that of the *Cristo del Perdón* in 1952, and that of the *Cristo de la Humildad* in 1955 (López Pérez 1984 : 16). Knowing what we know about the bloody excesses of the war, it seems appropriate that four out of five of the new brotherhoods were organized around images of the forgiving Christ.

The penitential brotherhoods of Andalusia—and all of its other social institutions—have been caught up in strife and violence at different mo-ments. It would be an error, however, to attribute their existence to a particular political regime. Franco has been dead since 1975, Spain is an industrialized, solidly democratic country and member of the European Economic Community, and *cofradías* remain extraordinarily popular in the south. People of diverse classes and political persuasions belong to them. In fact, many brotherhoods in smaller towns owe their splendor to the contributions of ex-*jornaleros* who migrated, prospered, and re-turned to assert their affluence in the time-honored ways (here again the pattern of work → salary → consumption). Governments and regimes come and go while *cofradías* continue to harbor and foment a frankly pre-capitalistic ideology—just the one I have described in this chapter. Every one of the values forged by medieval piety and consolidated during the age of Mañara is alive and well in today's penitential brotherhoods. They still provide the vehicle for the acquisition and display of individual and col-lective honor (one of many friction points with the ecclesiastical authorities). They still maintain a consciousness of solidarity among the *cofrades* who are alive and offer suffrages for those who are not. They still swear to uphold whatever attribute of the Virgin that has yet to be declared a dogma of faith. They still exert powerful but subtle influence on the rich to partially redistribute their riches. They are still the main and sometimes the only charitable institutions in many places. Above all, they still organize an *Estación de Penitencia* every year during Holy Week in which baroque images of the Crucified and His mourning Mother are accompanied through the streets by anywhere from a dozen to a thousand *penitentes*.

Virtually any *cofradía* could be cited to exemplify all of this and more. Let us take one at random—Córdoba's *Muy Humilde y Antigua Hermandad del Santísimo Cristo del Remedio de Ánimas y Nuestra Señora Madre de Dios en sus Tristezas* (the name itself is baroque). Founded in 1537, it almost disappeared during the *desamortización* and was reorganized in 1949. It has over 500 *cofrades* on its roster and treasures two "parental" icons, the seventeenth-century Christ and the eighteenth-century Virgin mentioned in its title. The brotherhood has its own *Casa de Hermandad,* publishes a trimonthly bulletin, and organizes spiritual exercises throughout the year. It arranges Masses for the souls of deceased members the first Monday of every month. It carries out constant charity for the needy, grants two scholarships, sponsors pre-matrimonial counseling, maintains a youth center for more than fifty poor children—many of whom sing in the *cofradía* choir—and holds a popular *Via Crucis* on Good Friday. Some 120 brothers participate in the regular *Estación de Penitencia,* clad in solid black tunics, *caperuzas,* scapularies, and sandles. This *hermandad* is exemplary in one final way, a good deal less edifying than the others: in 1962 and 1963 the brothers stayed home during Holy Week because of a grudge they were nursing against other *hermandades* (Gutiérrez 1978 : 95—102). But this is nothing; as we will see in the next chapter, Passional *cofradías* nourish passions that leave their own chaplains aghast.

Penitentiary Culture

In preceding pages I have attempted to situate the penitential ethos inside the larger context of Andalusia's decadence and social bipolarity. I have tried to show, in particular, how the penitential concept of charity typified by Mañara helped to stabilize this society and contributed to the formation of a veritable symbiosis of rich and poor. This symbiosis was evidently the work of many different men over the ages, above all men grouped together in institutions like the penitential brotherhood. The rich-poor symbiosis has been rich in cultural consequences: here I am referring not only to baroque art, but to the impassioned view of life, death, and the afterlife that baroque art exalts.

As we have seen, the Passion constitutes a key premise in the logic of penitence; Christ suffered to act upon Patriarchal Providence, thereby winning for humans the opportunity to do likewise (through the self-administration of physical pain or the symbolic sacrifice of suffrages). But we have hardly exhausted the contribution of the Passion to penitential culture. It is essential to recognize, for example, the extent to which the specific historical circumstances of Christ's death have functioned as a great mirror in which Andalusian society has contemplated itself over the centuries. This is especially true in the case of that segment of society Mañara was most concerned about: the underclass. In seeking to account for the fact that Holy Week has become the most important *fiesta* in Andalusia, Moreno affirms that in the events depicted by the processional *pasos,*

> the Andalusian people see the symbolic expression of their own experience as a marginal and oppressed people: hence the identification with a man who suffers unjustly, who is condemned without proof by the competent religious and civil authorities, . . . and who maintains his dignity, without recognizing any guilt nor feeling inferior but indeed very superior to his executioners. The suffering Jesus of Andalusian Holy Weeks symbolizes, for the simple people, for the Andalusian people proper, their centuries-old misfortune and oppression. [1982 : 231]

Naturally Moreno is not the first to notice that Andalusians victimized by circumstances relate to and identify with the supreme victim. Half a century ago, Cansinos wrote that the lower-class Andalusian "narcissistically recognizes himself in the myth of Jesus, witnesses his own passion and apotheosis, and fancies himself avenged of all his executioners" (1985 [1933]: 218). Cansinos even conjectured that in the patently anti-Semitic anathematization of Christ's executioners that takes place during Holy Week, the "Jews" really represent "the powerful, the rich, the *señores* that are martyrizing the proletarian Jesus" (219).

The Passion has been an apt symbol for people conscious of their own economic or political impotence. Strange as it may seem, this Passional symbolism has even remained valid in the case of Andalusians who opted to rebel. In centuries past, for example, numerous men rose up against the order of things and became outlaws, and subsequently myths. As with other great cultural artifacts of the south, the myth of the *bandolero* has its origins in economic stagnation and egregious social inequity. There really were *bandoleros,* of course, but what made them legends in their own time and myths in ours were the great masses of rural oppressed who were disinclined to rebel themselves but who were eager to sing the exploits of those who did. For this reason, the *bandolero* encarnates all of the virtues and values of the poor peasants themselves, including their circular and fatalistic world-design. The bandits were not looking for a new world or a new order for society; their goal was to make case-by-case readjustments of this one. A great many *bandoleros* ended up repenting and mending their ways (Gómez Marín 1972:29). Others were caught and killed, and here again the fate of Christ could be held up as a mirror. In fact, in the apprehension and execution of the most famous *bandolero* of them all, the civil authorities seem to have gone out of their way to underscore the Passional analogy.

According to historical documents assembled by Santos Torres (1987), Diego Corrientes Mateos was betrayed by a companion, arrested in an olive grove where he was resting unarmed with his band, treated with indignity, and executed in Seville by hanging on Good Friday of 1781 (60–69). Corrientes was only twenty-three years old at the time of death; he had already achieved a considerable reputation for unselfishness, hence his nickname, *el Bandido Generoso.* And, unlike other outlaws, his wholly nonviolent career was devoted almost exclusively to the smuggling of stallions, an activity for which he had developed a large network of collaborators in Andalusia and neighboring Portugal. He would never have been caught without the tenacity of Don Francisco de Bruna, an aristocrat who had accumulated so many judicial and executive titles in Seville that he was popularly known as *"El Señor del Gran Poder"* (38–39). The real Lord of Great Power was—and is—to be found in the church of San Lorenzo; it is a processional image of Christ with His cross and is one of the more important objects of devotion in all of southern Spain. Santos goes on to explain that the title was applied to Bruna because he was the very embodiment of absolute power (39–47). Even after documenting Bruna's reputation as a pitiless and arbitrary hanging judge, Santos still finds it incomprehensible that he would arrange for the young bandit to be executed on what for Sevillians is the holiest day of the year (67–70).

> Nevertheless, it must be recognized, a single manifestation of generous love was in the air that morning of the Good Friday of Seville. When the unfortunate one was taken out of the "Jail of *los Señores*," the loving hands of the brothers of the *Hospital de la Caridad* suspended him in the air to spare him the torment of being dragged before his hanging. An infinite charity of love of the brothers of Miguel Mañara . . . [a] sublime concept of Baroque spirituality that after a century was still being practiced by the brothers of his Hospital. [73]

Santos goes on to narrate in an increasingly mawkish style how the same brothers of the *Santa Caridad* lovingly carried the cadaver of Corrientes over to the "King's table" for the customary quartering (74–75). The respectable quantity of 307 Masses were said for his soul, bread was given out at the jail in his name, and the money left over from alms collected by the brothers was given to his grieving mother (80–81).

The legends that grew up around the death of the Generous Bandit are as instructive as the historical facts of the matter: folk work undertook to "Oedipalize" the relationship between Corrientes and Bruna, inventing chance meetings between the two men, acts of macho-style defiance, and even a love affair between the *bandolero* and the judge's niece (49–55). It can be affirmed in general that the oppressed classes of Andalusia have attempted to cope with authoritarian injustice by giving it, as it were, a "human face." That face is inevitably that of the father, the father who is out to control, castrate, judge, and punish. As a number of scholars have pointed out, God Himself has been envisioned in such terms; and as I will discuss in Chapter Four, the Passion according to Andalusia brings out this patriarchal fatalism in bold relief. Not even God the Son has escaped being assimilated to the punitive Paternal archetype; throughout Andalusia He is worshipped and feared under the appellative of "Our Father Jesus." What I have discussed in this chapter, of course, is the carrot that accompanies the stick, that is, the institutions and practices that have been on hand to reward conformity and submission to patriarchy or to a class structure perceived in patriarchal terms.

The brothers of the *Santa Caridad* carrying Diego Corrientes to keep him from ignominious dragging—something they habitually did with condemned criminals—is emblematic of the ethos of charity that helped to reconcile the losers with their "fate." For those criminals whose fate was not the hangman's noose but a jail term, another act of charity was available, one in which the prisoners were actively encouraged to see themselves in the mirror of Christ's Passion. It behooves us to look briefly into this practice, one of the most celebrated, dramatic, and emotive aspects of Passional culture, at once a canny escape valve for pent up hostility and an impressive demonstration of the symbiosis of the haves and the have-nots. I am referring to the *estación ante la cárcel*, whereby a penitential brotherhood brought its Holy Week procession to a halt in front of a penal institution (the word *cárcel* is applied generally to jails, prisons, and penitentiaries) and remained there while the prisoners sang anguished *saetas* to the processional images.

No complete study of this fascinating custom exists. As far as I have been able to discern, it dates at least from the first part of the nineteenth century and became traditional in towns large enough to have an administrative apparatus for the processing of the criminal element. In Seville, for example, prisoners were singing *saetas* from their cells by the 1830s (López Fernández 1981:77). In Jaén, the practice was instituted in 1865, the year in which an old convent was refurbished and made over into a prison to handle the increased "demand." Jaén's *cofradías* immediately began to include the new *cárcel* in their Holy Week itinerary and continued to do so until its closing in 1931.

> Upon these occasions the doors of the prison were opened and some of the inmates, secured with chains and shackles, begged for alms in front of the façade. The *cofradías* halted their images in front of the prison while the prisoners behind bars intoned *saetas* and chanted their laments. The scene was heartrending, very much in keeping with the customs of those days, and people gathered in droves at this place in order to directly experience this unique moment. [López Pérez 1984:179]

In many places, certain brotherhoods have "specialized" in charity for prisoners. Such is the case of Córdoba's *Hermandad y Cofradía de Nazarenos de Nuestro Padre Jesús de la Sentencia*, founded in 1944 by—appropriately enough—a group of lawyers. This *hermandad*, which boasts some 700 *hermanos*, has its headquarters in San Antonio de Padua Parish in the proletarian neighborhood of Miraflores, which also contains the Provincial Prison. Many of the brothers are involved in year-round acts of charity for the inmates of this institution and even hold religious services there during Lent. The *cofradía*'s titulary icon was sculpted by J. Martínez Cerrillo and portrays Christ in the act of being sentenced to die. He wears a beautiful purple tunic bordered in gold, His hands are bound with a golden cord, and with His serene and resigned countenance He is the very image of a model prisoner. Beginning in 1955, the brotherhood's maternal icon, the Virgin of Mercy, has been brought into the prison patio during Holy Week to enable the prisoners to sing *saetas* to her from their cells (Gutiérrez 1978 : 80–88).

Other kinds of charity toward prisoners have been practiced in other places. In Castro del Río (Córdoba), for example, huge baskets of food were distributed at the jail on Holy Thursday by priests "dressed up in their best and richest passion-purple cloaks" (Salido 1984 : 18). In many other towns it was common to grant some prisoner his freedom at the moment the procession appeared before the gates of the prison (Gómez Pérez 1984 : 17). In Málaga, the *Hermandad de Jesús el Rico* possesses the royal prerogative to free a prisoner every Holy Thursday. It was granted in the late eighteenth century by Carlos III after the prisoners helped carry the *pasos* through the plague-infested city, and has been renewed by Spain's current monarch Juan Carlos I. In 1988, the prisoner freed was a twenty-seven-year-old man serving time for the crime of sacrilegious theft; he came out of the jail dressed as a *penitente* and took up his cross behind the Nazarene (*Tele-Sur*, 31 March 1988).

In the previous chapter I cited the *copla* as a major vehicle of the emotion magic that characterizes the Andalusian way of being-in-the-world. This holds doubly in the case of the *saeta* and triply in the case of the *saeta carcelera* (*saeta* of the *cárcel*) sung by convicts. Unlike the *saetas* that are sung to narrate some specific moment of Christ's Passion, the *saeta carcelera* belongs to the larger category of *saetas afectivas*, which are sung to express intense emotion and which may be descended from the penitential verses popularized by Franciscan missionaries (Gómez Pérez 1984 : 35–38). Significantly, the development of the *saeta carcelera* is historically contemporaneous with that of the *copla flamenca*. They were almost certainly forged in the same milieu of oppression and misery. There is, for one thing, stylistic continuity between the two (the *saeta carcelera* employs the same rhythms and lugubrious melodial structures of the flamenco *martinetes* and *siguiriyas*). More important, there is thematic continuity. Early *coplas flamencas*, says Ortíz, all repeat the same message—poverty, crime, persecution, imprisonment, beatings, hunger, and lost freedom (1985:29), the grim legacy of a failure condition shared by Gypsies and down-and-out *Castellanos* alike. In reality, no strict line can be drawn between the early, noncommercial *copla flamenca* and the *saeta carcelera*, products as they are of the same social class and the same emotion magic. It is not hard to see how a history of mistreatment at the hands of authority would have made their singers especially receptive to the story of the Passion. The only difference, and it is not a great one, is that the *copla* calls upon human mothers for consolation and the *saeta* calls on divine ones like the *Virgen de la Esperanza* or the *Virgen de la Soledad:*

Virgen de la Soledad	Virgin of Solitude,
no te pases tan serena,	don't go by so serenely,
echa tu vista a la cárcel,	cast your eyes on the prison,
quita grillos y cadenas.	take away shackles and chains.
Por la reja de la cárcel,	Through the bars of the prison,
Soledad, dame la mano,	*Soledad,* give me your hand,
que somos muchos hermanos,	I have many brothers and sisters,
no tengo padre ni madre.	I have no father or mother.
Eres rosa de pasión	You are a passionflower
que por tu hijo sufriste	who suffered for your son
y pasaste gran dolor;	and went through great pain;
por mí lo pasó mi madre	my mother went through it for me
y ahora me veo en prisión.	and now I find myself in prison.
[López Fernández 1981:78]	

One of the emotional heights of Seville's Holy Week in years past was the stop made by Triana's *Hermandad del Santísimo Cristo de la Expiración* at the doors of the infamous *Cárcel del Pópulo*. A noted writer was on hand in 1927 to narrate the scene:

> Before the bars of the jail, a splendorous Virgin passes—the *Esperanza de Triana*. Disheveled heads and ferocious faces appear at the narrow little windows; hands soiled by crime reach out towards the image; blasphemous lips mumble a prayer; hardened hearts soften, and souls in pain pour themselves into *saetas*. . . . A shiver of intense emotion invades every last corner of the penal house. [From *La Semana Santa* by Luis Martínez Kleiser; cit. by Pineda Novo 1988:144]

A visit made by the *Virgen de los Dolores* to Jaén's prison in 1926 is commemorated in the following poetic prayer:

En las rejas de la cárcel	At the bars of the prison
fija tus ojos que lloran,	look how they are crying,
y los hierros de las rejas	and the iron bars
se van cubriendo de rosas.	are being covered with roses.
Se van cubriendo de rosas	They are being covered with roses
y cuando los presos rezan,	and when the prisoners pray,
tu dolor les va aliviando	your pain begins to lighten
el peso de las cadenas.	the weight of the chains.
[Cazabán 1984 (1926): 244]	

Obviously there is a vast stylistic difference between the anguished, rough-hewn *saeta carcelera* and the belletristic or oversentimental description of its performance (even as they coincide in their devotion to the Mother). There is an important element that can get lost in translation: dissent. The men who sang jail-house *saetas* did not find resignation any more palatable than the irascible poor of Mañara's age. This much is clear from a *saeta* sung during Holy Week of 1927 at the jail in Jaén:

No era la cruz del Señor	The cross of the Lord was not
tan grande como la nuestra,	as big as ours,
¡que entre todos la llevamos	we are all carrying it together
y no podemos con ella!	and we cannot handle it!
[Mendizábal 1984 (1927): 250]	

Mendizábal goes on to whitewash this irreverent but well-wrought *saeta* with a tender reference to the Christ of Love, but I think that the allusion to a burden more crushing than Christ's cross speaks for itself. A de facto cry of disconformity can even be heard in many of the *saetas* that call out to the Virgin, like the following one sung to the *Virgen de la Soledad* in Seville:

Dicen que me han de matar	They say they are to kill me
y me han de llevar al campo.	and take me out to the field.
¡Virgen de la Soledad	Virgin of Solitude
tapadme con vuestro manto!	cover me with your mantle!
[López Fernández 1981:78]	

Given the circumstances of their origins and the plight of the men who have sung them, it is not surprising to find a more or less manifest element of protest in many *saetas carceleras*. It will never be a call for pris-

Nuestro Padre Jesús del Gran Poder, sculpted in cedar by Juan de Mesa in 1620 (photo: Encarnación Lucas).

Dimas the Good Thief looks gratefully at the dead Christ in one of Seville's oldest and largest *pasos de misterio* (photo: Encarnación Lucas).

oners to rise up in mutiny and take over the prison, however. Like its sister, the *copla,* the *saeta* may complain about pain and rage against fate, but ultimately it will seek refuge in the consolation of the Mother, the benevolence of religious institutions, or the magic of its own intense emotion. The context in which the *saeta carcelera* is sung effectively limits its dissent and channels its rage. Herein lies the genius of the whole charitable practice of bringing Holy Week to convicts. The desperate and excessive emotionality of Andalusians rotting in prison is cannily harnessed for didactic purposes. The *estación ante la cárcel* puts into motion the very elements of the Passion itself: Fathers who are harsh yet just, Sons who complain but accept, Mothers who weep and console, and Good Thieves who get saved in the end. The crimes committed by men are like sins, and suffering will remove their stain. This fundamental link between penitential culture and penitentiary culture is aptly expressed in an anonymous *saeta* collected by Alcalá:

Llora tus culpas, cristiano,	Weep for your faults, Christian,
y confía en el Señor que,	and trust in the Lord who,
hasta con ansias mortales,	even in mortal distress,
supo hacer Santo a un ladrón.	could make a Saint out of a thief.
[Alcalá 1984 (1925): 240]	

The model is as pertinent to women as it is to men, thanks in part to the numerous images of Mary Magdalene that are carried through Andalusian streets during Holy Week. The prostitution of *la Magdalena* is not understood as a socioeconomic but a moral problem, and in the end faith raises her from the mud. She is the female equivalent of Dimas (the apocryphal name of the Good Thief).

The lessons instilled during a brotherhood's stop at a prison, therefore, did not stop at the prison. They were meant to be heard by all in attendance, convicts and *cofrades* alike. In making the *Estación de Penitencia* into one great act of charity, the *cofradía* system made a unique contribution not only to Passional culture but to bipolar Andalusian society, reinforcing ideological premises ultimately ascribed to by both poles. The sacrificial Christ has been the perfect catalyst for the rich-poor symbiosis, for He is simultaneously Lord and Master, poor and defunct, a powerful judge, an obedient Son, and a model prisoner.

Chapter 3

Social Psychology of the *Cofradía*

A Question of Identity

Spain was quick to get over Generalísimo Franco's death in 1975 but over-coming his life was to be another matter entirely. Problems swept under the rug during forty years of patriarchal dictatorship resurfaced with a vengeance; those relating to the cultural identities of Spain's regional communities (now called *autonomías*) were among the thorniest. Not surprisingly, nationalistic feelings ran the strongest in just those regions that had been subjected to the most intense pressure to abandon them: Catalonia and the Basque country. The situation of Andalusia, however, was quite different. Its well-known identity badges had not only been ex-empt from interference—they were promoted officially and unofficially as the *Spanish* ones par excellence. In this, however, as in so much else, the Franco regime was merely bowing to established practice. The identi-fication of Spain with Andalusia has been going on for at least 200 years; outsiders are to be thanked (or blamed) for putting the process in mo-tion. The eighteenth and nineteenth centuries produced no fewer than 858 Iberian travel narratives (Foulché-Debosc 1969), the majority of which devote far more attention to Andalusia than to anywhere else in the peninsula. As Bernal relates, travelers during the Age of Enlighten-ment designed their trips along the lines of scientific expeditions and sought to collect as much information as possible. They were succeeded by the diary-keeping soldiers and adventurers of the period of the Span-ish War of Independence, who in turn were followed by the Romantics, most of whom had already "seen" Andalusia before—in their dreams. Bernal points out how their perceptions were distorted from the start by mythic notions of a wild and beautiful landscape populated by bullfight-ers, bandits, smugglers, and voluptuous Gypsy dancers like Mérimée's Carmen (1985:21). The scientifically minded travelers of the preceding century had not failed to take note of the unjust and unproductive land tenure system, the disastrous state of public education, the debility of commerce, the slums, and so forth—all of this *before* the devastation wrought by the war with Napoleon. The Romantics, in the main, thirsted only for thrilling adventures and ignored the economic plight of Andalusia. Théophile Gautier, the most famous and frivolous of their number, comes close to congratulating the Andalusians for living "a thousand leagues from civilization" and for providing him with a never-ending series of novelistic anecdotes (1985 [1840] : 137). He glories in the miserable roads, the lack of creature comforts, the "brain-melting heat," and the terrible and mysterious dangers lurking all around (138). We know that in 1840 the streets of Seville were full of beggars, but Gautier only has eyes for the eyes of beautiful *señoritas,* their brilliant teeth, their fine noses, and their incredibly diminutive feet (153–155).

"The invention of Andalusia," as one investigator has called it (Heran 1979), was by no means in the hands of outsiders alone. For one thing, there were always plenty of natives who derived an income from reinforcing the foreigners' fantasies; for example, the main propagators of the rumors about bloodthirsty *bandoleros* were the armed guards who sold their protection to credulous types like Gautier (Bernal 1985 : 26). An additional symbiotic bond grew up between the fertile imagination of the writers and the inordinate pride of what we today would call "local boosters," who were pleased to see their sociocentrism confirmed by the awe or flattery of strangers. Nor can the influence of Spanish/Andalusian writers over their foreign counterparts be underestimated. The whole genre of travel literature, affirms Bernal, serves to gauge the growing European knowledge of native authors—many of whose narratives of popular customs, scenes, trades, and figures (*costumbrismo*) were incorporated wholesale into accounts of journeys (1985 : 27–28). A similar appropriation was carried out with local legends such as that of Mañara, who was thoroughly identified with the fictional libertine Don Juan by nineteenth-century writers like Mérimée, Dumas, and Latour (Bonachera and Piñero 1985 : 109–120).

As important as foreign or domestic authors were in the development of a certain romanticized image of the south, an examination of mid-nineteenth-century Andalusian painting reveals that the ideology and tastes of the landed bourgeoisie played a major role as well. In contrast to the pictorial *costumbristas* of Madrid who adopted a critical and ironic perspective on daily life in Spain, the painters of Seville preferred an idealistic and sentimental approach to their subjects (Reina 1979: 27–28). What began as a wholesome desire to exalt and preserve local singularity was eventually pressed into the service of a prosperous urban bourgeoisie in the years they were making their "great betrayal." Under their patronage, the image of the popular classes was slowly but surely purified of unpleasant class connotations and reduced to a fixed number of "types"—the *majo*, the *bailarina*, the Gypsy street vendor, the blind man reciting verses, or the *cigarrera*—each with his or her "typical" occupation, except for the *majo* whose personality was founded upon his alleged desire to avoid an occupation, caring only for his honor, his clothing, his dagger, his guitar, and his "aesthetic concept of existence" (Reina 1979: 60). The image of the "woman of Seville" was eventually identified with that of the young female workers of the *Fábrica de Tabacos,* a true exploited underclass. These *cigarreras* earned a meager five *reales* a day (although they could smoke or chew all the tobacco they wished) and proved on several occasions their capacity for violent protest. Little of this is visible in the numerous portraits of the archetypal *cigarrera* with the flower in her hair, the languor in her eyes, the colorful attire, and so on (74–75). The popular types were usually pictured in an appropriate setting—the street-side tavern, the fiesta, the cathedral, the bullring, and above all the great *ferias* (fairs) dear to the hearts of the absentee bourgeois landlords. All of this contributed, writes Reina, to "the negation of every critical aspect of reality" (76).

Significantly, one of the types that the Romantics admired the most, the *bandolero,* was virtually ignored by the idealizing painters of Seville. After all, how could there be plundering in paradise? It was not, of course, that the Romantics were attuned to the harsh socioeconomic conditions that drove men to a life of crime; they were simply out to celebrate the love of freedom and spirit of adventure they took to be the *bandolero*'s true motivations.

How did the selective reading of Andalusian identity described above come to symbolize that of Spain itself? Acosta Sánchez sees "the enormous weight of the Andalusian agrarian bourgeoisie in the apparatus of the Spanish State" as the principal factor; throughout the nineteenth century and into the twentieth, a disproportionate number of ministers, presidents, and dictators hailed from the south (1979: 63–64). Since dominant classes easily impose their ideas and tastes on society at large

(64), the oligarchy soon discovered that promoting Andalusian culture was the best means for promoting centralism and defusing incipient Catalan or Basque nationalisms. Small wonder, then, that an oligarchical and obsessively centralist regime like Franco's would continue and even intensify the manipulation of Andalusian singularity (64–69). According to Carr and Fusi, the pseudo-Andalusian "culture of evasion" was false and vulgar by definition, an opiate of the people, useful only for propping up the regime and "reinforcing the image of a generous, happy-go-lucky, temperamental Spain" (1985:120).

As if Andalusia's cultural identity had not suffered enough at the hands of Romantic mystifiers, idealistic painters, and political manipulators, yet another pernicious group has been pinpointed: foreign anthropologists. According to Isidoro Moreno, Andalusia has been subjected to a veritable "anthropological colonialism" (1984:98) that in many instances takes the form of an "acritical and mechanical application" of theories elaborated in vastly different sociocultural contexts (such as Anglo-American functionalism), which can tell us nothing about Andalusia (95). Moreno further resents the way in which Andalusian agrotowns have been utilized as training grounds for scores of American, French, and German graduate students who spend a year or two in the sun, take advantage of or even plagiarize the work of native scholars, and lose interest in the groups they study as soon as they receive a doctorate (94–95). Such remarks may strike us as unfair, but I judge them to be part and parcel of a crusading attitude shared by many Andalusian anthropologists of the post-Franco years. There is a consensus about grievances (too many foreigners, not enough money, and so on), and there is a consensus about priorities. To wit:

(1) All future research must be guided by the idea that Andalusia is an impoverished and dependent region of Spain,
(2) whose true identity has been expropriated or lost,
(3) but can be recovered and promoted through the efforts of social scientists in general and anthropologists in particular.

There can be little argument with the first of these propositions, already well-assimilated by—of all people—foreign anthropologists. Stanley Brandes, for instance, has shown how jokes, riddles, and other folk genres are employed by Andalusian men to prop up their self-image in the face of extreme social inequality (1980). No foreign or native scholar working today could seriously maintain a rosy image of life in the south. He or she will be quick to acknowledge the absurdity of Gautier and the veracity of Gautier's predecessors, people like Laborde or William Jacob, authors of invaluable descriptions of Andalusian decadence. The problems begin, in my view, with what many consider to be an automatic result of underdevelopment. It is widely held that the historical conversion of Andalusia into "the Sicily of Spain" inevitably occasioned the loss of its true identity, or its expropriation by a regressive bourgeoisie who sought to enhance its hegemony by force-feeding *toreros, cantaores,* and *bailaoras* to a docile public. Moreno speaks for all in damning the process by which Andalusian identity symbols were stripped of their socioeconomic connotations and "folklorized" for mass consumption (1984: 107). Santos urges his fellow Andalusians to "demythify" the old image, develop historical consciousness, and "recover" their genuine identity (1984:118–121). To one degree or another these researchers have fallen prey to a fallacious, naturalistic concept of identity, holding it to be something that can be lost or found, kidnapped or ransomed, mounted on wheels and carted off to Madrid or smuggled out of the country by cynical foreign anthropologists. Of course there was and is a quasi-official stereotype of Flamenco Spain. No stereotype has the power to subsume the culture from which it is derived, however; in the last analysis a stereotype is only a partial and selective "reading" of cultural complexity. The same holds true for an "identity"—always an artificial construct, a de facto invention. It is nothing given or eternal. Furthermore, the raw materials for identity invention are always at hand, that is, human groups in an environment. When a group has a will to forge an identity it will always find a way.

Let us take an example from a study produced inside the ideological coordinates of what has been christened the "new Andalusian anthropology" (González Alcantud 1984:143). In "Development, Underdevelopment, and Cultural Identity" (1984), Provanzal examines the role played by economic oppression in shaping the identity of Aguas Amargas, a small town on the coast of Almería. Established in 1897 as a wharf and railroad loading platform for a coal mining company, Aguas Amargas came to be populated by a marginal and miserable proletariat, which found unity in a common praxis in the context of capitalistic exploitation, regional dependency, and the international division of labor (156–157). The periodic tragic deaths of young longshoremen contributed greatly to the differentiation process, for the community began to retain the bodies and bury them secretly in defiance of the law (160). A general strike, however, was the key event, carried out in dramatic circumstances that made it the "central element of local history" and the "distinctive and definitive myth in relation to other places" (161). While the men took control of the installations and strikebreakers marched down from the north, the women bravely confronted the bayonets of the *Guardia Civil*. Provanzal stresses that the whole event has become so mythified that she was unable to find out how long the strike lasted; we are even left in the dark as to when it happened. Moreover, no two of her informants agree on who played the decisive roles (161). As it turns out, other types of confrontations of a more symbolic kind have helped to cement the community identity of Aguas Amargas: the locals carefully distinguish themselves from the people of nearby Carboneras, home of the evil eye; La Joya, full of narrow-minded rustics; and Níjar, all sanctimonious hypocrites (158–159). With neighbors like these, it comes as no surprise to learn that the men and women of Aguas Amargas have always preferred to find their wives or husbands inside their own municipal limits (158).

The point I wish to emphasize is this: as soon as an anthropologist carries out an in-depth study of identity-in-the-context-of-underdevelopment in a specific town in the south, we find that it has the same structure as all of the other kinds of crisis-provoked identity formation Spain has known (Mitchell 1988 : 11–37). The same elements of ecological competition, endogamy, esoteric-exoteric lore, and in-group jockeying for position are present; further, the class consciousness that Provanzal finds in the workers of Aguas Amargas is no more immune to mythopoesis than other kinds of group consciousness.

Again, there is no such thing as genuine identity. The distinction between genuine and spurious in cultural traditions has been thoroughly discredited (cf. Handler and Linnekin 1984). Identity cannot be lost or recovered, only invented again and again as the situation requires. What is the difference, then, between the identity-defining dynamics of the workers of Aguas Amargas and that of the anthropologists who study them? Both groups have their grievances, their enemies, their priorities, and their myths. Perhaps the anthropologists can be distinguished by their willingness to place their discipline, a most broad-minded and comparative one, at the service of narrow nationalism. They have even been told by a prestigious colleague, Salvador Rodríguez Becerra, that it is their social duty to do so:

> If research priorities exist, and we think they should be established, studies dealing with the nature and configuration of Andalusian culture must be among the first. Among the social sciences, anthropology is one of the appropriate ones to take up this problem inasmuch as the central concept of this discipline is that of culture. . . ; because of this it is in a position to approach the problems of the cultural definition of Andalusia and the configuration and delimitation of the Andalusian cultural area with certain techniques, certain methods, and certain theoretical concepts. We, the anthropologists of Andalusia, conscious of our obligations as social scientists and attentive to the demands of society, are willing to meet our responsibility. [1984 : 15–16]

It is not my purpose to disparage the social or political commitment of Andalusian anthropologists. Nor is it my intention to resuscitate the discredited dichotomy of the objective uninvolved observer and a reified passive otherness. Nor do I think that all social scientists are ethically bound to be neutral and politically impartial at all times (some assert that they cannot be even if they wish). If Andalusian anthropologists want to combine the study of cultural identity with its promotion, they are entitled to do so. Outside scholars will still have the right, however, to evaluate the new nationalistic monographs thereby produced. I am afraid that they will be found wanting.

In the first place, I do not believe that the Andalusian cultural area is co-extensive or continuous with the boundary lines of the new Comunidad Autónoma de Andalucía. Examples: *Cante jondo* does not restrict its domain to Andalusian provinces; for over a hundred years it has been popular *and* traditional in Extremadura, Murcia, and even the Balearic Islands. Tauromachy, though Andalusian in so many of its outward signs, possesses profound sociological roots all over the Iberian Peninsula. The cult of the Virgin (Andalusia is nicknamed "the Land of María Santísima") is adhered to with the same passion in Cuenca as it is in Almonte (González Casarrubios 1985 : 143–144). The only nineteenth-century author who was ever actually robbed by a *bandolero*, another Andalusian archetype, was the American Alexander Slidell—and it happened in La Mancha! (Bernal 1985:69). Andalusia is hardly the only area in southern Spain with a sizable Gypsy population, religious brotherhoods, and endless olive groves. And, unfortunately, the characteristics of underdevelopment that Santos lists are present in abundant quantities throughout the south; Andalusia has no monopoly on poverty, hunger, illiteracy, emigration, and so on. In view of all this, any attempt by an anthropologist or anyone else to delimit and demarcate the cultural area of Andalusia, as Rodríguez Becerra recommends, is bound to be arbitrary and patently misleading. The logic of the Andalusian defining project will always be vulnerable to a *reductio ad absurdum:* if we must have an Andalusian anthropology, of, by, and for the Andalusians, then we must have an Extremaduran anthropology, a Valencian anthropology, a Manchegan anthropology, and so forth, *ad absurdum.* Do the objects of anthropological inquiry respect the newly revised political map or the newly revived political anxieties of Spain? Do the Virgins of Jaén and those of Ciudad Real belong to different species? The local inhabitants would answer this question with a resounding "YES," of course, but anthropologists should be able to call spades spades. It is precisely for this reason that I employ a vague phrase like "southern Spain" in the subtitle of this book. My study is anchored mainly in Andalusia, true enough, but I have found nothing that authorizes me to build fences around it.

Secondly, we must not let ourselves be misled as to the extent of the current Andalusian identity crisis, or as to the degree of popular desire to exchange the old "regressive" identity signs for the unspecified but progressive ones that anthropologists recommend. As Caro Baroja (1957a: 273–275) pointed out years ago, the people of Spain have never been as concerned with nationalistic identity-defining as have their leaders or university professors. Optimism, self-esteem, and feelings of belonging have always been far stronger at the level of neighborhood or town than at more inclusive levels (266–269). For every anguished Ortega crying "My God, what is Spain?" there have been a thousand Juan Pueblos shouting "Long live our saint!" Like anywhere else in Iberia, the centennial and sometimes millennial communities of Andalusia have abundant resources available for the affirmation of local identity. When crisis threatens, as it often has, the appropriate "reading" is made and a given symbol is selectively highlighted once again. A typical example is the *Santo Rostro* treasured in Jaén, believed to be a remnant of the veil that Veronica pressed to Christ's face on the way to Calvary. Devotion to the relic has actually increased in the past few years and it remains the primary means for celebrating the identity of the people of Jaén today—believers and nonbelievers alike (López Pérez 1984 : 215–220).

More examples of the continuing strength of local identity badges could be cited, but it is identity at the *regional* level that most concerns the social scientists I have cited. But even here the Andalusians have not been waiting with crossed arms to be assigned a new identity. They have gone ahead and "recovered" the hoary *romería* of the Virgin of the Rocío (centered in Almonte, Huelva). There is no other item in the cultural inventory capable of drawing together hundreds of thousands of people from all over Andalusia—and beyond. With every year that passes by the event attracts new followers; students of the phenomenon concur in seeing identity definition as a central function (Comelles 1984; Díaz de la Serna *et al.* 1987). At both local and regional levels, then, religious symbols remain favorite vehicles of identity consolidation in the south of Spain. Nowhere is this more in evidence than during Holy Week.

Questions of identity are central to an understanding of Passional culture. Thanks to Aguilar, Briones, Moreno, and many other scholars, we know that penitential brotherhoods play a major role in cementing identities in Andalusia, at individual and collective levels alike. In reaction to the "official" religious interpretation of Holy Week, which was the only one to find its way into print for so many years, many modern researchers hasten to highlight the nonreligious aspects of the *cofradía* system; consequently, identity defining, sociocentrism, and sociality are dealt with the most in the current ethnographic literature. Significantly, interpretations of *cofradías* from the perspective of faith and from that of agnosticism both agree that emotion is the agglutinant. For the first, the operative emotions are those of piety, penitence, and pity; for the second, the only feelings that really count are those of group belonging, gregariousness, symbolic integration, love of disguise and festivity. I have no desire to be drawn into the battle of words currently being waged by the proponents of one perspective and the other in lecture halls, churches, university classrooms, pamphlets, homilies, and doctoral dissertations. In my view, both sides are laboring under certain self-imposed blind spots. The defenders of the official religious interpretation, for example, do not see how Andalusian emotionality is retrogressive enough to turn doctrine into de facto heresy (as I seek to show in Chapter Four). For their part, agnostic anthropologists overlook the fact that the many nonreligious elements they identify do not serve to make agnostics out of Andalusians, or to augment their rationality, reduce the raw supply of emotionality, or severe the Maternal umbilical cord; and religiosity in the south of Spain is nothing if not family-fixated irrational emotionality. At least this is what I hope to have demonstrated by the end of this chapter.

Warring Brotherhoods

Sociocentrism in the south possesses the characteristics of Spanish socio-centrism in general. In other words, it exhibits a great dependence upon religious identity symbols, it exerts a crucial influence over the lives and destinies of the members of the in-group, and it excels in the exasperation of intracommunity and intercommunity rivalries of all kinds (Mitchell 1988 : 11–56). If anything, Andalusian sociocentrism is even more heart-felt, irrational, and tribalistic than sociocentric feelings that prevail else-where in the peninsula. These allegations can be circumstantiated with special clarity in the *hermandades,* where the honor of every *hermano* is inseparable from that of the group, and individual identity is practically subsumed by the collective one—all under the watchful eye of person-alized icons that function simultaneously as mystical parents and as dif-ferentiating badges vis-à-vis rival brotherhoods.

There are even certain *cofradías* that surpass all others in this combative collective identity affirmation: those that are locked into a one-on-one, no-win rivalry with another *cofradía* of parallel size within the same agrotown. To understand the dynamics of these intense intracommunity conflicts is to appreciate the structuring power of passion in the south. Herein lies the value of Aguilar's prize-winning 1983 ethnography of Cas-tilleja de la Cuesta (Seville), a detailed case study of a situation that exists in towns all over southern Spain. Aguilar describes the relationship be-tween the two *hermandades* of Castilleja as one of reciprocal hostility operating at many different levels all year long and especially during de-votional manifestations of one kind or another.

> This antagonism is not limited to an exclusively religious or ceremonial plane, that is, in regard to the cults of each one, but is also reflected in other aspects of the town's social life. Confrontation is present not only at a symbolic level but

can also convert itself into real disputes between concrete persons. Any problem can act as a trigger for unleashing the latent hostility that exists between the two halves in which the neighbors of Castilleja are divided, and provokes more than one incident that can become violent and cause enmity between the families of the town. The reality is that a dispute between two people of different brotherhoods, no matter how unrelated it is to the religious sphere, is immediately channeled into a confrontation between the two halves, people taking the side of the individual who belongs to their own brotherhood. [1983 : 89–90]

The objective differences between the two *hermandades* can be summarized as follows. One has its headquarters in the church of Santiago located at the town plaza, calls itself "royal" and "illustrious," and possesses the triple patronage of Saint James the Moor-Slayer, Our Holy Lord of Remedies in the Holy Sepulcher, and Our Lady of Solitude. Its distinguishing color is red (hence the term *rojos* for the members). The exact year of its founding in the fifteenth century is uncertain, but it was definitely a few years before the founding of its rival—an important distinction in the minds of *cofrades* everywhere. Perhaps in compensation, the other *hermandad* calls itself "royal," "illustrious," and "pontifical." With its power base in the church of the *Concepción* on Calle Real, it treasures icons of the Immaculate Conception, Our Father Jesus of Great Power, and Our Lady of Suffering. Its color is sky blue (so its members are *azules*). The first brotherhood likes to style itself as more "of the people" and even "poor," while the second purports to be more "select" and even "aristocratic" (113–116).

In view of this labeling, it might be tempting to derive the rivalry from objective class differences, which are as sharp in Castilleja as they are in many other agrotowns of the south. In effect, antonymic epithets like rich/poor, conservative/progressive, landowner/landless, or right/left are frequently applied by Andalusians to their brotherhoods. But this conscious model does not correspond to the facts: agrotown *hermandades* are always "vertical," that is, they integrate people from every social class. As Moreno points out,

> If some community really did possess two semicommunal horizontal closed brotherhoods, each one embodying one of the antagonistic social classes of the town, the tension that this would originate would be capable of destroying not only the dual system of brotherhoods but also the minimum integration . . . that is essential for the very existence of local society. [1985a : 70]

Moreno is not happy with the way in which vertical *hermandades* cannily defuse class tensions and preserve the social peace:

> The symbolic negation of social reality acts in favor of the longevity of the latter, integrating people with diverse class interests into the same organization and producing an egalitarian ideology that carries out a false reading of reality. With this, class consciousness is objectively blocked and the degree of class conflict is reduced as it is transferred not only to a symbolic level but also to certain lines of opposition established in a different way, so that instead of hierarchical social categories and classes being perceived, above all one perceives *halves* that vertically divide the community. [39–40]

Moreno's reading of reality is plausible, but we must not lose sight of several facts. In the first place, the vertical *cofradía* system—even though it may function to shore up the status quo—was not imposed or invented by any one class. It is a popular creation, an anonymous product of the people themselves, people with a flair for building social support structures modeled on the hierarchical or patriarchal Andalusian family (more will be said on this later). In the second place, ethnographic evidence indicates that there is something inherently rewarding about symbolic, socially contained competition. All over Spain, even in northern towns where class differences are minimal, people like to divide themselves into rivalrous halves and fight it out with festive rituals. These traditional rivalries within towns pale by comparison with the feuds *between* towns, which are legendary both for their virulence and for the pleasing sensations of local superiority they provide. History has made Spaniards combative side-takers who thrive on the very idea of opposition. If some groups display a distressing knack for "falsifying" social reality by hiding objective differences, other groups falsify social reality by *inventing* differences where no objective ones exist. The rival aristocratic *cofradías* mentioned in Chapter Two may serve as an example: they were all filled by the members of one social class, blue-blooded men of the elite. Did that lessen their appetite for symbolic or real feuds of all types? Hardly— they simply agreed to disagree. In a less dogmatic moment, Moreno refers to the Andalusian tendency to "dichotomize everything" and to define politics as the struggle one band carries out to overpass another and get its way (1985a:85). Therefore, there is always some kind of dialectic involved. Moreno bristles not at the combative consciousness of the people but at their ignorance of the "real" enemies.

Meanwhile back in Castilleja, Aguilar finds that the popular distinction between the "poor" *rojos* and the "rich" *azules* does have some basis in social reality, since the *Hermandad de la Concepción* includes all of the families who run the lucrative local pastry industry. But it also includes the many lower-class citizens who man the pastry factories. While workers comprise the broad base of the *Hermandad de Santiago,* it also boasts brothers from "the highest point of the social pyramid" (117). Furthermore, the *pasos* and other ritual paraphernalia of the "poor" brotherhood are every bit as lavish as those of the other. The ability of the *rojos* to hold their own and even surpass the others in pomp is recalled in the following partisan lyric:

Qué callaos están los ricos,	How hushed the rich are now,
porque los pobres han ganao,	because the poor have won,
en misa y en procesión,	in Masses and in processions,
y también en alumbrao.	and in lighting effects too.
En la procesión del Carmen,	In the Carmen procession,
iban veintitres mocitas,	there were twenty-three girls,
en Santiago doscientas,	in Santiago two hundred,
y todas muy bonitas.	and all of them very pretty.
[116]	

The rivalry that pits one half of Castilleja against the other is several hundred years old but was sharpened in this century by the Church's decision to unify the two parishes for administrative purposes. Making the church of Santiago the parish seat only inflamed the group pride of the congregation-*cofradía* of the Immaculate Conception; hence, the parochial unification that exists in theory has only made local "differences" more irreconcilable. It has turned the job of parish priest into a precarious balancing act. As Aguilar relates, the slightest indication of partiality toward one of the *hermandades* will be enough to turn the other into an implacable foe, to the point that the average term of service for a priest in Castilleja is considerably less than in other parishes. One man of the cloth was hounded out for neglecting to tell the archbishop that the blue families expected to receive the sacrament of confirmation in their own church. Another found a dead cat hanging in his vestibule, with a note attached: *"Si no quiere verse como este gato, coja usted el hato"* (If you don't want to end up like this cat, start packing). The poor fellow wasted no time in arranging his transfer to another community. The current priest admits that he was spied upon for years before the people were finally convinced of his neutrality (92–109).

One of the things a priest has to be careful with in Castilleja is the color of his vestments: when saying Mass in the church of the Conception, he must avoid wearing the color red; in the church of Santiago at the plaza, he must eschew blue at all costs. Unfortunately, the hymnals and liturgical missals all have red covers—or had, that is, before they were torn off by an anonymous member of the blue brotherhood. Each *hermandad* employs its respective color on all of its emblems, ornaments, *pasos,* tunics, and so forth, while scrupulously avoiding so much as a hint of the other color. The color preferences and phobias of the families of Castilleja do not end there by any means, but actively determine the hue of virtually any belonging—flower pots, drapes, doors, the car, items of clothing, roof tiles, and so on (114–115).

Although the feud between *los rojos* and *los azules* is in force all year long, it is the Lenten cycle and especially Holy Week that provide the chief occasions for its expression. The solidarity of each in-group and its scorn for the out-group increase as the ritual calendar moves through Ash Wednesday, Palm Sunday, Holy Thursday, and Good Friday. Keen competition has ensured that the *pasos* carried through the streets of Castilleja are as ornate as the finest of Seville (125). Given the small size of the town, they must inevitably pass through the "territory" of the rival during the procession, that is, its church. Courtesy demands that a small delegation of the *hermandad* emerge from its church to hold a brief but painful "welcoming reception" for a delegation of the *hermandad* protagonizing the procession.

> It goes without saying that the act is one of the most problematic ones of the entire Holy Week in Castilleja, since nothing could be further from the truth than the cordial manners of one brotherhood for the other, and more so bearing in mind that the official representatives of one have no choice but to contemplate with absolute passivity the entire premeditated spectacle that the other carries out before them. The proof of this is that the courtesy receptions have been suspended for a long time, returning only five years ago. Until then, the doors of both churches remained closed while the other *cofradía* passed by. The cause of the suspension of this custom was precisely a confrontation that occurred one year when the Plaza came out to receive the Calle Real. The versions of what happened are very contradictory, but it seems that there were loud comments exchanged, and then words gave way to deeds, and then the

A solemn marching band accompanies one of Andalusia's numerous icons of Christ the Prisoner.

Baroque or neo-baroque *pasos de palio* shield the weeping Virgin from the sun in cities all over southern Spain.

situation degenerated into a veritable skirmish at the doors of the church in which even the *nazarenos* used their candles as blunt instruments. [Aguilar 1983 : 132–133]

The *cirio* or candle carried by a *nazareno*, incidentally, is usually a yard long and two or three inches thick, thereby making it a formidable war club. It is not the blunt instrument, however, so much as the musical one that has served as the major weapon in the long-standing feud between *los de la Plaza* and *los de la Calle Real*. "Band wars," as we might term the phenomenon, take place primarily on Easter Sunday in Castilleja. For a time the Plaza held the upper hand, for they boasted the services of the Ninth Infantry Regiment Band of Seville, a military marching band prized for its quality. So prized was it that the rival *hermandad* wooed it away several years ago. The *rojos* had no choice but to make up in quantity their deficit in quality, so they now field four bands on Easter Sunday in an effort to drown out their opponents. Experts in sociocentrism, the residents of Castilleja cunningly take advantage of the rivalries existing between the bands of different branches of the Armed Forces (mainly Infantería, Caballería, and Marina) to incite them to play better, or at least louder. This tactic backfired many years ago when the Cavalry band trampled citizens underfoot with their horses in its haste to occupy a strategic intersection (136–137). Today, musical expenses comprise the bulk of each brotherhood's Holy Week budget (146). The bands are hired to play on Easter Sunday, not to celebrate Christ's victory over death, as might be thought, but to accompany the apotheosis of each tribe's Mother figure.

The enemy-twin *cofradías* of Castilleja constitute a "model" example of sociocentric emotionality. Other Andalusian towns that correspond to the Castilleja model include Alcalá del Río, Olivares, Albaida del Aljarafe, Gerena, Benacazón, Coria del Río, Huévar, Salteras, Bollullos, Carrión de los Céspedes, Cantillana, and Setenil (Moreno 1985a : 69–77). Setenil, a town in the province of Cádiz, has been studied in some detail by González Cid (1984). The reciprocal antagonism of the two vertical, semicommunal *hermandades* could hardly be signified with more absolute terms, for one is "white" and the other is "black." The popular appellatives derive from the color of their respective penitential garments. In the beginning, there were only *blancos,* the members of the *Hermandad de la Santa Vera-Cruz* founded in 1551 (yet another instance of the "Franciscan connection"). Sometime during the nineteenth century a disaffected group of *blancos* broke away to form the black-robed *Hermandad de Nuestro Padre Jesús.* Oral tradition has it that an insult to the honor of the *Virgen de la Soledad* was the reason for the rupture (1984 : 375). Some sort of hindsight mythopoesis is surely at work here. It is not likely that the current maternal icon of the *negros* would have been profaned before her protégés existed as a group, for it is rivalry that leads to insults (real or imagined), not vice versa. Be this as it may, "band wars" have been fought in Setenil with special fervor. The high point—or the nadir—was reached when one of the competing *cofradías* introduced a troupe of American majorettes into their Good Friday *Estación de Penitencia* (377). Tired of such scandals, the bishop threatened to place the town under interdict and deprive it of the sacraments. Did the warring brotherhoods meekly bow to ecclesiastical ire and put an end to their excesses? No; they joined forces and informed the bishop that if they were not permitted to go on with their musical competitions they would no longer carry their *pasos,* either (378). Clearly the diocesan authorities had underestimated the extent to which each group's identity was enhanced by the rivalry and the lengths they were willing to go to in order to preserve their identities by protecting their rivalry from outside interference. Just as in Castilleja, the Church was eventually persuaded that the cure would be worse than the sickness, as the Spanish saying has it, and that truly popular religiosity cannot be legislated from above. The bishop finally agreed that the *blancos* and the *negros* could continue to disagree (380–381).

The Church never abandons hope, of course, of being able to guide the *hermandades* into a more spiritual direction. The outcome of this ongoing pastoral endeavor is inevitably related to the "political" acumen of a given priest in a given community. But given the degree of tribalistic emotionality in southern Spain, things will get out of hand sooner or later. Moreno cites a letter to the editor written by the priest of Palma del Condado (Seville), desperate and disgusted because of a fireworks battle staged by the town's warring brotherhoods (1985a : 90–91). Several rockets launched by one *cofradía* scored a direct hit on the roof of the rival group's chapel, thereby provoking a fire that left several people seriously wounded.

I do not wish to give the impression that Andalusian *cofradías* are incapable of policing themselves. In every brotherhood there is a mixture of highly vocal, excitable, and rivalry-obsessed individuals (known as *exaltaos*) and more temperate personalities who are usually open to the nudgings and suggestions and doctrinal directives of the *cofradía* chaplains. Positions of authority within the brotherhood tend to be occupied by cooler heads; but this does not mean that they abandon sociocentric emotionality, only that they sublimate it. Such sublimation, I contend, lies at the heart of eighty percent of everything that gets published on Holy Week in southern Spain—one hundred percent in the case of literary or poetic panegyrics. The great majority of newspaper and magazine articles dealing with the Andalusian Holy Week deal in reality with a particular brotherhood's version of Holy Week—its traditions, its icons, its ritual or cultural activities, and especially its Big Brothers and other prominent members. No *cofradía* worthy of the name will fail to edit a monthly bulletin or newsletter of some kind, and much of the material contained therein consists of out-and-out drumbeating or "historical" pieces that inevitably demonstrate that the *cofradía* is older, more authentic, more charitable, more devout, more popular, or just plain "better" than the others. Here again there is some degree of in-house policing, typically carried out by more serious historians. One in particular, Manuel López Pérez, has sought to defuse the major *causus belli* among the fourteen brotherhoods of Jaén, that is, *antigüedad* (the word itself equates antiquity with seniority):

> In Jaén, as in many other places, there has always existed an absurd rivalry among the *cofradías* regarding their *antigüedad*. Chronological pre-eminence, which normally entails certain privileges and distinctions of a protocolary nature, has even been the motive for serious feuds and absurd historical deformations. . . . To desire out of a puerile imitative spirit to add years, and even centuries, of *antigüedad*, elaborating picturesque theories that link our current brotherhoods with others long disappeared which, although they had the same name or gave cult to the same image, in reality lack a common history or any serious historical connection, is simply to disfigure history. And this is absurd. [López Pérez 1984 : 62–65]

The above denunciation, which as likely as not will fall on deaf ears, serves at least to show us that sociocentric emotional religiosity is not the exclusive terrain of brutish rural rocket launchers. After all, to elaborate a picturesque and self-serving theory about the origins of one's *cofradía* requires a certain degree of education or scholarly ability. Diverse means lead to the same end, however: the greater glory of the group.

It would seem that religiosity in the south is most "tribal" in Castilleja, Setenil, and all of the other small towns that are split into twin bellicose brotherhoods. It would seem reasonable to conjecture that in larger cities the *cofradías* would be more "civilized" or less beholden to hotheaded expressions of in-group identity. Nothing could be farther from the truth. Sociocentric religiosity remains essentially the same as we go from the two *cofradías* of Castilleja to the fourteen of Jaén to the twenty-eight of Córdoba to the fifty-six of Seville. The frame of identity reference changes from small town to urban neighborhood, but there is no lessening or dissolution of the bonds of in-groupness. Moreover, there is little difference in the forms for the venting of sociocentric emotions and invidious one-upmanship. If anything, the greater resources and sophistication of a city mean that the standard vehicles of group affirmation will be used with greater intensity. In Seville, for example, it is not enough for a *cofradía* to have its own band; it must also possess *marchas procesionales* composed especially for its use. The rivalry among the brotherhoods lies behind some of the most moving and imitated religious music in Spain.

The baroque or neo-baroque style of the *pasos,* and especially of the *pasos de palio* that transport the Virgins, is perfectly suited to the continual addition of materials and ornaments designed to make them a little better than last year and a little better than those of the rival. With the dutiful cooperation of the local press, each *cofradía* gives maximum publicity to these additions, which are known as *estrenos* or debuts. *Estrenos* announced by Seville's brotherhoods in 1988, for example, included new silver lanterns to illuminate the procession of *La Bofetá,* wrought by local silversmith Manuel de los Ríos; a diamond brooch by Carrasquilla for the Virgin's petticoat and a knocker by Marmolejo for her *paso de palio (Los Estudiantes);* sculptures of Saint John and Saint Stephen by Ribera for a *paso de misterio (San Esteban);* an embroidered hem for the congregation banner, a coif for the Virgin, and an assortment of silver-plated ornaments for her *paso de palio* by Manuel de los Ríos—all of this was announced by *Los Javieres,* a brotherhood known for its simplicity and austerity! (*ABC,* 29 March 1988, pp. 39–41). These are the *estrenos* of a few *cofradías* that hold their *Estación de Penitencia* on Holy Tuesday; a complete accounting of all *estrenos* announced by Seville's fifty-six *cofradías* would take up several pages. A small army of artisans derive their livelihood from the pious rivalry of the brotherhoods. *Estrenos,* some of which are extremely expensive and all of which are works of art, constitute the chief means for an *hermandad* to demonstrate that it is dynamic and competitive; for this reason, they constitute natural targets for malicious criticism. Evil tongues are active even during Holy Week.

Holy Week Players

Just as a vertical *hermandad* integrates people of diverse socioeconomic backgrounds, it also integrates people of diverse personalities and emotional styles. The penitential brotherhood boasts brothers of all kinds— rocket launchers, apprentice historians, poets, businessmen, those who can direct their collectively sanctioned boosterism into music or print and those who prefer to fight it out with *cirios*. Certain colloquial expressions have arisen to refer to some of these personality types; *capillita,* for example. This is the brother who knows every historical and artistic detail of the *cofradía* and its *pasos* and who will demonstrate his mastery of trivia to anyone who will listen. The *capillita* has his opposite in the *capirotero*. If the former is a kind of super-*cofrade,* the latter is distinguished by his lack of interest in anything outside of the penitential "disguise." The term is a derivation of *capirote,* the conical cardboard stuffing that gives the *caperuza* its unique shape. The ubiquitous *capirotero* has been the target of satire for many years. Muñoz y Pabón mocked him thus back in 1918:

> As soon as it was announced that such-and-such an *hermandad* had begun to distribute its tunics, he went to pick up his, and he brought it home and tried it on so that he could be admired by his wife, his sister-in-law, his mother-in-law, his little ones, and almost all of the neighbor women. [Cit. by Burgos 1982:76]

Moreno asserts that Seville's *cofradías* would lose four-fifths of their members if they could not dress up as *nazarenos* and enjoy all that this entails: to know yourself to be the center of attention, to recognize without being recognized, to be envied, to feel your velvet cape flapping in the wind (1982:109). In the case of those whose primary motivation is religiosity and not vanity or love of disguise, the *traje penitencial* shields them from the ego-bruising effects of "the cultural norm that men should not appear to be very religious in public" (110).

Motives other than religious ones would seem to predominate in men who opt for another variety of Holy Week costume, that of "Roman Soldier." Though far less common than the *nazareno*, the *soldado romano* has enjoyed a unique popularity in certain sectors of the population, that is, adults of the lower classes and children of all classes. His Holy Week mission is to accompany some *paso* of the dead or dying Christ, and his traditional form of organization has not been the *cofradía* but the squadron, the cavalry, the company, or the century. The Roman Soldier costume provokes snickers among the erudite for its blatant historical anachronisms—medieval mesh, sixteenth-century lace collar, capricious baroque plumes, sequins and pink hosiery like those of a bullfighter. But the outfit has been worn with great dignity and even arrogance. In Jaén, for example, to belong to the numerically restricted *soldados romanos* was one of the city's most coveted honors, and to be the very captain of the *centuria* was to win favor and respect at the top of the social pyramid (López Pérez 1984 : 212). In Seville, the Roman Soldiers are known as *armaos* (from *armado* or armed one) and have been permanently attached to the *Hermandad de la Macarena*. Tongue-in-cheek journalists refer to them as *católicos-apostólicos-romanos-sevillanos-macarenos* (*ABC*, 31 March 1988, p. 34). The extent to which these men identify with their Holy Week roles is reflected in numerous anecdotes. One *armao* had a widely talked-of quarrel with his wife regarding the appropriate name for their firstborn son (he insisted it be "Marco Antonio"). Another, a burly and somewhat violent man nicknamed "the Wolf," had committed some infraction of the rules during Holy Week; when he learned as punishment he would be forbidden to dress up as an *armao,* he broke down and cried like a baby (Marín 1986 : 33, 71). What does it feel like to be an *armao*? Miguel Fernández, a firetruck driver with twenty years of "service" as a Roman Soldier, claims that every time he dons his spectacular garb it feels as if he were getting ready for his first bullfight in the *Maestranza* (*ABC*, 31 March 1988, p. 65). As Burgos relates, the *armaos de la Macarena* draw their members chiefly from the fresh produce market on Feria Street (and the waiting list is lengthy); they follow the hierarchical designations of the Spanish rather than the Roman army and mark differences in rank by number of ostrich plumes stuck in their helmets: five for the privates, ten for the corporals, twelve for the second lieutenants, eighteen for the lieutenants, and an ostentatious twenty-one for the captain (1982:128).

In Puente Genil (Córdoba), the *soldados romanos* exist in order to escort men whose costumes are even more striking. In this locality, penitential brotherhoods are known as *Corporaciones Bíblicas* and the Holy Week processions do not contain *nazarenos* but *Figuras Bíblicas*. With their origins in the seventeenth century, these Biblical Figures are now more than 300 in number, each an ornate costume and mask representing personages of the Old Testament, the life, works, and Passion of Christ, or doctrines of the Catholic faith (Melgar and Marín 1987:40–42).

Despite such fascinating local variations, the dominant Holy Week garment remains that of *nazareno,* whose basic design allows for a wide variety of identifying color combinations. As discussed previously, those *nazarenos* who wish to put the accent on penitence will let their *caperuza* down, so to speak, by removing the cardboard *capirote.* One can still do significant penitence with the conical headgear in place, however, by simply removing one's shoes and trudging along barefoot for the eight to twelve hours that an *Estación de Penitencia* lasts. Hierarchical distinctions within the brotherhood are conveyed by the order of appearance and the right to carry certain insignia (the identity signs of the group in a literal sense). As evidence of the conservative nature of religious traditions in the south, the physical sequence of the procession has remained largely the same for over two hundred years. *Nazarenos* walk along ahead of a *paso,* while *penitentes* carrying their crosses come behind. The *paso* of Christ or the *paso de misterio,* which includes Christ and several other figures, always precedes—by several hundred yards in most cases—the Virgin's *paso de palio.* It is common to see groups of women clinging to the rear of the *palio* in completion of some promise made to María.

The *pasos* themselves are carried by groups of men known as *costaleros,* and their role is popularly regarded as the most heroic of all. It would certainly seem to be as physically demanding a role as that of the *penitentes. Pasos* weighing between two and three metric tons are transported on the backs of *cuadrillas* made up of thirty to fifty *costaleros,* normally hidden from view by a thick curtain surrounding the base of the *paso.* Claustrophobics need not apply: there is not a lot of "elbow room" under a *paso,* or ventilation, and in addition the men cannot even see where they are going. Every movement that the *cuadrilla* makes is controlled by the *capataz,* who for his part shoulders the awesome responsibility of moving the onerous, ornate *paso* out of the temple through streets broad or narrow for several hours and then back to the temple. The linguistic consequences of all this have been considerable. A specific word or phrase has been coined or co-opted for every detail of the *paso* and its underbelly, for every kind of lift or step that *costaleros* must execute in all kinds of terrain, for their clothing, and so forth. Thanks to Antonio Burgos, we know a great deal about the "folklore" of Seville's *costaleros* (1982 : 21— 66). The vocabulary varies, however, from province to province. In Jaén, for example, a *capataz* is called a *fabricano,* and a *costalero-cofrade* is called a *promitente* (López Pérez 1984 : 199—200).

The plebeian roots of this folklore are undeniable: *costaleros* were always drawn from the ranks of construction, agricultural, market, or dock workers who were already experienced in carrying heavy loads. Burgos dedicates his book to "the memory of the stevedores of Seville, who loaded *pasos* during seven days and ships the rest of the year" (1982 : 3). It was the tradition for a *cofradía* to hire a *capataz* and *cuadrilla* to carry its *pasos* during Holy Week for an agreed-upon amount of money. The evolution of the Spanish economy during the 1960s and early 1970s led to the downfall of this system; laborers with continually rising expectations grew ever more restive with the paltry sums they earned in a Holy Week *cuadrilla.* There was a transitional period that lasted from approximately 1975 to 1985 in which the old crews of mercenary *costaleros* were gradually replaced by enthusiastic teams of *hermanos* (a practice that had existed in Jaén since the 1940s). This process seemed to perplex secularizing observers like Burgos and Moreno. The former was bewildered by the growing "superimposition of the religious over the popular" (1982 : 13), as if they were two watertight categories, while the latter pondered the new *costalero*'s possible motivations:

> Reinforcement of *machismo* by the demonstration of strength and guts that carrying a *paso* implies? A way to increase the admiration of fiancées and girlfriends by endurance in a job "that only men can handle"? The emotion of feeling *his* Christ or *his* Virgin on his shoulders? An ego trip? A hobby, above all? [1982 : 152]

Moreno seems to assume that macho-style exhibitionism and religiosity are mutually exclusive, going on to take the side of the "true" *costalero* being wiped out by the vain and impetuous young and predicting "graver problems" than the ones motivating the change (i.e., the impromptu

A *nazareno* adjusts the *capirote* of his *caperuza* before the procession (photo: Encarnación Lucas).

strikes being staged by the "true" *costaleros*). Time has proved such ideo-
logically based misgivings wrong. By 1988, Burgos's comfortable "fossil
of popular traditions" had been completely renovated by the new breed
of not-for-profit *costaleros*. The young, well-trained volunteers were able
to perform striking street maneuvers with the *pasos*—hence their rapid
acceptance by the populace in general. The fact that the new *costalero-
cofrades* are known and loved by the *cofradía*'s members and devotees—a
situation that did not obtain with the mercenary crews of yesteryear—
has introduced a new degree of emotion into the *Estación de Penitencia*.
The emergence of the *paso del Gran Poder* from its temple in Castilleja, for
example, had always been a moving affair; a solemn silence in which only
the voice of the *capataz* and the footsteps of the *costaleros* could be heard
would always give way at the door to excited applause and hurrahs. But
Holy Thursday of 1982 was special,

> since for the first time the *paso* of Christ was to be brought out by young *cos-
> taleros* of the *hermandad*—people, therefore, with affective or family relation-
> ships with many of those who were present at the scene and who could not
> contain their tears of pride and emotion while watching them. Soon the scene
> was filled with ardent shouts directed to the Lord, such as "*¡Padre mío!*" or
> "*¡Jesús mío*, you are in the street!" and many more, punctuated by weeping,
> such as that of the lady who acclaimed the valor of the *costaleros* and repeated
> again and again, "*¡Padre mío*, your own sons are carrying you!" [Aguilar
> 1983:130]

The affective bonds that unite the men under the icon platform are as
strong as those that unite them with their adoring public. Long hours of
hard labor at close quarters develop a unique spirit of camaraderie among
costaleros. Like *cofrades* everywhere, they pay reverence to the memory of
their deceased brothers—especially when they die in the line of duty. On
Holy Wednesday of 1986, a *costalero* named José dropped dead of a heart
attack beneath a *paso* (that of the Christ of Health, as irony would have
it). The following year, his surviving comrades brought the *paso* to a halt
on the very spot where tragedy had struck. To the mournful accompani-
ment of a *saeta*, the Christ was *levantado a pulso*, the hardest and most
impressive way to raise a *paso*, millimeter by agonizing millimeter.

> In this simple way, the *Hermandad de San Bernardo* dedicated its best day of
> the year to the brother, the *cofrade*, the friend, the companion who had died
> under the Lord. What better place to die? [González del Piñal 1988:79–80]

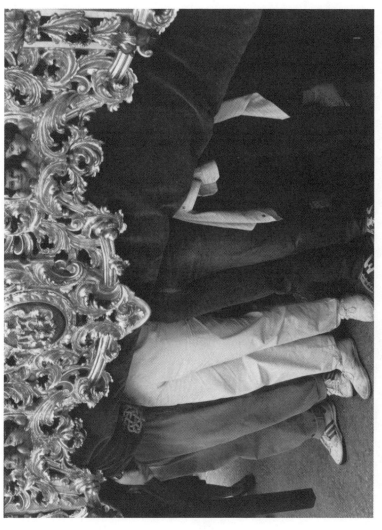

Costaleros move their feet in identical steps as they carry their ornate platforms through the streets.

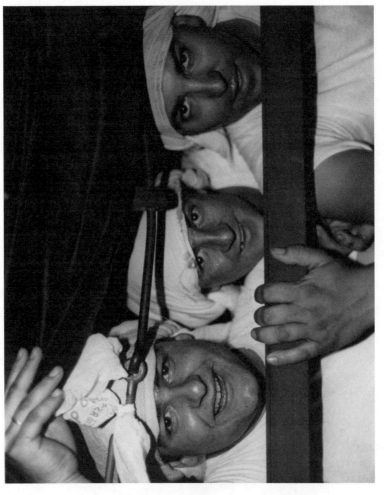

Carrying a *paso* is arguably the most arduous of Holy Week rituals. *Costaleros* need frequent breathers in order to carry on (photo: Encarnación Lucas).

Incidentally, this anecdote serves to demonstrate that, in some situations, manly exhibition of strength and religiosity are one and the same thing. Sex-role expectations in general, it can be added, are inseparable from popular forms of piety in the south; and when gender and piety are mediated by pain the results can be striking. The cultural prestige of the *Dolorosa* is a prime example of this (as I will discuss in Chapter Four).

If on the one hand the rivalry between *cofradías* makes for spectacular processions and superb works of art, on the other hand it functions to unify all the members of each *cofradía*. The emotional character of intergroup rivalry reinforces the emotional, nonrational, noninstrumental emotionality of companionship within each group. This sociality has been masculine, generally speaking; in southern Spain, men tend to prefer the company of men, and if the other men are their "brothers," so much the better. Nevertheless, there are places, such as Castilleja, where

> the real role of woman in the *hermandades* is very active; despite the fact that officially she can hold no office with the governing board, she possesses very significant functions in key aspects of their structures. For this reason, for women—or at least for those who are more involved with the activities of the *hermandad*—the characteristic of generalized sociability is equally valid. [Aguilar 1983 : 84–85]

To properly understand the role of "sisters" in the brotherhood, we must draw a careful distinction between organizational mechanics and psychological dynamics. In the former, women have been clearly subordinate, as subordinate as they have been in Andalusian institutions in general. In the latter, they have been crucial and occasionally preponderant. I will take up the psychological or psychosexual aspects of *hermandades* in the final part of this chapter. With regard to organizational mechanics, the traditional role of woman as "helpmate" in the *cofradías*, as well as the male attitude that made it possible, are manifest in the following statement:

> The *camarera* is a very old and classic institution in the *cofradías* of Holy Week. It was made necessary by the Baroque and very Andalusian custom of dressing the images. It was essential for someone to take care of the clothes and their cleaning, someone who knew how to put them on with grace and modesty and change them as often as needed. And no one was more appropriate than woman. Woman, with her constant and deeply-rooted devotion; with her delicacy and sense of detail; with her art of the needle and her gentleness in keeping the clothing clean and perfect. [Ortega Sagrista 1984b : 204]

The sheer quantity of robes, veils, dresses, capes, crowns, jewels, and other iconic appurtenances has given rise to special associations of women, normally the wives, mothers, and daughters of *cofrades,* who charge themselves with the care and dressing of the icon as well as the confection of new garments. Specialized varieties of embroidery and needlework that have disappeared in the rest of Spain survive in these groups of female Andalusians.

But times are changing. The recent incorporation of *nazarenas* (note the feminine ending) provides dramatic proof that popular religious traditions in southern Spain have not become fossilized. *Vera-Cruz,* considered one of the most austere *cofradías* of Seville, introduced *nazarenas* in 1987 and now has over fifty (*ABC,* 28 March 1988, p. 40). A dozen *nazarenas* marched with the *Hermandad de Santa Marta* in 1988 and over thirty with *Los Panaderos* (*ABC,* 31 March 1988, p. 32). As one female *cofrade* told me in Seville, there have always been clandestine female penitents, women who paid the *cuota de salida* in the name of their fathers or their uncles and then donned the penitential garb, their breasts dissembled by the ample folds of the *caperuza* and their hands protected from view by matching gloves. Therefore the above statistics refer to the formal and official participation of *nazarenas,* which has come about since the lifting of the ecclesiastical ban. Permitted or not, there are many male *cofrades* and a few female ones who are opposed to the very idea. While watching the *nazarenas* of *Vera-Cruz* file past in 1988, I heard several men grumbling about the diminutive crosses that some of the *señoritas penitentas* were carrying, and their low-heeled shoes, and the painted fingernails of one or two. Dynamic female *cofrades* have pressed for their rights since Vatican II with constancy and Job-like patience. And humor: a woman lecturing to a brotherhood in Granada reminded her listeners that women had shown more spunk than men during the crucifixion of Christ, since several women were present at Calvary and only one man—John—who had not even been able to keep his eyes open in the Garden the night before (cit. by Marín 1986 : 152).

The formal participation of women in the *Estación de Penitencia* will be a long drawn out process. For the foreseeable future, woman's role at the level of organizational mechanics will continue to be a pale reflection of her role in the psychological dynamics and overall emotional life of a *cofradía,* where intense feelings of individual and group identity can most often be traced to familial fixations of a most primary nature.

A Family Affair

Up to now I have reviewed the structuring power of sociocentric emotionality in the south, whereby rivalries between brotherhoods forge unities within them. It would be impossible to ascertain which came first, the rivalry or the unity; intergroup competition and intragroup sociability seem to be two sides of the same coin. The endless arguments about antiquity, band wars, color phobias, and ornamental one-upmanship discussed earlier are vehicles of the former, while the organization of the procession and the distribution of roles and costumes constitute a *cofradía*'s main occasions of camaraderie. Not all is brotherly love within a brotherhood, of course, but the consciousness of a common "enemy" is invaluable in defusing the personality conflicts that inevitably arise. Ultimately, all hinges upon clear-cut identity and its rewards.

It is crucial to bear in mind that a person's sense of identification with a given *hermandad* is by no means a function of formal membership. One does not have to don the penitential tunic or dress up as a *soldado romano* or play any role whatsoever in the organization in order to belong to it— or, more accurately, to belong to *Him* and to *Her*. For it is the loyal attachment to the images of Jesus and María that magnetizes the emotion and devotion of a *cofradía* and its public alike—to the point that in many cases a man's or a woman's psychosexual identity is permanently influenced by his or her relationship with a "parental" icon.

To begin with, the passionate rivalries of Castilleja and numerous other agrotowns with enemy-twin brotherhoods become fully understandable only when we consider the familial roots of image devotion. One is literally born into a *cofradía* in such places, that of one's parents. In the event one is the result of a "mixed" marriage, he or she will almost always be assigned to the *cofradía* of the mother. Such marriages are infrequent in towns that take their rivalries seriously, as they usually do. Each half tends to be endogamous and the informal social control of premarital friendships is considerable. If true love should blossom between a boy and a girl of opposing *hermandades*, it may soon wither and die from the menacing glances, sneers, and taunts that it elicits, especially during festal periods. Aguilar recounts the story of one complacent young man who put on the tunic of the rival *hermandad* in order to please his girlfriend. Recognized by his own relatives during the *Estación de Penitencia*, he paid for his treason with a humiliating public buffeting (1983:160). In towns all over the south, people can cite numerous examples of engagements that were broken up—sometimes on the very eve of the wedding—for going against the endogamous prejudices of the brotherhoods (Moreno 1985a:81).

Once the marriage is consummated and children have made their appearance, it is the mother who will cement their loyalty to a *cofradía* and especially to its images; if the primary image is a Virgin of any advocation, what might be called the "maternal connection" is redoubled. A veritable process of imprinting takes place and its effects are extremely durable, as seen in the case of the typical Castilleja infant:

> When he can scarcely talk, the mother teaches him to pronounce the name of the Virgin and her *hermandad,* and he is asked very frequently, especially in front of relatives and friends of the same *hermandad:* "Which do you belong to?" To which the child, already coached, invariably responds "I belong to ____!" provoking shouts of joy from all present and earning all kinds of kisses and demonstrations of affection. In this way, the child grows up with two foci of affection: his family, especially embodied by the mother, and his *hermandad,* and between both he distributes his love and affection with equal strength. From the beginning these two emotional foci become inseparable and thus any criticism or attack upon his *hermandad* will be felt as if it were directed against his family, against his own mother. [Aguilar 1983:88]

In the meantime, what is the father doing? Typically, the Andalusian father shoulders responsibility for the economic maintenance of the home while leaving nurturance and early childhood education almost entirely to his wife. Outside the home, he may join with other fathers in the economic administration of an *hermandad* whose main emotional agglutinant is a sacred female icon. The sacred male icon, meanwhile, is the object of a distanced and respectful veneration that largely reflects the empirical reality of fathers in the south. Both the empirical and symbolic levels of *cofradía* life, therefore, are "a family affair." Emotions follow suit: one is expansive and familiar with the Mother image, cautious and formal with the Father image (at least as a general rule).

Nowhere else in Spain does the somewhat unorthodox appellation of *Nuestro Padre Jesús* (Our Father Jesus) occur with such frequency as in the south. The "paternal connection" is redoubled in the case of *Nuestro Padre Jesús del Gran Poder,* an Andalusian cult par excellence. In the words of a popular *saeta:*

El más preciado clavel,	The most precious carnation,
el más justo Redentor,	the most just Redeemer,
el que tiene más poder,	the One who has more power,
¡ay! Jesús del Gran Poder,	Oh! Jesus of Great Power,
eres mi Padre y Señor.	You are my Father and Lord.
[López Fernández 1981:82]	

The image in this case is always the Nazarene Christ, clad in a luxurious Passion purple tunic and carrying a gigantic cross on one shoulder. A Christ by any name, of course, has more power than a Virgin. Whereas María is the one you go to for relatively small favors, consolation, pity, and spiritual affection, Our Father Jesus is kept in reserve for matters of life and death. The Virgin is the supernatural go-between, pleading for paternal benevolence in much the same way as a terrestrial woman mediates between her children and their authoritarian father. By a happy theological ambiguity, Jesus is also María's Son, and He always gives in to His Mother like any good Andalusian son of any age; that is, if there is no objection from the Father of Our Father Jesus. The familial-supernatural chain of command is set up like this: People ↔ Virgin Mother ↔ Fatherly Son ↔ Fatherly Father. If there is a mystery here, it must be traceable to the mysterious inner logic of patriarchy in a Catholic clime.

The popular liturgy of Holy Week processions is utterly consistent with the above schema. The motions that the Sevillian town of Marchena puts its *pasos* through on Good Friday may serve as an example: the *costaleros* under the image of *Jesús Nazareno* literally turn His back to the crowd assembled at the town plaza; then the men under the *paso de palio* of the Virgin bring it as close as possible to the other one. A *saetero* then sings the first explanatory *copla:*

Jesús nos vuelve la espalda,	Jesus turns His back on us,
pero su Madre le implora	but His Mother implores Him
que mire a los pecadores,	to look toward the sinners
aunque ella se quede sola.	even though she is to be alone.

At this point the *paso* of Christ is turned around to face the crowd. And the scene is immediately glossed by the second *saeta:*

Volviendo la cara al pueblo	Turning his face to the people
y respetando a su Madre,	and respecting His Mother,
nos echa la bendición	He gives us His blessing

y pide al Eterno Padre
que nos conceda el perdón.
  [López Fernández 1981 : 44]

and asks the Eternal Father
to concede us His pardon.

In Castilleja, where Virgins are both the instruments and the objects of partisan passions, the *Cristo del Gran Poder* possesses the power to cross *cofradía* boundary lines. The people of the Santiago parish feel more devotion for the Nazarene Christ of the Calle Real congregation than they do for their own dead Christ in His sacred urn; many *rojos* are therefore present in the crowd when the *azules* bring out their *Gran Poder* for His agonic journey through the streets (Aguilar 1983 : 131–132). Along with the greater power of the Father figures, it is their greater distance that facilitates the transcending of sectarian emotion. For the same reason, invidious comparisons between Christs of different groups are not common. It is also significant that, in Castilleja and indeed all over the south, dying Christs are more powerful than dead—or resurrected—ones.

The Mother figure is another matter entirely, possessed of another sort of power. In southern Spain, whenever there is need of group affirmation at any level—*hermandad,* city, county, or region—some icon of the Virgin is likely to be involved. The ever-growing cult of the *Virgen del Rocío* provides ample proof of this. Naturally, María's power to unite is a correlate of her power to divide; at the level of tribalistic passion, it will often be a case of my-Virgin-against-yours. It is not the virginal so much as the maternal aspect of María that makes this possible, a result of early childhood identification with a real nurturing female and subsequent projection of same onto a given Marian cult until the end of one's days. A *saeta* sung to the *Virgen de Soledad* of Castilleja is revealing in this respect:

Soleá, yo a ti te quiero,
porque al nacer me enseñaron
a quererte con locura,
y me apuntaron de hermano,
y hasta el día que me muera,
no me pierdo un Viernes Santo
sin ver tu cara morena.
  [Aguilar 1983 : 88]

Soledad, I love you,
because at birth they taught me
to love you madly,
and they enrolled me as a brother,
and until the day I die,
I will not miss a Good Friday
without seeing your brunet face.

The long-term effects of such imprinting on individual personality orientation have only begun to be studied. In a fascinating monograph, Moreno hypothesizes that it may be a contributing factor in the larger-than-expected number of effeminate men found in Andalusian agro-

Andalusians learn to identify with their parents' *hermandad* at a very early age.

towns. Moreno begins by correlating the sex of a given sacred image with the differing systems of ascription whereby a child is assigned at birth to the *hermandad* of the mother or that of the father; he reasons that when a male child is born into the *hermandad* of his mother and its principal icon is one of the Virgin, he may come to have marked feminine personality traits. In those cases where a female child is automatically assigned to the *hermandad* of her father and the tutelary image is Christ (alias Our Father Jesus), she may well end up as a tomboy. Such effects will tend to be neutralized when a matrilineal ascription system is attached to a male icon or when a patrilineal system is oriented toward a female icon (Moreno 1985a: 147–165). Since the matrilineal form is by far the most common throughout Andalusia (153), it is reasonable to assume that psychosexual identity formation will be slanted in a feminine direction for men and women alike.

The potential implications of all this are striking. Gilmore and Gilmore interpreted Andalusian *machismo* as the struggle to "disidentify" with the powerful Andalusian mother (1979); but what happens when the mother figure has a supernatural hold on one's identity? Perhaps some men will give up without a struggle. The matrilineal ascription system is in force in Castilleja and may well lie behind an effeminate, fervently religious class of young men known as *maricas*. (As opposed to a *maricón*, or homosexual, a *marica* is a sissy or milksop. The prefix "*mari-*" seems significant in this context of overwhelming Marianism.) Despite their aberrant personalities, or perhaps because of them, *maricas* have an important role to play in Castilleja's *hermandades*

> since they are considered to possess the feminine quality of "good taste" as much as women, and can even surpass them in this respect. For this reason, each *hermandad* designates one of them, assisted by several more and some woman, to prepare the images, the *pasos,* and the general decoration of the church for any important ceremony. [Aguilar 1983: 125]

One such ceremony is the dressing of a Virgin, something that no brotherhood's board of directors could bear to supervise or even dare to observe. As one man explained while hurrying out of the church of Santiago, "It's something I can't help, I can't watch them undress the Virgin, I can't be here when I know they are going to change Her" (179). *Vergüenza* in the sense of shame-modesty is augmented by the fear of sacrilege. In nearby Seville, it was held that no one—meaning no man—had ever been able

An eighteenth-century *Mater Dolorosa,* typical of the hundreds of virginal/ maternal icons that anchor identities throughout southern Spain (photo: Encarnación Lucas).

It takes forty-eight men to carry this *paso de misterio* through crowded streets at daybreak on Good Friday. A Roman cavalryman and Simon the Cyrene accompany an image of Christ making His third fall (photo: Encarnación Lucas).

to see the *Virgen de los Reyes* without her clothes; the only one who tried had been struck blind instantly (Guichot 1986:117). Not that there is much to see, however; since the sixteenth century, dressable icons of the Virgin consist only of a sculpted face and hands attached to a simple wooden *candelero* (González Gómez 1985:130).

The image is real enough for the *maricas* of Castilleja. One night Aguilar stayed behind in the church with another woman and four *maricas* pledged to the service of the Virgin of Solitude. It took them hours to choose the clothing, put it on, and adjust it:

> In the first place they proceeded to undress Her, and immediately they began to argue about which clothes would be the most appropriate. One had the feeling that they were talking about a living being when they would nonchalantly say things like "Today let's put on the blue outfit with the white mantle that goes so well with Her." . . . When all was finished, the one who had done most of the work could not repress a last spontaneous gesture, and before getting down from the altar he drew close and kissed the Soledad, exclaiming "*¡Ay, qué guapa estás!*" [Oh, how lovely you are now!], a phrase that the others seconded with enthusiasm and conviction. [1983:179–180]

It is undoubtedly their intimate relationship with the maternal icon that lies behind another socially sanctioned role of the *maricas*. For when the images are being carried through the streets on Easter Sunday, these men become the most vocal exalters of the charms of their Virgin and the most unabashed critics of the Virgin that belongs to the rival *hermandad*. *Maricas* get away with shouted comments that are warmly applauded by all those with too much *vergüenza* to shout themselves. The slogans run the gamut from "*Viva* the pride of Castilleja!"—by which the wrong Virgin is subtly left out of the picture—to more direct comparisons like "*Viva* the one with the oldest *palio!*" to overtly catty allegations like "*Viva* the one without the Carnival dress!" or "*Viva* the one that's not pasty-faced!" (134–143).

I believe there is an emotional continuum between the antics of matrilineal *maricas* and the pious feminoid masochism of other men whose expressive vehicle is not the *viva* but the sermon, the poem, or the *saeta* (I will develop this idea in the next chapter). The emphasis now is on the passionate identification of all kinds of people, not just *maricas,* with Passional parental icons. The main issue is that of identity and its rewards: to glorify a given advocation is to glorify your own mystical Mother or Father, supernatural guarantors of your own identity and dependable dispensers of favors. When individual personality anchors itself in partisan emotionality, the results can be anything from sublime to childish. "I come every afternoon to pray to my *Gran Poder,*" said one Sevillian woman to another. "He's the most miraculous image in all Seville." "You can say what you want," replied the other, "but wherever *my* Christ is, no other is as miraculous." The first shot back: "You think so, eh? That image you're talking about couldn't even cure a cold!" (Marín 1986:22). This is a true story. So is another Marín recounts whose central figure is the Virgin known by the same name as the neighborhood she protects, the *Macarena.* The Virgin was returning to her basilica one Good Friday at the end of the *Estación de Penitencia,* mounted on her sumptuous *paso de palio,* slowly making her way through the adoring multitudes. A Jesuit priest watching the scene was so overcome by emotion that he could not help shouting, "*Madre mía,* if you are so beautiful, what must the one in heaven be like?" A *nazareno* standing by turned around and heatedly replied, "Would you get out of here? The one in heaven is uglier than this one!" (27).

To glorify a given maternal or paternal icon is to glorify the devotional in-group that one happens to belong to—by no means limited to an *hermandad.* The group and the image are actually felt to belong to one another, which is why so many advocations are in the possessive case. In Córdoba, for example, *El Cristo de los Hortelanos* (The Christ of the Vegetable-Gardeners) is a Nazarene Christ with a special mechanism in His arm that allows Him to bless the gardens of His protégés. *El Cristo de los Esparragueros* was the special devotion of a neighborhood populated by wretched asparagus-pickers; the hoary icon is adorned with an old-fashioned natural hair wig (Gutiérrez 1978:121, 158). It is the same feeling of mutual possession that makes so many popular *saetas* sound like *vivas* in a more aesthetic guise:

Virgen de la Macarena,	Virgin of the *Macarena,*
la más bonita y graciosa,	the prettiest and most gracious,
para alivio de penas	for the relief of sorrows
tienes la cara de rosa.	you have a pink face.
¿Dónde vas paloma blanca	Where are you going white dove
tan triste y afligida,	so sad and afflicted,
llorando con tanta pena,	weeping with such sorrow,

si por ti damos la vida
los hijos de la Macarena?

when for you we'd give our lives
the children of the *Macarena*?

Madre mía de la Esperanza,
honra de los trianeros,
es tu cara más bonita
que la de los macarenos.
  [López Fernández 1981:81–82]

My Mother of Hope,
honor of the *trianeros,*
your face is prettier
than [the Mother] of the *macarenos.*

Mírala por donde viene
la Virgen de los Dolores,
la que se lleva la gala
de todas las procesiones.

Look, here she comes
the Virgin of the Pains,
the pride and joy
of all the processions.

Anda con Dios, Madre mía,
Reina entre todas las mujeres,
que eres la más presumida,
que hasta los presos te quieren.
Anda con Dios, Madre mía.
  [Martínez Ramos 1984:245]

Go with God, my Mother,
Queen among all women,
you are the sauciest,
and even the prisoners love you.
Go with God, my Mother.

Sooner or later, the desire to exalt the feminine finery and graces of the Mother figure will produce slightly grotesque *saetas* like the following:

De las alas de un mosquito
hizo la Virgen su manto,
y le salió tan bonito
que lo estrenó el Viernes Santo
en el entierro de Cristo.
  [Martínez Ramos 1984:245]

From the wings of a mosquito
the Virgin made her mantle,
and it turned out so pretty
that she wore it on Good Friday
at the burial of Christ.

Like any other Andalusian collectivity, Gypsies affirm their group identity through their paternal and maternal protectors:

Parroquia de Santiago
orgullo debe tené,
porque encierra en tu aentro
lo mejó de tó Jeré,
a Nuestro Pare der Prendimiento.

Parish of Santiago,
you must be proud,
for you guard inside you
the best of all Jerez,
Our Father of the Arrest.

Ere vara de azucena,
ramo de rosa y clavele,
hija de Joaquín y Ana,
prima de Santa Isabel
y en er cielo soberana,
¡Angustia, la má gitana!
  [Plata 1984:50, 57]

You are a sprig of white lily,
bouquet of roses and carnations,
daughter of Joaquín and Ana,
cousin of Santa Isabel
and in heaven [you are] sovereign,
[Our Lady of] Angustias, the
  Gypsiest!

The sacro-familial nature of group identity in southern Spain has always spelled trouble for secularizing political modernity. Although the problem has traditionally been presented in terms of left versus right, it can be argued that the issue for the people involved is that of sacred versus secular authority. People whose sociopsychological stability is based on their loyalty to supernatural parental protectors will naturally resent any attempt by mere terrestrial authorities to limit the sacred authorities' sphere of action. In Andalusia such attempts have been forthcoming from both the Left and the Right, and the results have been the same: a revival of the classic Andalusian fear of domination by other groups and a net increase in sociocentric emotionality. Under duress people will cling to their absolute Maternal and Paternal authority symbols more fervently than ever. A number of examples can be cited to show that popular religion in the south is genuinely apolitical, as apolitical as emotion itself, or conversely that politics can be a continuation of religious passion by other means.

During the 1930s the penitential brotherhoods were caught in the middle of the increasingly vicious struggle between rightist and leftist fanatics. The Government banned Holy Week processions in some areas of Spain in 1932, ostensibly to keep extremist violence in check; a better way of provoking anti-Republican sentiment could hardly have been found. What happened in Castro del Río, a small town in the province of Córdoba, was typical: on Good Friday the entire population was crowded into the parish church, waiting for authorization to begin the traditional procession with their beloved maternal icon, the *Virgen de la Soledad*. Permission never came. Popular fervor was running high and it was only a matter of time before a large group of the locals rushed forward, shouldered the Virgin, and made for the door. Priests shouting caution were overruled by everyone else. An eyewitness describes what happened in the street:

> Despite its breadth the street is not wide enough for the hundreds of *castreños* that accompany their Mother. The moment is one of confusion. Some people applaud, others cry, others laugh. One hears no processional music or *saetas*. At the Meléndez house on Corredera Street the applause and the vivas become more ardent still. A secret policeman, one of two that had been sent in those days to Castro, took out his pistol with the intention of firing. He never had a chance. A group of men, with several of the Meléndez among them, valiantly fell upon his arm. [Salido Bravo 1984:17]

The following year, in Seville's Plaza de San Lorenzo, crowds waiting in vain for the Christ of Great Power to emerge from the church were moved to tears by a spontaneous *saeta:*

Descubrirse, hermanos míos,	Hats off, my brothers,
vamos a hincarnos de rodillas,	let us get down on our knees,
que ahí dentro está el Gran Poder,	for there inside is the Great Power,
honra y gloria de Sevilla,	honor and glory of Seville,
que no nos lo dejan ver.	and they won't let us see Him.
Honra y gloria de Sevilla,	Honor and glory of Seville,
¿cuándo te volveré a ver?	when will I see you again?
[Marín 1986 : 38]	

It might at first be thought that it was the clumsily anticlerical politicians of the Second Republic that the *saetero* was referring to when he sang "*they* won't let us see Him." But as Moreno has demonstrated beyond the shadow of a doubt, it was the *cofradía* governing boards in Seville themselves that cajoled and threatened their members into boycotting the processions (1982 : 180−214). Most of the Big Brothers, it seems, were in league with reactionary forces bent on weakening the government. It was authority on the far Right, therefore, that was effectively blocking the traditional journey of *Nuestro Padre Jesús del Gran Poder* through the streets of Seville. For Moreno, this makes all the difference; for popular religiosity, it makes no difference. For the people involved, the issue was not the ideology of power but who had it—Christ or "the authorities." This, of course, is one of the great themes of the Passion itself, and the downtrodden masses of the south have been acutely attuned to it. As I hope to show later, the harsh and arbitrary exercise of authority has been a major factor in the evolution of what has been termed "the Passion according to Andalusia." Significantly, in Moreno's paean to the *Hermandad de la Estrella,* the humble neighborhood *cofradía* that stood alone against the fiats and calumnies of the (right-wing) authorities, there is more than a touch of righteous Passional indignation.

There is no better way to manipulate group passions than to tell the group that some other group is trying to manipulate it. This explains the success of a *saeta* that was sung to the Virgin in 1934 in Seville and spread like wildfire throughout the south. It was apparently motivated by President Azaña's incautious remarks about Spain no longer being Catholic.

Han dicho en el "banco azul"	They have said in the "blue bench"
que por ser republicana	that because she is Republican

España ya no es cristiana.	Spain is no longer Christian.
¡Aquí quien manda eres Tú,	Here the one in charge is You,
Estrella de la mañana!	Star of the morning!
[López Fernández 1981:83]	

Melgar and Marín offer this version and another that ends with *¡Madre de Dios Soberana!*—"Sovereign Mother of God!" (1987:91–92). If such verses sound like pure demagoguery, it is because they are: *pure* demagoguery that can only stir up passion by telling people exactly what they want to hear. The people of Seville, Córdoba, and the other places where this *saeta* was sung wanted to hear that their identity was intact and still sustained by the *highest* authority, an Authority to be respected by all worldly authorities. During Lent of 1988, the *Hermandad de la Macarena* sponsored an "Act in Exaltation of the *Saeta*" in their beautiful mini-basilica; one of the exalters ended his harangue by citing the above mentioned *saeta* and he brought down the house. I had never seen such wild cheering and applause in a church before, and I assure the reader that the crowd assembled there was ninety percent proletarian.

All over the south, and especially in the larger cities, the purest demagoguery has been institutionalized in the form of the *pregón* or proclamation, a speech given as a preliminary to the Holy Week processions in which some local celebrity with a flair for oratory fans the flames of sociocentric religiosity. During the 1950s, reports Moreno, the most successful *pregoneros* of Seville were carried out on the shoulders of their impassioned listeners like so many triumphant bullfighters (1982:70). Would-be demagogues had better make sure, however, that they are in tune with the sentiments of their listeners. In 1981, Spanish president Leopoldo Calvo Sotelo visited Seville during Holy Week to have his photo taken with *cofradía* Big Brothers and make some political capital off the popular processions. Standing on a balcony overlooking Adriano Street, the president smiled and waved his hand to the people in the street below who were waiting to see the *paso de palio* of the Virgin of Pity. When the Virgin finally appeared, a man named Luis Cabrera sang the following impromptu *saeta*:

Escucha bien, Madre mía,	Listen well, my Mother,
la plegaria de mi cante.	to the prayer of my song.
Te pido con toda mi alma	I ask you with all my soul
que bendigas y protejas	to bless and protect
al Presidente de España.	the President of Spain.

The *saetero*'s efforts were rewarded with a massive chorus of boos, hisses, and insults, which were quickly extended to the man on the balcony as well (Melgar and Marín 1987:93; Moreno 1982:178–180).

Can the popular disgust with the politicized *saeta* be described in terms of Right or Left? I think not. People resented the very idea that a mere president could somehow usurp the protagonism of an *Estación de Penitencia*. It is one thing for an *hermandad* governing board to curry favor or garner influence, quite another to gain popular sentiment. Holy Week is nothing if not sentiment. The tribalistic emotionality I have discussed in this chapter is inseparable from the rivalrous affirmation of difference, the drawing of boundaries, and, above all, the designation of authority—*divine* authority that is considered more real than any secular power and implies bonds as strong as those that tie sons and daughters to mothers and fathers. The need to know who you are and where you come from will not go out of style easily in family- and neighborhood-oriented Andalusia. Even in the Sevillian *barrios* most devastated by progress, the sacred image is the one thing that people who have moved elsewhere will return to see again and again (González del Piñal 1988:76). Identity is indeed of the essence, identity conceived of in defensive, highly emotional, sacro-familial terms. Sociocentrism is a basic feature of the emotionality that animates Andalusian culture in general and Passional culture in particular. As we will see in the next chapter, passionate feelings of ingroupness have even produced some remarkable distortions in the narrative of the Passion itself.

Chapter 4

The Passion Retold

Romance Catholicism

If I have presented my case effectively up to now, the reader will be persuaded that emotion is a powerful thing in southern Spain. Historical and material decadence seems to have given it a free hand in shaping crucial areas of culture in its own image. Emotionality that arises in reaction to a failure condition carries the seeds of magical beliefs within it; the seeds of emotion magic then flower into the *copla*, popular concepts of fate or popular ways of manipulating it, death rituals, pious legends, *machismo*, and so forth. Negative emotions like fear and guilt animate penitential ideology and institutions, and emotional ties to the family govern group dynamics and image devotion. In view of all this, to assert as I will here that emotionality governs the way Andalusia retells the Passion should not elicit surprise. Nevertheless, surprises are in store. In the street liturgy of Holy Week we will find the supreme achievement of emotion magic. The many facets of Andalusian emotionality that I have discussed will all be seen at work, not only in mechanical but also in genuinely creative ways. What has been created simultaneously reflects and feeds back into Andalusian life and society in numerous ways.

Unlike the divine variety, human creativity does not take place in a vacuum; it must begin with a stock of themes and a supply of narrative or dramatic techniques. To properly situate what many have called "the Passion according to Andalusia"—the textual/theatrical nucleus of Passional culture—it behooves us to briefly consider the general differences between religious and secular storytelling. Here my thinking has been oriented by Northrop Frye, for whom these differences are a matter of authority, consensus, or function, *not* of structure (1976:8). As part of their social development, certain stories adhere to one another and take root in a particular culture for purposes of explanation and identity. Frye uses the word "myth" for such stories and contrasts them with the more nomadic genre of folktales (9). It is the essential structural similarities of both nomadic and sedentary stories, meanwhile, that makes "mythic imperialism" possible, that is, the process whereby an ascendant society's central body of myth expands by absorbing all manner of local legends and apocryphal tales. Even folktales, however, can come to stick together, absorb other tales in an encyclopedic manner, and eventually cross the threshold from the fabulous to the mythical (12–13). In time, cultural evolution can give birth to a veritable mythological universe, which Frye defines as "a vision of human reality in terms of human concerns and hopes and anxieties; it is not a primitive form of science" (14). Here he coincides with those scholars who emphasize the primacy of emotional factors in mythmaking, an approach I share wholeheartedly. Frye subsequently formulates his main thesis:

> We saw that there is no structural principle to prevent the fables of secular literature from also forming a mythology, or even a mythological universe. Is it possible, then, to look at secular stories as a whole, and as forming a single integrated vision of the world, parallel to the Christian and biblical vision? This is the question implied in the "secular scripture" of my title. . . . Romance is the structural core of all fiction: being directly descended from folktale, it brings us closer than any other aspect of literature to the sense of fiction, considered as a whole, as the epic of the creature, man's vision of his own life as a quest. [15]

Frye devotes the rest of his remarkable essay to a study of the main motifs of romance, his "secular scripture."

Having hereby distinguished between the mythological universe of religion and that of romance, it can now be observed that, at least in the case of Spain, the two realms have not been parallel so much as coincident. In Iberian discourse of all kinds, written and authoritative as well as oral and traditional, the creator-oriented spirit of the Bible and the creature-comforting ethos of romance have been virtually indistinguishable, to the point at which we might do well to coin the term "Romance Catholicism" for the hybrid mythological universe that has evolved thereby. We can go further: Spanish Romance Catholicism can be seen as not only a verbal order and an imaginative structure but an entire complex of values and behavior patterns that have oriented or played themselves out in the lives of real men and women. Where can one draw a sharp distinction, for example, between religious and warrior values during the many centuries of struggles waged by the chosen people

(Spaniards) and God's own enemies (Moors)? Had not Spain suffered an almost Old Testament–style "fall" due to the lechery of King Rodrigo and/or the temptations of Florinda? To what other nation had God given the chore of Christianizing a New World? To an extent unparalleled by any other nation of Europe, Spain had fulfilled its bellico-religious dreams, and thousands of individual Spaniards had seen their great fantasy realized—"to serve God while doing what they wanted" (Fernández Suárez 1961:196).

Contrary to what had happened in the Holy Land, the Christians of Iberia had won out over the heathens, and while a disappointed Europe turned away from the *chanson de geste,* an old-fashioned ethos of Christian knighthood continued to flower and bear fruit in Spain (cf. Amezcua 1973:27–29). The fictional adventures of gallant warriors with names like Amadis, Belianis, Cristalián, Esplandián, Palmerín, or Tirante were extraordinarily popular throughout the peninsula and were still being reprinted well into the eighteenth century (Gayangos 1963:lxiii–lxxxvii). (That Cervantes dealt the death-blow to the genre with *Don Quixote* has been a persistent critical fiction.) As is well known, the "will to romance" of the *conquistadores* led them to perceive what they found in terms of chivalric novels and even to bestow novelistic names like "California" on the lands they ruled.

Naturally there were moralists who reviled chivalric romance as un-Christian; they were outnumbered by the priests who published chivalric novels *a lo divino* (Gayangos 1963:lvi–lx). As Caro points out, the average sixteenth or seventeenth-century Spanish Catholic was rarely inclined to turn the other cheek; touchy pride, defiance, and dueling were the norm in life and popular literature alike (1985:446). The enthusiasm Spanish friars felt for martial exploits apparently knew no limits (437). As is common knowledge, the Jesuit order was founded along military lines by an ex-soldier and passionate admirer of chivalric romance, Ignacio de Loyola. Teresa de Avila, the great mystic and reformer of the Carmelite order, was an early enthusiast of *libros de caballerías,* by her own guilt-ridden admission (Sánchez de Cepeda 1922 [1565]: 8–9). In their religious writings, both saints—along with their predecessors and followers—continually employ metaphors drawn from the twin worlds of knight-errantry and courtly love (Rougement 1984:164–169). According to Baruzi,

In Spain, the authors of chivalric novels as well as those of mystical treatises are characterized by the same realism when they forego the sentiment of the marvelous for one of more familiar and more emotive intimacy, as well as the way they tend to put the human and the divine on the same plane, whether by contemplating the divine with profane eyes or considering the human with a divine interpretation. [Cit. by Rougement 1984:166–167]

Rougement devotes considerable effort to drawing a fine casuistic line between the language of the Spanish mystics and that of the "courtly heresy" from which it derives (169–176 *et passim*).

Santa Teresa, incidentally, exemplified another theme dear to romance and Catholicism alike: virginity. When her coffin was opened in 1584, two years after her death, the nuns were astounded to find the cadaver as fresh and soft as the day she died. In the words of a contemporary biographer,

Just as Our Lord kept her entirely free of dishonesty with perfect virginity, after death he kept her from the slightest corruption; and He forbade the worms to touch she whom the ardors of dishonesty had not. [Cit. by Silverio de Santa Teresa 1922:xx]

The saint's left forearm was cut off and, still uncorrupted, found its way to Franco's deathbed in November of 1975 (Carr and Fusi 1981:1). Here again the striking historic continuity of the Spanish faith in relics; here also a connection to Frye's universe of romance, where virginity represents integrity, immortality, and a magical redemptive or curative quality (1976:73–87). Let it not be thought that I have wandered too far away from modern Andalusia; Brandes discovers a similar rationale in his Monteros informants:

Virginity is a symbol of the new, the pure, the good; it stands for *el colmo de la posibilidad*—"the height of potentiality and possibility." It therefore can be converted into a thousand beneficial things for the future. For this reason, "the act of deflowering in and of itself is bad, because it terminates the possibilities for the future; a whole series of potentialities that the virgin represents are lost." This is why the Virgin Mary herself is so important in Monteros, for she stands for permanent purity and permanent hope. [1980:181]

The difference between the virginity of a regular woman and that of the Blessed Virgin is none other than autonomy—the prime obsession of Andalusians. A human virgin has to struggle: she is subject to desire, temptation, provocation, hormonal drives. María, however, is above all that. She is not only *Purísima* but *Serenísima,* unperturbable, free. To the extent that virginity represents a kind of autonomy in the south, it is a cultural ideal devoutly to be cherished.

The "Virgin of Avila," as Santa Teresa has been called, can be aligned with hundreds of other female and male saints and hundreds of thousand of nuns and priests who have cherished their chastity for love of God and in emulation of the Virgin Mary. The Marian cult itself can be seen as the Church-sanctioned replica of the medieval ethos of courtly love (Rougement 1984:115–116). If Our Lady is the heroine of a divine romance, it can hardly be surprising that the romance-minded gallants of Spain served her with special ardor, identifying the Lady's unbesmirched honor with their own. In effect, Marianism is a prime element of the Romance Catholicism that has held sway in Spain in general and Andalusia in particular. The passionate defense of the doctrine of the Immaculate Conception is of course the prime example of this. This concept had its origins in popular piety and found support among the medieval theologians who were intent on deifying Mary, as opposed to the ones bent on humanizing her; it held that not only Christ but also His Mother herself had been conceived in a stainless manner. It therefore implies the belief in the perfect virginity or at least "closed uterus" of Saint Anne, Christ's grandmother. The doctrine met with success among a number of monastic and knightly orders of the Middle Ages, and went into decline at the same time as they did; it was revived in Spain, however, during the same period that saw the renovation and historical reinforcement of romance ideals of all kinds. Spaniards in all walks of life became passionate defenders not of a complicated theological postulate but of the figure of *María Inmaculada,* alias *la Purísima,* a super-virgin and powerful personalized symbol of a vigorous and intact national integrity. Her cult was closely allied to the success of the so-called *Reconquista.* The conqueror of Andalusia, Ferdinand III (San Fernando), attributed his victories over the Moors to the *Inmaculada;* Ferdinand and Isabella trusted in her aid to conquer Granada in 1492; she was also the preferred devotion of Carlos V, who in 1527 encouraged the founding of *hermandades* with the *Inmaculada* as the tutelary image. The aristocrats of Seville promptly heeded the recommendation of the Emperor (Jiménez Sampedro 1988:15). Even the enlightened despot Carlos III made the Immaculate One into the patroness of Spain in 1761 (Llompart 1968:226–227). In the meantime, Spanish theologians had defended the cause, without success, at the Councils of Basilea and Trent.

To steadfastly maintain a doctrine at variance with the official Church is technically heresy, of course, but a Church that needed Spanish arms to fight the good fight of the Counter-Reformation could not be troubled by technicalities. Besides, Spaniards had always been "more papist than the pope," as the Spanish idiom puts it. Their Marian zeal was the perfect antidote for the anti-Marian iconoclasm of the protestants, for it implied only mania, not reform.

Chivalric by definition, Romance Catholicism was thoroughly quixotic when it came to Our Lady. The penitential brotherhoods of Andalusia have been the primary exponents of this gallantry in search of a Marian cause. For three centuries, every new member swore an oath to uphold the truth of the Immaculate Conception. But when Pope Pius IX promulgated the edict known as *Ineffabilis Deus* in 1854, the belief became binding dogma for all Catholics and the victorious *cofradías* were left without a cause. They immediately took up the defense of the notion that María had been taken up *body and soul* into heaven. Brothers swore a new oath to this effect until 1950, when it too became dogma. Now, the majority of *hermandades* are pledged to uphold the idea of María's "universal mediation" (Moreno 1985a : 27; Castillo Martos 1988 : 36). The quixotic defense of the *Inmaculada* has hardly waned, however; brotherhoods and clergy alike are now united to keep her feast day of December 8th, a legal holiday in Andalusia. The battle has been won in Seville; elsewhere, *cofradías* are threatening to suspend their Holy Week processions to protest the secular affront to the honor of the *Purísima*.

The attempt to account for Andalusia's special fervor for the *María Inmaculada* lay behind an intriguing if not altogether reliable theory proposed by Giménez Caballero in 1927. For this noted proto-fascist belletrist, the cult of the *Purísima* was essentially a reaction to the amorous amorality of the Renaissance symbolized by Don Juan, an expert remover of virginities and the first to lament the loss of lost women (1927:161). It was Don Juan, or more exactly the repentant Don Juan, symbolized by Miguel Mañara, who created "the myth of the Immaculate Conception" out of frustration and boredom with the weakness of real women (166–171). *La Purísima* was pictured as a woman of sexual plenitude, aged twenty to twenty-five years, but one that was "definitely redeemed" and beyond all soiling; her cult was the exaltation of virginity carried out by men who had been led to doubt it by their own lust (176–178). Reproduced below is the diagram Giménez used to illustrate his theory (188):

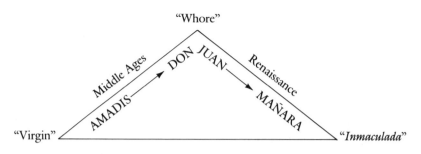

The Estimation of Woman from the Middle Ages to the Renaissance

As evidence for his theory, Giménez cites the numerous "scholarships" that Mañara arranged for young women who wished to preserve their purity in convents (185). In reality, however, the Big Brother of *la Santa Caridad* was just as willing to make women wives as nuns. His use of evidence is shaky and his chronology is skewed; but Giménez is on the right track regarding the androcentric devaluation of female sexuality and concomitant hyper-valuation of virginity. He ought to have mentioned, in addition, that one of the primary functions of a redeemed woman is to redeem men, that is, to save them from the wrath of an exacting patriarchal God. The myth of Don Juan in its definitive Spanish form is instructive in this regard: the Sevillian libertine kidnaps the virginal Inés out of one-upmanship more than lust; her father shows up to defend her honor (i.e., *his* honor), Don Juan slays him, flees, and Inés dies of grief. Her magical purity thus preserved, Inés becomes the *ánima* dressed in white who saves Don Juan's soul from hell at the last moment (Zorrilla 1986 [1844]). The Don Juan myth is a classic example of Spanish Romance Catholicism. If we were to remove the structure of romance, we would be left with a dry disquisition on the value of contrition. If we remove the Catholicity, making Don Juan into a rational atheist à la Molière or an operatic hero à la Mozart, we end up with socially irrelevant fiction.

What lends an aura of social authenticity to this famous Catholic romance is the fact that all of the characters are Andalusians and the action revolves around classic Andalusian concerns—hubris, arbitrary authority, *señoritos* and their servants, blasphemy, virginity, convents, dueling, funerals, death-as-punishment, repentance, forgiveness, and maternal succor. In this regard, traditional Andalusian society has been the natural habitat for all the archetypes of Romance Catholicism and the natural setting for its literary or dramatic vehicles. For Joaquín Marco, the popular literature of Spain is "radically conservative" (1977 : I, 50). The creators and conveyors of popular romance consciously adhered to established forms and formulas. The blind men who transmitted semi-oral traditional literature in the form of the *romance de ciego,* for example, always began their verse narratives with an invocation to the Virgin and always ended with a moral. The religiosity of popular balladry was not just a question of form:

> The world of popular literature constitutes the model of an ideal society based on traditional Catholic religious principles. Although violence, vengeance, or ferocious satire form the coordinates of behavior for the main characters of chapbooks, these in general seek to offer the reader or the listener a school of proper habits. The attitude of the chapbook, in this sense, coincides with Spanish plays or with the picaresque novel. The elaboration of the imaginary world is carried out in accordance with morality. The authors of chapbooks confer upon them the general moralizing tone that has abounded in Spanish literature since the 16th century. But passions boil behind this backdrop. [Marco 1977 : I, 89–90]

In his seminal study of Spanish/Andalusian *romances de ciego,* Julio Caro Baroja emphasizes their religious character and explores the story lines that emerge in consequence. For one thing, the heroes are in continual conflict with infidels or with "horrible and sacrilegious Jews, like those of the popular *pasos* of Holy Week" (1969 : 121). For another, the twin themes of divine wrath and Virginal compassion, the latter as the prime antidote for the former, are repeated ad nauseum (122–126). Suffering and death constitute another great area of preoccupation (127). The blind poets were particularly fond of tales about men who commit some horrible sin (usually parricide or incest), repent, engage in extravagant penitence, and eventually achieve expiation. In these pseudo-hagiographical narratives, the function of "fate" is often assigned to the devil, who tempts or tricks the Oedipal saints into sinning against their will. Speaking of the devil, an ancient French legend of Satan's son became one of the most popular romances of nineteenth- and twentieth-century Spain. It narrates how one Roberto el Diablo loots, murders, rapes, and burns his way through life until his mother tells him the truth of his diabolic birth. Struck with piety, he travels to Rome to seek the

Pope's pardon and goes on to become a bastion of the Catholic faith (Flores 1985:53–55). There are, finally, numerous anonymous texts that recount recent miracles worked by popular patron saints, the ransom of captives from North Africa with the aid of some Virgin, and martyrdoms depicted with every gory detail imaginable (Caro Baroja 1969: 132–133).

In general, Spanish popular literature gives a religious twist to romance and a romance twist to religion. The truculence, cruelty, oversentimentalism, anti-Semitism, and general obsession with sexual crimes are so many instruments of moral didacticism in the hands of chapbook authors. If men and women were not wayward, after all, there could be no story to begin with and no moral at the end. As Caro puts it,

> The themes adjust themselves to the capacities of a public avid for dreadful tales, persuaded that the dramas of life are what most give it meaning, whether or not the protagonists of these dramas are saints or sinners: and if they are saints who were sinners before, so much the better. [1969:133]

Thus, it is not so much a question of the particular genre or form that the dramas are expressed in, but the beliefs and values that make them appealing in any generic guise. Cansinos has found the same worldview at the heart of the Andalusian *copla*, where

> sin will sometimes occupy the place of sanctity or be confused with it, and destiny will pour a facile absolution over it all. The fall of Man and Woman, fatefully swept away by the passions, constitutes the preferred myth of the *copla*, as it is of Romantic art. Mary Magdalene and the Good Thief are its principal characters. [1985 (1933): 63]

As a total imaginative order and value complex, Romance Catholicism does not confine itself to any one genre. In Andalusia, Romance Catholicism has achieved its supreme expression not in chapbooks or *coplas* but in the verbal and visual street liturgy that has grown up around the most gripping story of all—the death of God. The Passion has undergone a profound transformation in the south; it has been infused with many of the stylistic techniques and themes that structure the *romances de ciego*. Crudity, sensationalism, patriarchal fate, maternal benevolence, devilish Jews—all these features can be found in the Andalusian version of the Passion. In addition, the mystical love rhetoric of centuries past seems to be alive in many of the *saetas* people sing to the *pasos*. And the *pasos* themselves, as will be seen, are mute but highly expressive narrative vehicles.

The Passion According to Andalusia

The Passion of Christ need not be narrated in a passionate way. The original evangelical texts themselves are models of sobriety and a matter-of-fact manner of exposition. The New Testament certainly contains the seeds of emotion, but it is up to a particular Christian culture to nurture them in light of its own sociohistorical circumstances. Many versions of the same story thus become possible. Certain moments will be highlighted here and ignored there; apocryphal details will appear and disappear from one age to another. Even within the same culture, the version of the Church will inevitably be at variance with the folk or popular version.

In southern Spain, the popular or "street" version of the Passion is often a far cry from scripture, depending upon the street. In some towns, "folk work" has reigned supreme; in others, the official Church has achieved, with great effort, a meager degree of standardization. The various popular versions can be collated to form a "Passion according to Andalusia" that is idiosyncratic, richly syncretic, and heterodox in a dozen different ways. Not that I consider myself a watchdog of doctrine: I use the term in a nonjudgmental, empirical sense. In my view, the whole Andalusian approach to religion was and is enough to provoke a schism. This has clearly not occurred, but for reasons that have everything to do with Church geopolitics and nothing to do with the empirical reality of street liturgy, whose errors are there for all to ponder (though few do). To be sure, some of these errors are just that, meaningless mistakes that are made in oral transmission. One popular *saeta* of Córdoba, for example, goes against canonical and apocryphal traditions alike in depriving Christ of the chance to carry His cross:

Entre juncos y una fuente	Between rushes and a fountain
un carpintero acabó	a carpenter finished
una cruz pesada y fuerte.	a strong and heavy cross.
Al Calvario la llevó	He took it to Calvary
para enclavar a un inocente.	to nail down an innocent man.
[Melgar and Marín 1987:38–39]	

In the same province, a living representation of the Passion, which was instituted in the year 1600 in Iznajar, had accumulated so many doctrinal and historical absurdities by 1750 that it was banned—only to resurface a few years later (Melgar and Marín 1987 : 151–152). Notwithstanding such rare birds, the incoherence of the majority of popular texts is only apparent, reflecting underlying social pressures or psychological needs that are perfectly comprehensible.

The Passion according to Andalusia, that is, Holy Week street liturgy, has evolved over many centuries, selectively retaining the memory of many kinds of oral and written texts. In roughly chronological order, the most important ones are (1) the New Testament, (2) apocryphal legends, (3) liturgical ceremonies of the Church, (4) the miracle plays and *autos sacramentales* of the Middle Ages, (5) the *romancero* or ballad corpus of the Passion, (6) the *coplas* that were sung during the *Via Crucis* and other kinds of penitential rituals, (7) Holy Week sermons, (8) devotional tracts, (9) representations of the Passion known as *mandatos* or *sentencias* that were staged by certain brotherhoods, and (10) the spontaneous, anonymous *saetas afectivas* that people began to sing around the middle of the nineteenth century. The New Testament is still available, of course; one can also read *The Golden Legend* and the old religious dramas. Devotional rituals are still held in churches and sermons are still preached. The formative period of street liturgy is over, however, and except in those towns that maintain the fascinating custom of the *mandato,* the chief narrative vehicles of Holy Week are now the *saeta* and the *paso.* What these narrate is distilled from all of the sources listed above.

If the *saeta* and the *paso* are the oral and visual "texts" of Andalusia's romance of the Passion, their natural context is the Holy Week *Estación de Penitencia.* Indeed, the climax of Holy Week emotion is the right *saeta* sung in the presence of the right *paso* at the right moment. At such times, the scholarly distinction between *saetas narrativas* and *saetas afectivas* tends to break down. For expository purposes, however, it behooves us to bear this distinction in mind. The *saetas* I cite in this part of the chapter are of the narrative type, having their origins in a longer poem, *romance,* or *mandato;* in the following section I will deal with those *saetas* that have been forged by certain kinds of superheated sentiment and that present special problems for analysis.

A few years ago, an erudite *cofrade* of Puente Genil (Córdoba) came up with the theory that the *saetas* sung in that locality during Holy Week had been translated directly from the Latin version of the Passion according to Matthew. This enabled him to affirm that his home town had anticipated the vernacular reforms of Vatican II by five centuries (cit. by Melgar and Marín 1987:29–30). Although he was able to find several *saetas* that corresponded closely to the Latin text, I believe his theory owes more to sociocentric drumbeating than to the facts (it was even presented in the form of a *pregón,* the sociocentric instrument par excellence). In any town's *saeta* corpus, including that of Puente Genil, there are far more deviations from the evangelical text than there are coincidences. As will be seen, not a few of these distortions can be traced precisely to self-aggrandizing in-group pride.

A great deal of the Passion according to Andalusia, in fact, begins in apocrypha and goes on from there. This is as true of the visual narrative forms as it is of verbal ones. Thanks to a recent discovery, we now have a good idea of the kinds of popular literature that guided the great makers of Passional images in sixteenth- and seventeenth-century Andalusia:

> The list comprises a series of theoretical books on mathematics, geometry, architecture, and perspective, but the bulkiest catalog is constituted by pious and devotional readings that describe in a lively and impressive way the scenes of the Passion, accentuating the expressive and the emotive. And it is these treatises and books of religious and spiritual formation where the *imaginero* found his inspiration to carve the processional images. And here reside the differences between the sculptor and the *imaginero,* for even though every *imaginero* is a sculptor, not every sculptor is an *imaginero.* While it is enough for a sculptor to have a technical formation and thematic inspiration, the *imaginero* must have . . . a decidedly sacred formation. In sum, an *imaginero* is a sculptor specialized in the realization of religious images who in addition feels identified with the feelings of popular spirituality. [Palomero 1987:60]

The extraordinary development of Passional art is perhaps the most famous aspect of Holy Week in southern Spain. Few people realize the extent to which *imagineros* studied and agonized over every detail of Christ's agony in order to combine aesthetic appeal with commonly held beliefs. The size and shape of the crown of thorns, the folds of the *sudario,* the height of the column Christ was scourged at, the number of floggers, the number and length of the nails required for crucifixion, whether the right foot should be on top of or underneath the left, how much blood was spilled—these and dozens of other issues were involved. According to Aroca, the great majority of Golden Age and post–Golden Age *imagineros* waited until they were middle-aged before attempting the most demanding image of all—the *Crucificado* (1987:87).

Since in larger cities most of the *saetas* now sung are of the non-narrative or affective type, the *costaleros* carrying the images also bear the burden of the narration. This is especially true with the onerous *pasos grandes de misterios* whose life-sized statues reenact some episode of the Passional drama (cf. Bernales 1985). Not that the episodes are presented to the people in sequential order during Holy Week, however, in capital cities like Córdoba, Jaén, Málaga, Granada, or—least of all—Seville. As Moreno notes,

> It is as if the *pasos* of the Passion had been shuffled and no longer had any logic. And they do not, of course, from the perspective of a simple spectator who sits in a chair on Sierpes Street or in the Cathedral to passively watch a kind of commemorative movie of the death of Jesus Christ. But they do have an order, which is not that of the Gospels but of Seville: that which expresses the *antigüedad* of each brotherhood and the continuity of its procession on the same day of the week. [1982:30]

Apart from the time-honored *cofradía* timetables Moreno mentions, it can be affirmed that the people of Seville and other cities know their version of the Passion backward and forward, and therefore the lack of sequential order does not mean a lack of coherence. In Seville there are enough *pasos* to tell the story several times over, almost, and some crucial moments are repeated again and again.

The visual riches of large cities can be contrasted with the verbal wealth of Marchena, Cabra, Puente Genil, Doña Mencía, and other towns in the provinces of Seville, Córdoba, Cádiz, and Jaén. In effect, writes López Fernández,

> in the Holy Week of Seville we meet up with the great *imagineros* who have given marvelous shape to every one of the *pasos* or mysteries of the Passion. In Seville all is for contemplation, from the Entry of Jesus in Jerusalem to the Holy Burial, and including the Last Supper, the Prayer in the Garden, the Arrest, the Kiss of Judas, Jesus before Caiaphas, before Herod, before Pilate, the Presentation to the People, etc., etc., and a multitude of scenes with Nazarenes, Crucifieds, Descents, Calvaries, *Piedades,* and Virgins. . . . By contrast, in medium-sized and small towns, with only two or three mysteries represented by the Nazarene, the Crucified, the Holy Burial, and the [Virgin of] Solitude, we have enough to interpret all of the scenes of the Passion of Christ, unfolded by means of the actions staged in a *mandato* where the most diverse evangelical and biblical personages appear and march alongside the few images available. [1981:34]

This haunting icon of Christ tied to the column was completed by Francisco Buiza in 1974. The golden rays emanating from the head are known as *potencias* (photo: Encarnación Lucas).

Nuestro Padre Jesús de la Salud, by Francisco de Ocampo, has carried His cross through the streets of Seville since the early seventeenth century (photo: Encarnación Lucas).

Local legend has it that any young woman who plays Veronica during Seville's Good Friday will die within a year (photo: Encarnación Lucas).

"Our Father Jesus Deprived of His Garments"—Christ patiently waiting to be crucified—was sculpted by Antonio Perea in 1939 (photo: Encarnación Lucas).

The agonic *Cachorro*, sculpted by Gijón in 1682 and restored three times since, is at once the height of baroque art and the object of passionate devotion in modern Seville.

As might be expected, these performances of popular liturgy retain the chronological order of events (and have even added a few for good measure). López Fernández offers convincing evidence of the veracity of theories proposed by Rodríguez Marín, Mas y Prat, and other folklorists who argued that in the beginning the *saeta* was never an isolated *copla* but formed part of a longer composition in romance octosyllabic meter (51–53). In practice the text of a *mandato* is one long *romancero* or corpus of *romances;* the one currently performed by the *Cofradía de Nuestro Padre Jesús Nazareno* in Marchena (Seville) has 468 stanzas (1981:65).

In what follows I will treat southern Spain's Holy Week as one macrotext in which *saetas, pasos,* and *mandatos* alternate as narrative vehicles. As a general observation, it might be said that for every inch of scriptural foundation, Andalusian street liturgy will take a mile. The motif of prophecy may serve as an initial example. As is well known, the Evangelists are at pains to show us that all Christ said and did was in completion of one prophecy or another. One of the crucial points of the Passion was that it had been foreordained from all time and announced when Christ was a baby:

> Led by the Spirit, an old man named Simon took the baby Jesus in his arms and told Mary that "This child is chosen by God for the destruction and salvation of many in Israel. He will be a sign from God which many people will speak against and so reveal their secret thoughts. And sorrow, like a sharp sword, will break your own heart." [Luke 2.33–35]

By the sixteenth century, the theme of the Holy Child predestined to die on the cross had become a staple of Andalusian iconography and it had undergone a certain telltale permutation. In Seville, a sculpture of *el Niño Jesús* was carried every Holy Week by a now defunct brotherhood; the image was that of a child eighty centimeters tall, blessing the instruments of crucifixion and *pointing towards his horoscope* (Bernales 1985:87). As Andalusia slides into decadence and fatalism, what began as prophecy becomes astrology and ultimately fortunetelling, as evidenced by a nineteenth-century *romance* that was extraordinarily popular throughout the south. In this case, it is no longer Christ's presentation in the temple but His very day of birth that serves as the occasion of the predictions:

Una gitana se acerca	A Gypsy woman draws near
al pie de la Virgen pura;	to the foot of the pure Virgin;
hincó la rodilla en tierra	she knelt down
y le dijo la ventura.	and told her fortune.

"Madre del Amor hermoso, —así le dice a María—, a Egipto irás con el Niño y José en tu compañía."	"Mother of beautiful Love, —thus she spoke to María—, to Egypt you'll go with the Child and Joseph in your company."
Mirando al Niño divino, le decía enternecida: "¡Cuánto tienes que pasar, lucerito de mi vida!	Looking at the divine Child, moved to compassion she told him: "How much you will have to pass, little light of my life!
"La cabeza de este Niño, tan hermosa y agraciada, luego la hemos de ver con espinas traspasada.	"The head of this Child, so beautiful and charming, in time we are to see it transfixed with thorns.
"Las manitas de este Niño, tan blancas y torneadas, luego las hemos de ver en una cruz enclavadas.	"The little hands of this Child, so white and well-shaped, in time we are to see them nailed to a cross.
"Los piececitos del Niño, tan chicos y sonrosados, luego los hemos de ver con un clavo taladrados.	"The little feet of this Child, so tiny and rosy, in time we are to see them drilled with a nail.
"Andarás de monte en monte, haciendo mil maravillas; en uno sudarás sangre, en otro darás la vida.	"You will go from mount to mount, working a thousand wonders; on one you will sweat blood, on the other you'll give your life.
"Morirás en vera cruz levantada en el Calvario, que a tanto te obligará ese tu amor extremado."	"You will die on the true cross raised up on Calvary, for to this much you'll be obliged by your extreme love."

The whole style of this ballad is premonitory of the decidedly maternal filter through which Andalusians perceive the sufferings of Christ as a grown man.

In Doña Mencía, a small town in the province of Córdoba, every Holy Week procession is accompanied by men known as *rezaores,* who take turns chanting long Passional *romances* of uncertain origin. Each change of voice and stanza is signaled by the blare of trumpets. In one of these traditional ballads, Christ's foreknowledge of His fate is rendered in particularly graphic terms:

Un jueves, ya por la tarde, siendo las cinco y dos cuartos	One Thursday, along towards the afternoon, it being five-thirty

y según dice la historia	and according to history
el veinticinco de marzo,	the twenty-fifth of March,
se juntaron a un convite,	they gathered at a dinner party,
tan dichoso y deseado	so lucky and desired
para dar fin a las obras,	in order to finish up the work
de tantos siglos pasados,	of so many past centuries,
donde el Cordero Divino	where the Divine Lamb
vio un cordero degollado	saw a lamb with his head cut off
que para hacer el convite	that was there for the dinner party
estaba allí desangrado . . .	with the blood drained out . . .
en un asador de palo,	on a wooden spit,
figura que a Cristo hizo	a sight that made Christ
estremecer por un rato.	shudder for a while.
[Melgar and Marín 1987 : 137]	

The evangelical "Do this in remembrance of me" with which Christ instituted the Mass is rendered by this *romance* as an invitation to celebrate the torments of His Passion with yearly processions (138).

Psychological/narrative mechanisms put in motion by sociocentrism characterize the next part of the Andalusian romance of the Passion. Here I am referring not to boosterism but to projection, polarization, or what Girard has termed "magico-persecutory thought" (1982 : 80–83). These devices have played an important role in the development of myths and folktales all over the world. Projective thoughts and words can also lead to deeds, of course, whenever a group has a critical need to identify its hidden enemies and exorcise them. In Spain, as in other countries of Europe, in-group solidarity has often been won at the expense of one conspicuous minority, and the story of Christ's death has been used to justify this tendency. Centuries of tradition are on the side of the *sermón del paso* of Puente Genil when it affirms that

Encomiensa la pasión	The Passion begins
con lo mal que se portaron	with the bad behavior of
aquellos perros judíos	those Jewish dogs
con Jesú quera tan santo.	with Jesus who was so holy.
[Melgar and Marín 1987 : 117]	

Like many other stories, the Passion has a built-in "bad guy" (Judas); but only the historical development of Christianity can explain why the actions of one tormented man helped to make scapegoats of an entire people.

The figure of Judas looms very large in the Passion according to Andalusia. As I discussed in the last chapter, both individual and group identities in southern Spain tend to be formed along intensely emotional, sacro-familial lines; when Judas betrays Christ, he betrays (and symbolically slays) the Father of the group. Such an Oedipal crime has to be exorcised along with the criminal. To vilify the man who turned in Our Father is to project and expel one's own unspeakable urges. At the same time, a natural villain like Judas polarizes the inner tensions of an ingroup and permits their expression in what must be a very satisfying way for socially tense agrotowns. Like the medieval Jew, Judas is readily identified with the devil in Passional romance; the perfect target for the release of anger and hate, he simultaneously helps to keep anti-Semitic sentiments alive even today. All over Andalusia, *saeteros* try in vain to keep Judas from making his evil bargain:

Detente Júa, detente,	Stop, Judas, stop,
no vendas a tu Maestro,	don't sell your Master,
que treinta monea de plata	thirty pieces of silver
no valen er reino der cielo.	are not worth the Kingdom of Heaven.

    [Plata 1984:51]

Once the die has been cast, *saeteros* in Lucena, Baena, or Cabra ache to get their hands on the reprobate:

¡Ven acá Juas traidor!	Come here, traitorous Judas!
Enreoso y embustero.	Troublemaker and liar.
Tu vendiste al Señor	You sold the Lord
solo por treinta dineros.	for just thirty moneys.
[Melgar and Marín 1987:47]	

The contempt Judas arouses has even led the *saeta* corpus to *mentar la madre* (mention one's mother), the ultimate insult in southern Spain:

¿Quién sería la madre	What kind of a mother
que parió a Judas?	would give birth to Judas?
¡Qué hijos tan indignos	What despicable children
paren algunas!	some give birth to!
[Plata 1984:17]	

That Judas acted as he did was of course preordained from all time. God the Father arranged it and Jesus prophesied it: "I tell you, one of you will betray me" (Matthew 26.21) and "One who dips his bread in the dish with me will betray me" (26.23). What happened next is narrated by a *saeta* that was described as "absurd" and "grotesque" by the folklorist who collected it:

Se quedó el Apostolado	The Apostles were left
hecho mármoles de piedra	like marbles of rock
llenos de terror y espanto.	full of terror and fright.
Y Judas con risa fiera	And Judas with a savage laugh
metió la mano en el plato.	put his hand in the dish.

    [Published by M. Alvarez in 1915, cit. by Melgar and Marín 1987 : 30]

Doña Mencía's Passional romance pictures "that damned Judas" rounding up a large group of fellow traitors and heading for Gethsemane "with damaged hearts and bronze innards"; Judas "hikes up his skirts" in order to walk faster, but his "atrocious thoughts" and "clouded vision" make him stumble all the way to the garden (Melgar and Marín 1987 : 138). The Arrest of Jesus (el *Prendimiento*) is a major moment of the Passion according to Andalusia. Since only Judas knows where to find Jesus, he is the leader in the sense of "guide." Another romance makes him the leader in the sense of "chief":

Estando el Rey Celestial	While the Celestial King
en el huerto de la oración,	was in the garden of the prayer,
vino Judas infernal	infernal Judas came
con un lucido escuadrón	with an elegant squadron
de ellos siendo el capitán.	with him as their captain.

    [58]

The seizure of Christ has been a favorite theme for both *imagineros* and the brotherhoods that contract them, such as Seville's *Real e Ilustre Hermandad del Santísimo Sacramento y Cofradía de Nazarenos de Nuestro Padre Jesús de la Redención en el Beso de Judas*. Every Holy Monday, forty-eight of the brothers carry a gigantic *paso* that pictures the moment when Judas targeted Christ with a kiss in the presence of John, James, Peter, Andrew, and Thomas. The *paso* also includes an olive tree, four huge gold-plated candelabras, and an ornate mahogany base. The images date from 1958 and are the work of Castillo Lastrucci, the most important *imaginero* of the twentieth century. Christ is dressed in white and Judas is portrayed in a brown robe with a green purse ostentatiously attached to his cingulum, and he strains to reach the cheek of the Master with pursed lips. Like so many other iconographic details, the notable difference in the statures of the two statues reflects the influence of St. Bridget of Sweden, the fourteenth-century mystic who claimed to have vivid visions of the Passion. In one of them the Swedish saint observed that Judas was considerably shorter than Christ (cit. by Palomero 1987:77).

According to Matthew, a remorseful Judas went off and hanged himself (27.3–5). According to Luke, Judas fell to death in the field he had bought with his ill-gotten silver—"he burst open and all his insides spilled out" (Acts of the Apostles 1.18). In either case, the traitor got off too lightly for the Spanish folk, who have preferred to stone, shotgun, and burn him in effigy for centuries, usually on Easter Sunday (Mitchell 1988:95–99). The towns and cities of Andalusia have participated in these activities with relish. During his *Wanderings through Spain* in 1872, A. J. C. Hare witnessed a representation of the Passion in Granada that began with the Last Supper and ended with the descent of Judas into hell, complete with claps of thunder and flashing blue lights; the enthused public demanded to see the same scene again and again. Hare reports that the Archbishop of Granada had tried in vain to have the whole spectacle prohibited (1985 [1873]: 202). Such examples could be multiplied ad infinitum.

The magico-persecutory logic of Passional romance has not balked at attributing the treason of Judas to his Jewishness; the arch-traitor is only the archetypal representative of a race that is low, double-dealing, cruel, and fickle by nature:

Juntito a los olivos,
esos judíos traicioneros
a mi Jesús de mi arma
ya se llevan prisionero.
  [Plata 1984:35]

Right next to the olive trees
those traitorous Jews
are already taking away prisoner
my Jesus of my soul.

Judíos tended las capas
para que pase Jesús
y aluego en el Viernes Santo
la daréis muerte en la cruz.
  [Melgar and Marín 1987:61]

Jews spread your capes
so that Jesus can pass by
and then on Good Friday
you'll give Him death on the cross.

Los que en la Cruz te clavaron
eran de muy mala sangre;
no tuvieron compasión
viendo llorar a tu Madre.

  [Alcalá 1984 (1925):241]

The ones who nailed you to the
  Cross
were of very bad blood;
they had no compassion
watching your Mother weep.

It is tacitly understood that Jesus, His Mother, the Apostles, and all of the other "good guys" were somehow non-Jews. In effect, only bad guys are given notably Semitic features by *imagineros* (Roman soldiers are not generally considered bad guys). This does not mean that Andalusians are not willing to play the role of "evil Jew" when tradition so demands. In Pozoblanco (Córdoba), the man who plays Judas is a kind of master of ceremonies who goes all over town accompanied by a Roman Soldier and a Trumpet-Blower in order to round up the other players and stage the arrest of the *paso* of Jesus (Melgar and Marín 1987: 109–110). In years past the people of Cabra put on a folk drama with images of the Nazarene, the *Virgen de los Dolores,* Veronica, and Saint John. The *judíos de rostro* (groups of men wearing grotesquely Semitic masks) hid behind the walls of a ruined castle and on a given signal rushed forth to "attack" the Nazarene, waving their white-gloved hands in the air in mock frenzy. The moment is recalled in a local *saeta:*

Ya asomaron los judíos	Now the Jews have appeared
por esa calle infernal	in that infernal street
para prender al Señor	to seize the Lord
y entregárselo a Caifás.	and turn Him over to Caiaphas.
[57–58]	

Magico-persecutory projection is a prime aspect of the primary emotionalism that has shaped the Passion according to Andalusia. Once Jesus has been betrayed into the hands of the authorities, a new phase of the romance begins, one in which patriarchal or father-fearing fatalism comes to the fore. Anti-Semitism will persist, of course, alongside other emotional forms of in-group assertion. Moreover, in the increasingly graphic description of Christ's traumas, anonymous narrators will seek to traumatize their listeners, liberally applying aesthetic canons that mix equal amounts of pathos and bathos. The treatment Christ receives at the hands of His captors provides an initial opportunity:

Una soga en la garganta	A rope around His neck
y otra lleva en la cintura,	and another around His waist,
atadas sus manos santas	His holy hands tied
con tan fuertes ligaduras	with knots so strong
que hasta a las piedras quebranta.	that they would break rocks.
[Martínez Ramos 1984: 245]	

Lest it be thought that hyperbole confines itself to the lyrics of the unlettered, I reproduce one of the verses sung in the yearly novena to *Nuestro Padre Jesús Nazareno* in Jaén:

Con cordeles anudados,	With knotted cords,
Con abrojos y cadenas,	With thistles and chains,
Rompen tus sagradas venas	They rupture your sacred veins
A golpes descompasados.	With extravagant blows.
Los Cielos quedan pasmados	The Heavens are left stunned
Viendo así a su Criador.	Seeing their Creator in this way.
[López Pérez 1984 : 224]	

A higher level of vocabulary or greater skill with composition does not necessarily guarantee a lessening of melodramatic effects. Lenten rituals sponsored by the Church abound in them. Still, such *tremendismo* is best illustrated in the folk renditions of the Passion preserved in places like Doña Mencía:

En un calabozo oscuro	In a dark dungeon
sucio y mal formado	dirty and badly shaped
lleno de miles de insectos	full of thousands of insects
estuvo Cristo aguardando	Christ was waiting
por término de dos horas	for a period of two hours
con grillos y encadenado	shackled and chained
con el corazón ardiendo	with His heart burning
un amor divino y santo	in divine and holy love
aguardando la sentencia	waiting for the sentence
de ese falso tribunal	of that false court
del presidente Pilatos. . . .	of President Pilate. . . .
[Melgar and Marín 1987 : 144]	

The appearance of Christ before the Council of the High Priest is a moment of high drama in the Gospels. An indeterminate number of witnesses testify falsely against Him, but their internal contradictions render them ineffectual (Matthew 26.59–60; Mark 14.55–56). A peculiar twist is given to this episode in Puente Genil, however, in which the testimony of the false witnesses—now a folkloric three in number—becomes nothing less than crucial:

El Templo temblar se vio	The Temple was seen to tremble
cuando los falsos llegaron	when the false ones arrived
y la ley de Jesucristo,	and the law of Jesus Christ,
todos tres la renovaron.	was renewed by all three.
Los tres testigos romanos	The three Roman witnesses
decidieron la condena	determined the verdict
y entre soldados tiranos	and amidst tyrannous soldiers

Cristo sucumbió la pena
para salvar a los humanos.
   [Melgar and Marín 1987:49]

Christ yielded to the punishment
in order to save humanity.

This curious bit of heterodoxy can be traced directly to sociocentric drumbeating. The above *saetas* have been placed in circulation by The False Witnesses, one of the numerous Passional men's clubs of Puente Genil that seek to assert their prominence by exaggerating the importance of the biblical figures their group identities are founded upon. Each club has its *cuartel* or quarters where the members sing their identity-promoting verses all year long (cf. Caro Baroja 1957b).

In numerous towns throughout the south, long and rambling *romances litúrgicos* are chanted in the streets on Holy Thursday or Good Friday. They are composed of anywhere from three to a dozen speeches variously known as *pregones* or *sentencias* and are delivered by two principal characters, Pontius Pilate and an angel. According to one Evangelist, an angel appeared to Christ at the Mount of Olives and comforted Him (Luke 22.43). With this "inch" of scriptural foundation, the liturgical romances have taken a mile. They are full of truculence, pious sensationalism, anti-Semitism, and incongruity. The very idea of an angel appearing alongside Pilate might seem to be an unnecessary garbling of the Passional narrative. Nevertheless, there must be some powerful sense in this apparent nonsensicalness for it to have prospered and survived in so many different places. The centerpiece of these oral traditional works is the *Pregón del Angel,* wherein the winged messenger proclaims divine will to the assembled populace and makes it clear that God the Father sentences God the Son to be sentenced by Pilate: What follows is a composite text assembled from multiple variants (Melgar and Marín 1987:119–131):

Esta es la justicia de Dios, irrevocable.
Del arcano de Dios inexcrutable.
Cúmplala, pues, la cándida inocencia,
la más áspera y rígida sentencia.
Manda, cual justo juez, el Padre Eterno
(no estorbando el precepto amor paterno)
que hoy el amor hermoso sea preso
siendo por un juez, llamado Poncio Pilatos,
sentenciado a muerte de Cruz y azotado,
coronado de espinas y blasfemado
lleve pesada Cruz, hasta el Calvario,
caminando con ella voluntario

y que sea pendiente de un madero
sin quejarse, el mansísimo Cordero
viéndole allí su Madre Dolorosa
afligida mortal triste y llorosa.
Manda así, tu Padre Soberano
te abran tu santo pecho
con un hierro inhumano,
con una lanza terrible y peligrosa,
un soldado de la gente hebrea,
mala y furiosa
que expire Cristo Dios, luz de la luz
y que su vida dé en la Santa Cruz
que es preciso padezca tales penas
quien toma sobre sí culpas ajenas
y pues sólo el amor la causa ha sido
muera de enamorado el ofendido.
Manda el Eterno Padre
que quien tal quiso tal pague.

This is the irrevocable justice of God.
Of the inscrutable secret of God.
Fulfill it, therefore, candid innocence,
the harshest and most rigid sentence.
The Eternal Father, like a just judge, decrees
(paternal love not hindering the precept)
that today beautiful love be made prisoner
being by a judge named Pontius Pilate
sentenced to death on the cross and whipped,
crowned with thorns and blasphemed,
to carry a heavy cross all the way to Calvary,
walking with it voluntarily
and be hung from a beam
without complaining, the most gentle lamb
seeing Him there His Grieving Mother
a sad and tearful afflicted mortal.
Your Sovereign Father also decrees
that your holy chest be opened
with an inhuman iron,
with a terrible and dangerous lance,
by a soldier of the Hebrew people,
evil and furious
that Christ God expire, light of the light
and give His life on the Holy Cross
for it is indispensable that he suffer such pains
he who takes upon himself the guilt of others

and since only love has been the cause
may the offended one die enamored.
The Eternal Father decrees
that He who so desired pay thusly.

If I were a vulgar Jungian, I would seize upon this *sentencia* to prove that
the Arian heresy of Iberia's visigothic invaders survives in the collective
unconscious of rural Andalusians. As depicted by an angel with presum-
ably privileged information, the Father and the Son are hardly on equal
footing. The Passion is portrayed not in terms of consensus but of fiat; it
is obedience, above all, submission to the harsh decrees of a remote *Padre
Eterno* who will not let sentiment stand in the way of "justice." What
Christ goes through, therefore, is a punishment that is legitimated by human authorities in one way and the divine authority in another. Such a
discourse might make psychological sense for people accustomed to the
hardheaded attitudes of human fathers and the pitiless actions of a law
perceived in patriarchal terms. But note the paradox: Christ has been sentenced to die voluntarily. He has been ordered to submit to punishment
of His own "free will." The meager measure of autonomy that is mus-
tered up for Him thereby, however, ultimately springs from a fatal weakness for humankind. His suffering and His death are His just deserts for
having loved sinners. His is to be a love-death (a theme dear to the hearts
of heretical Cathari and Spanish mystics alike). Christ does not want to
suffer—He says so Himself in the garden—but His love is too great for
Him to choose another course. God the Father does not want to make
His only Son suffer, but His need to exact retribution is too great for
Him to act otherwise. This takes us back to a controversy older than the
Arian one: the Greeks had never been able to make up their minds as to
whether the gods were above fate or as bound to it as miserable humans
(Nilsson 1964 : 171–172; Tripp 1970 : 246). All manner of old unresolved
conflicts come alive in these *romances litúrgicos*. Forgotten heresies are actualized, ancient debates are reopened, and half-repressed Oedipal dynamics resurface. I do not believe that any of this is gratuitous; and I am
inclined to rule out the influence of a collective unconscious and rule in a
mode of consciousness that perceives the universe in terms of punitive
fatalism and recasts the Passion accordingly.

Whatever His own degree of autonomy, the Celestial Father—always
according to Andalusia—delegates authority to an earthly judge who like
Himself is not in a position to show mercy, not even when his apocryphal

but predictably merciful wife requests it, as in the following *saeta* traditional in Jaén:

De su mujer, el consejo,	The counsel of his wife
Pilato escuchar no quiso	Pilate refused to listen to
y, lavándose las manos,	and, washing his hands,
te entregó a los asesinos.	he surrendered you to the murderers.
[Alcalá 1984 (1925): 240]	

In keeping with the magico-persecutory spirit of Doña Mencía's folk *mandato*, Pilate finds his prisoner to be guilty of witchcraft and subsequently orders Him to be flogged

con instrumentos de hierro	with instruments of iron
con juncos verdes y garfios	with green rushes and hooks
y en pena de sus delitos	and in penalty of his crimes
también será coronado	he will also be crowned
con penetrantes espinas.	with penetrating thorns.
Lo firma Poncio Pilatos.	Signed, Pontius Pilate.

Somehow the scourging takes place in the house of Caiaphas; due to His natural modesty, Christ undresses as slowly as He can, and when the floggers finally set to work, every rivulet of His blood triggers a release of souls from Limbo (Melgar and Marín 1987: 139–141). In Castro del Río, one of the many *saetas del Santísimo Via Crucis* calculates the effects of the scourging:

A una columna enlazado	Roped to a column
azotes muy desiguales	very uneven lashes He
recibió y quedó llagado	received, and the Sacred Pontiff
el Pontífice Sagrado	was left ulcerated
con cinco mil cardenales.	with five thousand bruises.
[55]	

In their urge to play to the emotions, two *saetas flamencas* collected by Plata resort to grammatical diminutive or awkward conceits:

Amarrao a una columna	Hitched to a column
le escupen y agofetean	they spit on Him and slap Him
y lo coronan de espina,	and crown Him with thorns,
y la sangre le chorrea	and the blood runs down
por su carita divina.	His little divine face.
Llegó a sudá sangre pura	He came to sweat pure blood
de pasá tanto quebranto,	from enduring such affliction,

y tomó er coló der lirio
su cuerpo de marfí santo.
  [Plata 1984 : 31]

and His body of holy ivory
took on the color of the lily.

Another collected by Alcalá chooses a different means to reach the same end:

Cuando tus sienes benditas
con espinas traspasaron,
un perrito compasivo
vino a lamerte las manos.
  [Alcalá 1984 (1925): 240]

When your blessed temples
were pierced with spines,
a compassionate little dog
came to lick your hands.

Imagineros who have sculpted the scourging for processional *pasos* have often exaggerated the ugliness of Christ's floggers to the point of caricature; Bernales attributes this to the influence of medieval mystery plays (1985 : 84–85). In contradiction with known Roman practices, Christ is always seen tied to the column with arms in front; Aroca affirms that "without doubt this posture is more aesthetic" (1987 : 30).

Dramatic tension increases with pain itself as Christ takes up His cross and sets out for Calvary. As might be imagined, Christ's journey through the streets has been a particularly appropriate theme for street liturgy, verbal and visual. With the exception of the *Dolorosa* and the *Crucificado*, the *Nazareno* is the image most often carried along during an *estación de penitencia*. The *imagineros* of Seville, for example, have created ten different masterpieces that depict the Nazarene before, during, or after one of His falls (Bernales 1985 : 70–82; Palomero 1987 : 100–121). In many cases, the Nazarene is the central figure of a *paso de misterio* that might also include Simon the Cyrene, Veronica, a soldier, a Jew, and others. One of the *saetas* collected by Plata was almost surely created to describe a *paso* of this kind:

Jesús mío Nazareno
que vas sufriendo y penando,
y ese maldito judío
de tu cuerpo va tirando.
  [Plata 1984 : 32]

My Jesus Nazarene
you go along suffering and aching,
and that damned Jew
is there pulling at your body.

A *paso* that portrays Simon helping with the cross has elicited another *saeta* in which Christ asks

¿Quién me ayuda a llevar
este maero tan pesao?

Who will help me to carry
such a heavy crossbeam?

Que traigo los hombros muertos
y el cuerpo descoyuntao.

For my shoulders are dead
and my body is dislocated.

Yo no puedo seguir más
al pueblo pido clemencia.
Si yo mismo he de pagar
lo que mi Padre ordenó
para el mundo remediar.
　[Melgar and Marín 1987 : 63]

I cannot go on any longer
I ask the people for clemency.
I myself am to pay
what my Father ordered
in order to help the world.

Helping Christ to carry His cross, incidentally, is one of the conscious rationales employed by penitentes to explain their own cross-carrying. Simon's intervention is described by another *saeta* sung in one of Puente Genil's Passional men's clubs and considered "unfortunate" and "vulgar" by Melgar and Marín:

Lleno de polvo y sudando
va caminando Jesús.
Como un gusano arrastrando
ya no puede con la cruz
y un hombre le va ayudando
　[49]

Covered with dust and sweating
Jesus goes walking along.
Crawling like a worm
He can no longer handle the cross
and a man is helping Him.

To make way for the coming of Veronica, Andalusia's Passional narration goes out of its way to describe the lamentable condition of Christ's face. This ubiquitous and wholly apocryphal theme has reached a maximum point of development in Jaén's traditional *Canto Doloroso Al Santísimo Rostro de Nuestro Redentor,* which first describes how "a Jewish hand armed with iron" strikes Christ's innocent cheek with such force "that it bursts into blood," then notes that the crown of thorns "breaks the divine temples," and finally presents us with Christ in the streets—

Al Calvario va llagado
y las mejillas llorosas,
con salivas asquerosas
y el Rostro acardenalado,
Denegrido y afeado
Va, que el verlo es un dolor.
　[López Pérez 1984 : 232–233]

Ulcerated He goes to Calvary
and the tearful cheeks,
with disgusting spittles
and His face bruised,
blackened and made ugly
He goes, and it hurts to see Him.

Here, sensationalism is bound up with sociocentrism. Jaén has a vested interest in the shape of Christ's face because it has the privilege to possess one of the folds of the veil with which Veronica cleansed it. A cathedral was even built to house this famous *Santo Rostro de Jaén,* and erudite locals have attested to its authenticity (215–220).

At last Christ arrives at Golgotha. Not content with the succinct Synoptic "they crucified him," the Passion according to the people fills in the gory details. The following *saetas* are heard all over Andalusia and have even attached themselves to the *mandato* of Doña Mencía:

Cuando al Calvario llegaron	When they got to Calvary
con el Jesús Nazareno,	with the Nazarene Jesus,
al punto lo desnudaron	they immediately undressed Him
la cruz en tierra pusieron	put the cross onto the ground
pies y manos lo amarraron.	and bound Him hand and foot.
Los clavos que previnieron	The nails they made ready
para poderlo enclavar	in order to nail Him down
sin puntos los dispusieron	without points they arranged them
y por no poder entrar	and since they would not go in
golpes y mas golpes dieron.	they hit them again and again.
[Melgar and Marín 1987:143–144]	

Saeteros in Cabra add another five lines that in spite of their brutality enclose a finely felt folk irony:

Con tal fuerza el inhumano	With such force the inhuman one
los crueles golpes le daba	was striking the cruel blows
que se le escapó de la mano	that the hammer flew out of
el martillo, y blasfemaba	his hands, and he blasphemed
sobre su Soberano.	about his Sovereign.
[64]	

The Passion according to Andalusia not only is inventive of new details but can recreate Scripture with vigor and economy:

Despréndete de esos clavos	Detach yourself from those nails
y bájate de la cruz,	and lower yourself from the cross,
le decían los soldados.	the soldiers said to Him.
Tú que dices que eres Dios	You who say you are God
y que del cielo has bajado.	and have come down from heaven.
Perdónales, Padre mío,	Forgive them, my Father,
a los que me han enclavado,	those who have nailed me down,
lo que han hecho no han sabido,	they know not what they have done,
deben de ser perdonados	they should be pardoned
porque no me han conocido.	because they have not known me.
Al mirarse en tal estado	Seeing Himself in such a state
con gran voz al Padre llama,	with a loud voice He called the
su rostro al cielo elevado.	Father,

¡Dios mío! ¡Dios mío! clama,	His face upturned to heaven.
¿por qué me has desamparado?	My god! My God! He shouts,
	why have you forsaken me?
Y habiendo Cristo probado	And Christ having tasted
la hiel que a beber le dieron,	the gall they gave Him to drink,
exclamó muy fatigado:	exhausted he exclaimed:
los decretos se cumplieron,	the decrees have been fulfilled,
ya está todo consumado.	now all is consummated.
Padre Eterno, pronunciaba,	Eternal Father, He pronounced,
mi espíritu os encomiendo,	to you I commend my spirit,
y dando las boqueadas	and giving His last gasps
el pecho se le iba hundiendo	His chest was caving in on Him
y la cabeza inclinaba.	and His head was nodding.
Ya comienza su agonía	Now His agony begins
el pecho se le levanta,	His chest heaves,
se le afila la nariz,	His nose sharpens,
se le aprieta la garganta.	His throat tightens.
¡Ya está próximo a morir!	Now He is about to die!
[López Fernández 1981:71–73]	

Compared to the melodramatic and sometimes maudlin exaggeration of Christ's torments, which we noted in earlier stages of the Passion according to Andalusia, the moment of death itself is treated with deference. These last two *saetas* (from the traditional *quintas* of Marchena's *Hermandad del Santísimo Cristo de San Pedro*) are a model of self-control and realism. They are in perfect concordance with the Andalusian *Crucificados* themselves, as will be seen. But the story that is steeped in fatalism cannot end without the completion of every last prophecy:

¿Dónde vas, ciego Longino?	Where are you going, blind
¿Qué es lo que han ordenao?	Longinus?
Voy a cumplir mi destino	What is it they have ordered?
alanceando el costao	I am going to fulfill my destiny
de ese Cordero Divino.	by lancing the side
	of that Divine Lamb.
[Melgar and Marín 1987:63]	

According to John (19.31–37), the Jewish authorities wanted to keep the Sabbath especially holy and therefore requested Pilate to take the bodies down from the crosses. Pilate agreed, and his soldiers went and broke the legs of the two bandits in order to precipitate their death by suffocation.

"But when they came to Jesus, they saw that He was already dead, so they did not break His legs. One of the soldiers, however, plunged his spear into Jesus' side, and at once blood and water poured out" (33–34). Strange as it may seem, this lancing of the dead Christ offers one last opportunity for sensationalism, and *saeteros* in many localities of the south have exploited it to the maximum. A typical example from Castro del Río:

Lleno de furia un soldado	Full of fury a soldier
al cadavre Santo avanza	advances on the Holy cadaver
y de furores armado	and armed with furors
rompió su santo costado	broke the holy side
con el golpe de una lanza.	with the blow of a lance.
[Melgar and Marín 1987:57]	

The relatively sophisticated meter and vocabulary of Marchena's *sextas* do not save them from patent absurdity:

Con mano alevosa, impía,	With a perfidious and impious hand
un atrevido soldado, sin temor,	an impudent soldier, without fear,
al Dios que la luz envía	opened up the glorious side
le abrió el glorioso costado:	of the God who sent the light:
¡qué dolor!	what pain!
[López Fernández 1981:74]	

In contrast to what might be expected, Andalusian images of the Crucified cannot be described as sensationalistic. Unlike the sculptures of certain Castilian *imagineros,* southern Christs are not contorted, strained, spasmodic, recriminatory, or excessively bloody. This is not because the *imagineros* of Andalusia were out to please the refined tastes of a cultivated minority. For one thing, the whole point of baroque religious art is to impress and appeal to the emotions of the vast majority. For another, the sources I have consulted all stress that Andalusian *imagineros* were— and are—totally in touch with popular sentiment, tastes, and beliefs (Aroca 1987:12–15; Bernales 1985:88; Palomero 1987:60–63 *et passim*). In addition, every *cofradía* is highly vigilant of the popular acceptance or rejection of the images their *costaleros* carry through the streets. A *paso* of the Scourging made by Joaquín Bilbao, for example, was brought out for the first time in 1914 by Seville's *Hermandad de las Cigarreras.* According to Palomero, the monumental corpulence and crudity of the Christ gave rise to a number of satirical *saetas* that compared the sacred image with the obese paymaster of the Tobacco Factory; the mortified penitential brotherhood was eventually obliged to replace the image at great expense (1987 : 72–73).

It is therefore reasonable to assume that Andalusian *Crucificados* look the way they do because the people so desired. Truculent effects have been as rejected for visual representation as they have been tolerated or sought after in verbal representation. Since the image is a more direct and fascinating way to grasp the sufferings and death of Christ, perhaps people were determined that it be not only realistic but also exemplary, the latter requirement serving to restrain the former. In contrast with the *saeta,* which is sung to narrate some episode of the Passion, the image is designed not merely to tell a story but to be an object of veneration and worship. No *saeta* can be placed on an altar during Lent to receive the reverent kisses of the faithful.

A detailed examination of Andalusian Christs lies beyond the scope of this study, but it might be instructive to consider one that is broadly representative of them all—the *Santísimo Cristo de la Expiración,* nicknamed "*el Cachorro,*" sculpted by Francisco Gijón in 1682, and currently the most popular image of the Crucified in all of Seville.

> The representation is that of a brunet man, tall and strong, with Andalusian traits and proper facial features. All the signs of death are present in an intense manner, indicative of the death rattle giving way to a movement that contorts the figure; and this dramatic effect is sharpened by a *sudario* divided into three parts, worked with unusual agitation of folds and chiaroscuro effects. But in reality a minute description of the formal elements of the image seems sterile; the concept that animates it transcends the image and reaches the spectators and the faithful, so it is enough to look upon it and let the emotions be felt. [Bernales 1985 : 66]

As in every other aspect of Passional culture, emotion is of the essence in the Passional image. But the *Cachorro*'s fatal diagnosis merits a second opinion: according to Antonio Hermosilla Molina, a Sevillian doctor who has specialized in the examination of dying Christs, Gijón's sculpture is a model example of medical realism in that it portrays "the preliminary termination of vital neurological functions that through hyperventilation are reaching the critical point, with abolition of reflexes and functions. There is no pain, there is no spasm" (cit. by *ABC,* 1 April 1988, p. 65). Due regard should be paid to the *imaginero*'s genius for drama and eye for clinical accuracy, and yet another factor must be cited to understand the total impact of the *Cachorro*. In the view of another scholar, Gijón has not allowed the elements of pathos and realism to eclipse the religious message of his great *Crucificado:*

> There is no doubt that it is God Himself nailed to the crossbeam. Neither the blood of the Garden of Olives, nor the betrayal, nor the flagellation, nor the jeers, nor the flight of the disciples, nor the despoilment, nor even the crucifixion, have managed to defeat Him. There is no physical or moral pain capable of subduing His grandeur. Bearing with strength upon the nail in His feet, Jesus stiffens to commend His Spirit to the Father. He does it with the gallantry befitting God. [Aroca 1987:186–187]

In effect, the *Cachorro* is the archetypal Andalusian Crucified because He is dying gallantly, with elegance, aplomb, and grace. In a culture historically obsessed with how to die, how Christ dies is of crucial importance. Only if He does it properly, it seems, will people be able to reap the thaumaturgic benefits they have needed so desperately. In the final analysis, the *Crucificados* of the south are only moderately bloody because they must appeal to hope as well as to visceralness. As far as Andalusia is concerned, it is Christ's infinite capacity for suffering and His model death that make not only salvation but also a host of lesser favors available, not the least of which is the gratifying play of emotions Bernales speaks of. Ironically, Christ's Resurrection three days later leaves most Andalusians cold.

Mater Dolorosa

Up to now I have discussed how factors like sociocentrism, anti-Semitism, sensationalism, and fatalism have informed the way Andalusians retell the Passion of Christ. Remarkable as some of the deviations may seem, however, what we have seen of street liturgy so far cannot in general be considered wildly divergent with Catholic tradition. It might almost seem as if people in the south had merely developed certain tendencies already present in either the Gospels or standard apocryphal legends. Yet there is one episode that has remained strangely undeveloped in southern Spain, precisely the one that might be thought the most important of all from the standpoint of faith. I am referring to the Resurrection. In comparison with the sheer amount of culture derived from or devoted to the diverse incidents of the Passion and Death of Christ, the theme of the Risen Christ (*Cristo Resucitado*) has elicited little culture and less interest in Andalusia. Church authorities have been the first to recognize and attempt to redress this regrettable omission. Their efforts have hardly been crowned with success. In some places bishops resorted to prohibiting the Holy Saturday processions in a vain ploy to oblige people to join in the Pascual vigil (*ABC*, 2 April 1988, p. 46). Elsewhere they have fomented the creation of *hermandades* charged with the carrying of an image of the *Resucitado* on Easter Sunday morning. Such an *hermandad* was finally created in Seville in 1982, and the comments made by one of its brothers in 1988 betray its frailty:

> Regarding my *hermandad* I can say that I wish it were just another Sevillian *hermandad*. Because when we decided to put it on the street, following the dispositions of the Council [Vatican II], we knew we were attempting something very difficult in this city. Even so, we are getting the new generation to see us as something normal and not as something shocking, which is what happens, understandably, with older *cofrades*. In Seville there have been several experiments of this type over the centuries, but not one managed to jell. [Cit. by *ABC*, 30 March 1988, p. 66]

As Burgos put it bluntly several years ago, "for the popular theology of Seville, the Resurrection has nothing to do with Holy Week" (cit. by Moreno 1982 : 61). The same must hold true for Jaén, where the *Ilustre Cofradía del Señor Resucitado* is not a *cofradía* at all but a procession organized from above by the *Agrupación de Cofradías* "in order to complete the Holy Week cycle" (López Pérez 1984 : 129). It first appeared on the streets in 1952 with a *paso* of the *Resucitado*. In 1955 an image of "Our Lady of Victory" was introduced, only to be retired two years later for lack of popular demand (129–130). In most other Andalusion localities, no attempt has ever been made to include the Risen Christ in Holy Week processions.

The peculiarly inconspicuous role that Andalusia assigns to the Resurrection presents a problem not only for the Church but also for the psychology of storytelling. For Northrop Frye, the myth of Christianity is a complete romance because it ends happily, complementing its falling action with rising action (literally, in this case) (1976 : 88–92). Even assuming that Christ's rising from the tomb was pure fiction, it clearly represents the optimistic *will to romance* that people stubbornly oppose to negativity of all kinds and death in particular. If the happy ending is truncated, then what we have is an incomplete romance or tragedy along classic pagan lines. This leads to two obvious questions: Why does street liturgy the length and breadth of Andalusia truncate the Passion to end in death, desolation, and mourning? What has happened in the south to quash the normally irrepressible human desire for a happy ending?

The answer to these questions, in my view, will depend on the interpretation we give to another facet of southern Spain's street liturgy, perhaps the most striking of all: the protagonism of the *Mater Dolorosa*. If the insignificance of the Resurrection is a scandalous "sin of omission," then the predominance of the grieving María errs on the supply side. In fact what has happened in Andalusia goes well beyond even the apocryphal tradition, to the point that it becomes perfectly valid to speak of a Passion of María parallel to, intertwined with, theologically subordinate but popularly equal to that of Christ. Here we find, perhaps, not only the key to the missing Resucitado but also crucial clues for an understanding of Andalusian religiosity as a whole.

Beginning with the more general and moving toward the more specific, the factors that have contributed to the present importance of the *Mater Dolorosa* can be summarized as follows. (1) The most general factor is European Romance Catholicism, the backdrop against which the *mythos* and the *ethos* of Marianism have developed. (2) What holds for Europe holds doubly for Spain and triply for Andalusia—"land of *María Santísima*." One has only to think of the quixotic defense of the Immaculate Conception, or of deeply rooted social values of female honor, virginity, maternity, and so forth. (3) Devotional practices popularized by different religious orders take us into the specific terrain of Passional Mariology. Here, once again, the Franciscans enjoyed a preeminent influence over people of all social classes. In his best-selling *Subida al Montesión* (1535), Fray Bernardino de Laredo developed the theme of María's com-passion

> with heartrending pathos, describing the physical union and participation of María Santísima in the torments that destroy the holy body of her son unto death. In this sense, for Laredo, the passion of María is . . . a singular union between Mother and Son in which "Christ gave His sacred body to the cross, but always accompanied by the most triumphant divinity, while the Virgin, body and soul, was nailed to the cross with her tender heart and with all her being." . . . Likewise, the Franciscan poet Fray Ambrosio Montesino had sung

in some deliciously expressive verses that Jesus and María, the "most beloved" of the Father, were

"atados en un amor	[bound in one love
y penados en un dolor	and tormented in one pain
y en una cruz abrazados"	and embraced on one cross.]
[García de la Concha 1988a : 46]	

The mystical/erotic ring of all this is no accident, if we bear in mind that the Franciscan order was the great historical link between the love rhetoric of the twelfth-century troubadours and the language of mysticism of later centuries (Rougemont 1984 : 163, 343–344). García de la Concha goes on to cite a long list of Franciscan, Augustinian, Dominican, and Jesuit preachers who fomented the passionate devotion to María's Passion in sixteenth- and seventeenth-century Andalusia (1988a : 46). Another order of mendicant friars, known as *Servitas,* were successful promoters of the same message during the eighteenth century in Catalonia, Valencia, and all over the south (González Gómez 1985 : 130–131). The teachings of St. Antonio María Claret, a Spanish archbishop and founder of the Claretian order, were greatly influential in the latter part of the nineteenth century. As the apostle of the "filial consecration to the Heart of the Best of Mothers," Claret propagated the practice of the rosary as the shortest route to said Heart (Gutiérrez Serrano 1988 : 112–114). He was encouraged in his endeavors by direct personal messages from heaven, such as the one received on 6 December 1862–"Antonio, do what my Mother tells you to do" (cit. by Gómez Marín 1972 : 71). Four years later he watched in astonishment as a crucifix and a portrait of the Virgin drew near to each other in his rectory (72). In thanks for such divine signals, Claret adopted "María" as a middle name and penned numerous prayers like the following:

> I, Antonio María Claret, would like to have all the lives of men to employ them in the service of the Mother of God. . . . I wish to die and shed all my blood out of love and reverence for María, Virgin and Mother of God. I desire that Jesus grant me the grace and strength I need in order that all of my members be tormented and cut off one by one out of love and reverence for María, Mother of God and mine also. Let it be done, let it be done. [Cit. by Gutiérrez Serrano 1988 : 115]

It would not be hard to see a link between this pious masochism and what Preston calls "the earthy aspects of mother worship"—self-mutilation, blood sacrifice, and so on (1982:339). Or perhaps the archbishop merely spoke the same language of mystical Marianism spoken by Fray Bernardino, Fray Ambrosio, and the other preachers cited above. Metaphorical and metaphysical masochism abounds in Andalusian poetic compositions, which contribute in their own way to Passional culture. José Vega's ode to the *Dolorosa de San Juan* may serve as an example. In the final lines the poet gushes,

Y, de fervores y emoción deshecho,	And, melted by fervors and emotion,
yo gozaré sufriendo, enternecido,	I will enjoy suffering, touched,
el dolor penetrante y encendido	the inflamed and penetrating pain
de los siete puñales de tu pecho.	of the seven daggers in your breast.
[Cit. by López Pérez 1984:123]	

Vega is ostensibly referring to the daggers of grief that symbolically pierce the *Dolorosa*'s heart during the Passion. One can only wonder whether the ongoing taste for such tingly metaphors can ultimately be traced to the matrilineal ascription systems that might have feminized scores of young male *cofrades* throughout Andalusia (Moreno 1985a: 147–165).

(4) In any case, the purveyors of Passional Mariology from the sixteenth through the twentieth centuries were either directly involved with or influential over the practices of Andalusia's penitential brotherhoods. Claret, for example, was a brother of both the *Hermandad de la Santa Caridad* and the *Cofradía del Silencio*. Thanks to the *cofradías,* says González Gómez, the *Mater Dolorosa* is the most important Marian advocation in Seville and many other cities and towns (1985:121). Since it was in the Passion of Christ that the finest qualities of His Mother were realized, brotherhoods organized to give cult to the first immediately began to give a Passional interpretation to older, originally non-Passional Marian advocations. In many cases, antique icons with placid expressions were fitted with masks that retained the facial features but transmuted them into the appropriate expressions of grief or pity (García de la Concha 1988b:35). Castillo Martos accurately summarizes how the cult of the *Mater Dolorosa* fits into the patriarchal scheme of the Passion:

> This advocation as an object of piety and cult contemplates not only the Woman as disconsolate, discouraged, and tearful for what was happening to Jesus, but also full of pity, never murmuring a word against those who affronted her Beloved and filled with love and resignation to the plans of God

that she accepted from the first moment until she stayed, in an attitude of submission and charity, at the foot of the cross on Calvary. [1988 : 36]

The street liturgy of Holy Week has ceaselessly added onto this gender-related nucleus of submissive compassion, creating distinct Marian advocations for every moment of Christ's ordeal. Guided by the *cofradías,* Passional Mariology in Andalusia has become a complex of images, *pasos de palio,* rites, beliefs, *saetas,* and above all emotions. People feel the Passion of Christ through that of His Mother, people console the Mother as she attempts to console the Son. Affecting as His torments are in themselves, people find them much more affecting when filtered through María (who suffered the very same torments vicariously, according to legions of preachers).

(5) This brings me to the next factor in the development of Holy Week Mariology. For Andalusians, the *Mater Dolorosa* is just that, a grieving mother; the images that *costaleros* carry through the streets are natural symbols for all the worldly mothers who can only weep and despair in their impotence while the world witnesses pain and death upon their loved ones. Naturally no people has a monopoly on maternal sentiment. Yet few peoples expect as much from their mothers as Andalusians do—for reasons detailed in previous chapters—more so, in fact, than any human mother can give, try as she may, but that felt to be within the power of a humanized icon. The icon is humanized through a massive projection of one's own indestructible maternal imago. This in turn has led to a veritable idolization of the Maternal images that *cofradías* treasure and put on the streets during Holy Week.

In contrast with the varied artistic masterpieces of *Nazarenos* and *Crucificados,* the sculptures of the *Dolorosa* are monotonously alike (for an uncommitted observer); nevertheless, they are the greater objects of ingroup fervor. It is not that people are indifferent to art, by any means; it is precisely the conscious awareness that it is a work of *art* that prevents their idolatrizing a well-wrought image of Christ. There will be veneration, of course, and in the case of the greatest veneration there will be a tendency to tell or believe some folk legend regarding the uncanny origins of the image. Jaén's *Nuestro Padre Jesús Nazareno,* for example, is said to have been sculpted overnight by a mysterious *imaginero* befriended by peasants (Vega Gutiérrez 1984). Such legends do not lose sight of the fact that the image has been fashioned or created in some way. With the graven image of the Mother, however, a different sort of psychology takes over, one that takes its cue from durable unconscious idealizations and is therefore all too willing to forget that "she" is only a carved and painted face and hands attached to a wooden frame. But more than one *imaginero* has carved and painted the face with his own mother in mind (López Pérez 1984:103), and anthropomorphizing *maricas* rush in to dress and undress their Mother where most men fear to tread (Aguilar 1983:179–180).

Like everyone's maternal imago, the Maternal image never ages— added proof of its divinity. The anecdotes I cited in the last chapter give an idea of the extent to which people behave as if the divinity and the icon were one and the same. The opportunities for idolatry, therefore, will be as numerous as the idols themselves. The Doleful Mothers of southern Spain run into the hundreds and are worshipped under appellations like the Virgin/Our Lady of the Encarnation, of the Star, of Solitude, of the Greatest Grief, of the Greatest Grief in her Solitude, of Hope, of Angels, of Tears, of Water, of Anguish, of Succor, of the Helpless, of Charity, of Refuge, of Consolation, of Health, of Pity, of Mercy, of Bitterness, of Crowned Bitterness, of the Seven Griefs, of the Greatest Grief and Pain, of the Good End, and so on. The cult of Our Lady of the Swoon is now defunct (González Gómez 1985:136–142; García de la Concha 1988a, 1988b).

(6) The final and most culturally specific factor of all in the making of the Andalusian *Mater Dolorosa* is the so-called *saeta afectiva*. Unlike the *saetas* discussed earlier, the affective variety seeks not to tell a story but to arouse emotion in as intense a way as possible. Inasmuch as the affective *saeta* is sung directly *to* a Passional image (rather than *about* one), it is the perfect vehicle for the idolatrous cult of the grieving María. In its urge to sym-pathize with her Passion, emotive lyrics fall into additional forms of heterodoxy, not the least of which is the overshadowing of the Resurrected Christ.

Attuned as it is to occasions of exquisite grief, the *saeta afectiva* has made the most out of the apocryphal encounter between the Nazarene and His Mother on Bitterness Street. From Marchena, Jaén, and Castro del Río, respectively:

Hijo y Madre se han mirado, Son and Mother have seen each
¡qué confusión! ¡qué tormento! other,

hasta la tierra un momento
en lágrimas se ha bañado.

[López Fernández 1981:68]

what confusion! what torment!
even the earth for a moment
has bathed itself in tears.

En la caye e l'Amargura
Cristo a su Madre encontró.
No se pudieron hablar
del sentimiento y doló.

[Alcalá 1984 (1925): 239]

On Bitterness Street
Christ found His Mother.
They couldn't speak to each other
out of sentiment and pain.

Cuando madre e hijo se vieron
sobre aquella turba impía
de dolor desfallecieron,
y al decirle "¡Madre mía!"
hasta los astros gimieron.

[Salido 1984:59]

When mother and son saw each
other
above that impious mob
they fainted from pain,
and when He said "My Mother!"
even the stars moaned.

In a number of small towns throughout the south, street liturgy calls for the *costaleros* carrying the image of the *Dolorosa* to attempt to bring her close to the image of *Jesús Nazareno,* only to be blocked by a group of plumed, lance-wielding Roman Soldiers. As an amateur poet of Puente Genil relates,

Se pone er pelo de punta
ar presensiar este cuadro,
porque se escuchan lamentos
y suspiros prolongaos
y las mujeres soyosan
y después suerten el yanto.

[From *El Sermón del Paso* by Agustín Rodríguez; cit. by Melgar and Marín 1987:117–118]

One's hair stands on end
when watching this scene,
because laments are heard
and prolonged sighs
and the women sob
and then begin to weep.

The "maternal connection" latent in all affective *saetas* is manifested with finesse in the following example from Córdoba:

A verte, Señor aquí,
vengo de Santa Marina.
Lo quiere mi madre así.
Esa que llora y camina
descalza detrás de tí.

[Melgar and Marín 1987:104]

Here, Lord, to see you,
I've come from Santa Marina.
My mother wants it this way.
The one that's crying and
walking barefoot behind you.

One *saeta* collected by Plata eloquently expresses the com-passion of María:

En la calle la Amargura	On the Street of Bitterness
el Hijo a su Madre encuentra	the Son meets His Mother
el Hijo lleva la cruz,	the Son carries the cross,
¡pero a su Madre le pesa!	but it weighs heavy on His Mother!
[Plata 1984 : 24]	

Affective *saetas* have developed every possible metaphor of pain in their efforts to convey adequately the enormity of María's suffering. The *Mater Dolorosa* is pictured as burdened, weighed down, crushed, exhausted, consumed, weak, faint, and, above all, penetrated with swords or daggers.

Al ver clavado en la Cruz	Seeing the innocent Jesus Christ
a Jesu-Cristo inocente,	nailed to the Cross,
el corazón de Madre	the Mother's heart
sintió fatigas de muerte.	felt mortal fatigue.
Eran los golpes certeros	The well-aimed blows
que Jesu-Cristo sufría,	that Jesus Christ suffered,
puñales que atravesaban	were daggers that pierced
el corazón de María.	the heart of María.
[Alcalá 1984 (1925): 241]	

Numerous popular lyrics refer to the Virgin's tears. The following *saeta* achieves a nice conceit with devotional overtones:

¡Quién hubiera recogido,	If only someone could have
para formar un rosario,	gathered, to form a rosary,
las lágrimas que la Virgen	the tears that the Virgin
lloró en el Monte Calvario!	cried on Mount Calvary!
[Alcalá 1984 (1925): 241]	

The great majority of icons of the *Mater Dolorosa* have crystal tears running down their cheeks, sometimes with inlaid pearls. *Saetas* often allude to them:

Esas lágrimas preciosas,	Those precious tears
que te ruedan por la cara,	that roll down your cheeks
se paran en tus mejillas	stop at your cheeks.
¡no hay paño con que limpiarlas!	No cloth can clean them!
[Melgar and Marín 1987 : 103]	

Many *saetas* take the form of an exhortation to the *costaleros* carrying the image of the *Dolorosa:*

Costaleros, costaleros,	Costaleros, costaleros,
llevarla a poquito a poco	carry her little by little
y tirar por lo derecho,	and turn towards the right
que no se le claven más	so that the daggers in her breast
los puñales de su pecho.	do not stab her even more.
[Melgar and Marín 1987:104]	

The hour of desolation finally arrives:

A la vera de la Cruz	At the side of the Cross
sola en mundo te ha dejao.	alone in the world He has left you.
Te darán un Hijo muerto	They will give you a dead Son
y tres clavos ensangrentaos.	and three bloodstained nails.
[Melgar and Marín 1987:64]	

Christ's Passion comes to an end with His death, but the Passion of María is only beginning. Of the numberless *saetas* sung to the Virgin or Our Lady of Solitude, perhaps the traditional *samaritanas* of Castro del Río best express the popular feelings aroused by the *Mater Dolorosa* as she fulfills her final destiny:

Con el corazón lloraba	She was weeping with her heart
porque lágrimas no había	because there were no more tears
y en la Santa Cruz besaba	and on the Holy Cross she kissed
aquella sangre vertida	that flowing blood
que su hijo derramaba.	that her Son was spilling.
No llores Madre querida	Do not cry dear Mother
que ya no tiene salvación.	there is no longer any use.
Tu hijo perdió la vida	Your Son lost His life
partiéndote el corazón	breaking your heart
y dejándote afligida.	and leaving you afflicted.
Llevas los párpados rojos	Your eyelids are red
de tanto y tanto llorar.	from crying and crying.
Se están secando tus ojos	Your eyes are drying up
y no paras de pisar	and you keep stepping on
sangre, espinas y abrojos.	blood, thorns, and thistles.
Tienes el rostro encarnado	Your face is flushed
de la sangre de Jesús,	from the blood of Jesus,
será que te ha salpicado	it must have spattered you
estando al pie de la cruz	at the foot of the cross
al lancerarle el costado.	when they lanced His side.
Ya no hay consuelo en su vida	Now there is no comfort in her life
porque lo lleva en sus brazos	because she carries Him in her arms

Mediterranean funerary practices, as filtered through medieval mystics, transformed the descent from the cross into a *Lamentación* or Pietà and María into *Nuestra Señora de la Piedad* (photo: Encarnación Lucas).

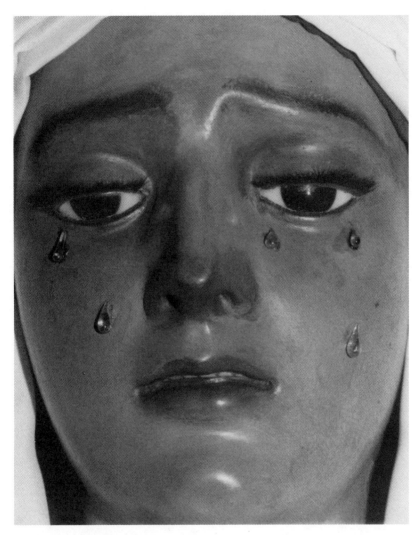

The archetypal Andalusian *Mater Dolorosa* (photo: Encarnación Lucas).

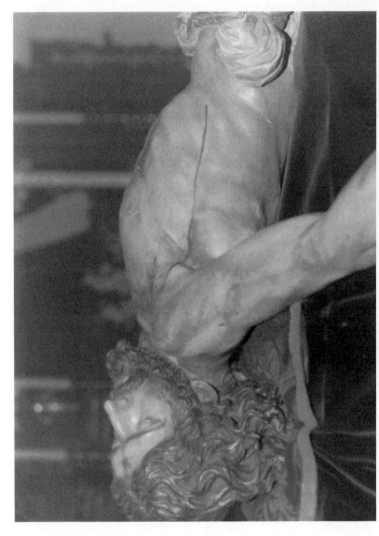

The Christ that is laid every year upon María's knees was sculpted by Ortega Bru in 1950 (photo: Encarnación Lucas).

muerto. Y quedó afligida,	dead. And she was left afflicted,
con el alma en dos pedazos	with her soul in two pieces
va muy triste y dolorida.	she goes along very sad and pained.
Un lucero se apagó	A bright star went out
al ver tu cara de pena.	seeing your face of sadness.
Madre mía del amor	My Mother of love
sangre diera de mis venas	I would give blood from my veins
por consolar tu dolor.	to console your grief.
Cuando preso lo seguía	As a prisoner she followed Him
en sus mayores tormentos,	in His greatest torments,
lo seguía en su agonía.	she followed Him in His agony.
Y hoy lo va siguiendo muerto,	Today she is following Him in death,
llena de dolor María.	full of pain, María.
[Salido 1984:57–58]	

One will search these verses in vain for some glimmer of light, hope, or optimism. So far as popular tradition is concerned, the story of the Passion ends here, in utter *Soledad*. It is not really an end, therefore, since María is left to sorrow eternally. The plot line of the Passion according to Andalusia can be summarized as suffering, death, burial, and suffering without end. If the people do not wish to spoil this story with a joyous Resurrection, they must have some powerful reasons.

That Andalusians cannot bring themselves to believe in such a far-fetched thing as a man rising from the dead is a possibility that I think we can rule out. If anything, the whole tendency of religiosity in the south is to believe too much, not too little; skepticism is not a facet of Passional culture. The numerous interlocking romances of Romance Catholicism thrive on improbable, magical, miraculous, and awesome events of all sorts, and the ability of a god-man to conquer death hardly strains the limits of romance credibility. It is precisely when we situate the theme of Christ's Resurrection within the coordinates of romance that we begin to make progress: In terms of overall narrative structure, the Resurrection would stand for the recovery of reality, identity, and serenity; the end of anxiety and alienation; the defeat of tyranny and illusion (cf. Frye 1976: 54). The Resurrection would be a standard ascent theme, the logical end of Frye's "cyclical movement of descent into a night world and a return to the idyllic world" (54). Andalusia's romance of the Passion deviates from the norm in that it does not end happily; it seems to remain trapped in the night world, haunted by images of a grieving mother searching for her Son and her serenity in vain.

Ya viene la Soledad,	The *Soledad* is coming,
Madre del mayor dolor,	Mother of the greatest pain,
llorando porque no encuentra	crying because she cannot find
a Aquél que nunca pecó.	the One who never sinned.
[Alcalá 1984 (1925): 241]	

If this is the ending that people value and prefer, then it would be plausible to assume that they find the night world to have special meaning and relevance to their *own* world, or, more exactly, to their own world-design. In effect, in the denouement of the Passion according to Andalusia we can find the final ironic achievement of emotion magic.

The absence of the *Resucitado* and the omnipresence of His grieving Mother are perfectly coherent with all of the other changes, deviations, and inventions that emotionality has effected in the narrative of Christ's death. The Passion according to Andalusia, in my view, represents the cultural culmination of the fixative and fatalistic Andalusian way of being-in-the-world. The emotional mode of consciousness has been able to shape vast areas of religious and secular culture alike because it has something to offer in exchange for lack of autonomy, nongrowth, and ego-stifling dependence: itself. By and large, Andalusians have found emotion to be its own reward, one that is as habit-forming as any other panacea. It stages a magic comedy of impotence for itself, luxuriating in maladaptive but guilt-assuaging beliefs of other-directedness, of ferocious Fatherly Fate and infinitely nurturant Lady Luck (especially the luck of Our Lady).

Nevertheless, it would be a mistake to interpret the Andalusian indifference to the Resurrected Christ as indifference to redemption. The whole penitential ideology underlying Passional culture is dedicated to the removal of sin through suffering—because it is suffering that removes sin, not Resurrection. Miraculous benefits accrue to the sacrifice of the Son, not to His restoration, which for southern Spain's Passional narration has the status of an afterthought. Redemption-through-suffering is the part of the catechism that Andalusians have learned by heart. They did not invent the concept, but they have developed it to the point that other considerations are blurred. They have rewritten the Passion accordingly: the whole point of the *Mater Dolorosa* is to preserve redemptive suffering. Someone must take up the torch of suffering that Christ passes on when He passes on. In Passional context, the *Purísima* can purify sinners because she is capable of *infinite* pain. How else could she save so many sinners or assist men and women at the hour of their own agony? Without María, there would literally be no limit to rough Patriarchal justice. If María's sufferings were to come to an end by restoring her Son to her, that would be nice for her but disastrous for all the people who count on her endless suffering capacity as a fount of grace.

The passionate character of the Passion according to Andalusia is actualized in every performance of an affective *saeta*. It is in these moments that emotion is at its most intense, immediate, and magical. The *saeta* is the super-*copla* as it restructures reality in accordance with sentiment (cf. Fernández and Pérez 1983 : 22–23). The *saeta* thrives upon the strongest dose of pathos imaginable—that evoked by a mother grieving for her son—and consoles even as it magnifies the pathos. Every net increase in suffering—a tear here, a dagger there—is a net increase in grace, in thaumaturgic capacity, in salvation. In the moment a *saeta* is being sung, as all students of the Andalusian Holy Week concur, popular emotionality reaches its climax. Listening to a *saeta*, one can feel saved, one has the consciousness of being saved. What you feel is what you get, to paraphrase the colloquialism. Saved, in the last analysis, by sentiment itself.

There is a gender-based bias here, clearly enough, a reflection of cultural expectations regarding the role of woman in general and mother in particular. But if Moreno's study of gender identity in the brotherhoods proves anything, it is the extent to which both men and women identify with the maternal (1985a : 147–165). This identification is implicit in each of the three great facets of the Andalusian *Mater Dolorosa:* imago, idol, and role model.

With this in mind, the *saeta afectiva* can be defined as an artistic weeping directed toward the Super-Mother. It is no more theological than a child's cry—everyone's first experience of emotion magic—as it conjures up the maternal imago and simultaneously casts a spell over its hearers. It is no accident that the Andalusians most reduced to a state of helplessness created the most emotive maternal incantation of all—the *saeta carcelera* (discussed in Chapter Two). In a sense, all *saetas* are *carceleras* in that they are sung from the prison house of emotion. In the final analysis, the consumers and producers of Passional culture are not imprisoned by their historical circumstances—oppressive and stifling as they have been—

but by the incarcerating emotionality they have fled to, one that effectively prevents their ratifying the Resurrection or any other optimistic, forward-looking ascent theme. The present moment is everything, and if that moment can be made magical, so much the better. The history of Passional culture is the history of men and women determined to forget history and save themselves in exquisite moments of emotion.

Glossary

agricultor: farmer or peasant.

ángel: ("angel"); an ineffable grace or talent that one is born with and which supposedly manifests itself in many different ways.

ánima: soul; soul in purgatory.

ánimas benditas: "blessed" souls recently released from purgatory and in a position to reward those who prayed for them.

antigüedad: ("age"); seniority.

armao: (from *armado* or armed one); term used in Seville for those who play the role of "Roman Soldier" in a Holy Week procession.

azules: ("blue ones"); members of the *Cofradía de la Concepción* in Castilleja de la Cuesta.

bandolero: member of a *bando* or mounted gang of thieves.

blancos: ("white ones"); members of the *Hermandad de la Santa Vera-Cruz* in Setenil (Cádiz).

Cachorro: ("puppy"); name popularly given to a masterful image of the crucified Christ sculpted by Gijón in 1682 and now identified with Triana, a working-class neighborhood of Seville.

capataz: the man who controls the movement of a *paso* by giving voice commands to the *cuadrilla.*

caperuza: the hood of a penitential garment.

capillita: the brother who knows every last detail of the history and the by-laws of his brotherhood.

capirote: the piece of stiff, cone-shaped cardboard that fits into the *caperuza* of a *nazareno.*

capirotero: a somewhat derisive term for a brother whose loyalty to a brotherhood is entirely based on the thrill of dressing up like a *nazareno.*

cárcel: any jail, prison, or penitentiary.

cigarrera: any woman employed by a *Fábrica de Tabacos* to make cigars or cigarettes.

cirio: the large candles carried by *nazarenos* during the *Estación de Penitencia.*

cofrade: any member of a *cofradía.*

cofradía: strictly speaking, any association of laymen and/or women organized for any purpose under the advocation of some Christ, Virgin, or patron saint. In general usage, however, the term is synonymous with a *Cofradía de Pasión.*

Cofradía de Pasión: a *cofradía* whose main purpose is the yearly commemoration of Christ's Passion with a procession, a *Via Crucis,* or other rituals.

copla: an anonymous lyric poem three or more verses in length to be sung in a great variety of rhythms and melodies.

copla flamenca: any *copla* sung in a Gypsy-Andalusian or pseudo–Gypsy-Andalusian style.

costaleros: men who carry *pasos* during a procession and who are normally hidden from view by a thick curtain around the base of the *paso.*

costumbristas: nineteenth-century writers and painters who sought to portray the *costumbres* (customs) and personality types peculiar to a given region of Spain.

Crucificado: any image of the crucified Christ sculpted in cedar or some other noble wood by an *imaginero.*

cuadrilla: a crew of *costaleros.*

curanderos: folk healers whose treatments are based on a combination of faith, suggestion, and natural remedies; if female, *curanderas.*

desamortización: disentailment.

Dolorosa: any advocation or icon of the Virgin Mary in her role as the condemned or crucified Christ's sorrowing mother.

duende: ("fairy" or "elf"); a mysterious, involuntary quality believed to take possession of a performer (most often of flamenco music or dance) and infuse his or her performance with a unique, quasi-magical emotional power.

echadora: in Andalusia, a lower-class woman who knows how to *echar las cartas.*

echar las cartas: ("to cast the cards"); to purport to read someone's fortune from cards dealt at random from a Spanish deck.

endemoniadas: ("bedevilled ones"); Spanish women of the nineteenth and twentieth centuries who gathered on a given religious feast, worked themselves into a swooning trance, performed miracle cures, and made enigmatic prophecies.

estación ante la cárcel: pause made by a Holy Week procession at the doors or inside the central courtyard of a penal institution.

Estación de Penitencia: any public procession in which a *cofradía* marks the Passion of Christ with *pasos, nazarenos, penitentes,* and so forth.

estrella: ("star"); a celestial agent or force that controls and/or presides over one's life.

estrenos: ("debuts"); alterations or additions made by a *cofradía* to any item in its inventory of Passional paraphernalia.

fario: an invisible aura that accompanies a person everywhere, auguring either good or ill for the bearer and those whom he or she has dealings with.

fiesta: any festival celebrated in connection with a given date on the Church-year calendar.

gracia: grace; heavenly favor; flair.

hermandad: ("siblinghood"); largely synonymous with *cofradía,* this term includes the concepts of both "brotherhood" and "sisterhood."

hermano: ("brother"); male member of an *hermandad* (a female member would be an *hermana* or "sister").

Hermano Mayor: ("Big Brother"); the head of the *hermandad.*

imaginero: sculptor of religious images.

Inmaculada: ("the Immaculate one"); María in her aspect of having been born without original sin.

jornaleros: landless agricultural workers who are paid a *jornal* or daily wage for their labor on another's estate.

latifundista: the owner of a *latifundio* or large estate.

machismo: the mystification of masculinity carried out by men caught up in some kind of failure condition.

majo: a lower-class man of nineteenth-century Spain characterized by a cocky demeanor, sideburns, and clothing designed for sex appeal. The *maja* was his female counterpart.

mal fario: an aura of evil omen.

malage: a Gypsy-Andalusian term for accursed one.

malas lenguas: ("evil tongues"); anonymous gossipers.

mandas pías: bequests made to a religious institution.

mandato: ("mandate"); a recital/performance of the Passional narrative.

marica: sissy; milksop; effeminate man.

Mater Dolorosa: Latin term for María as the sorrowing, grieving, pained, or mourning mother of Christ; by extension, any icon of the same.

Mitwelt: German term used by phenomenological and existential psychologists to refer to the social sphere of human being-in-the-world.

nazareno: in common parlance, any man who participates in an *Estación de Penitencia* dressed in a penitential tunic and *capirote*.

negros: ("black ones"); members of the *Hermandad de Nuestro Padre Jesús* in Setenil (Cádiz).

Nuestra Señora: Our Lady.

Nuestro Padre Jesús: Our Father Jesus.

paso: any platform designed for the transportation of Passional images through the streets.

paso de misterio: a *paso* that has several figures (as opposed to just Christ or the *Mater Dolorosa*).

paso de palio: a *paso* with a canopy (used only for icons of the *Mater Dolorosa*).

penitente: in common parlance, any man who dresses in a penitential garment without the *capirote* and carries a cross of varying size in a Holy Week *Estación de Penitencia*.

pícaro: In sixteenth-, seventeenth-, and eighteenth-century Spain, any lower-class individual for whom the end (eating) always justified the means (guile and trickery).

pregón: proclamation or announcement.

pregonero: person who delivers a *pregón*.

pro remedio animae: [Latin] for the sake of souls in purgatory.

pueblo: the common people.

Purísima: ("the Purest"); advocation or icon of María as the purest of all women.

real/reales: antique Spanish monetary unit of widely varying value.

refrán: any Spanish proverb.

refranero: Spanish proverb corpus.

Resucitado: any image of Christ that portrays Him as rising from the dead.

rojos: ("red ones"); members of the *Hermandad de Santiago* in Castilleja de la Cuesta (Seville).

romance: folk or popular poem of any length using octosyllabic meter and either consonant or assonant rhyme.

romance de ciego: any *romance* composed or hawked by a blind man. Also known as a "blind beggar ballad."

romance litúrgico: any doctrinal or liturgical narrative creatively misrendered in a *romance* format.

romancero: a corpus of *romances* of any type or theme.

sabia: ("wise woman"); Andalusian term for a *curandera.*

saeta: ("arrow"); a Passional *copla.*

saeta afectiva: a Passional *copla* whose primary purpose is to evoke emotion rather than narrate. In practice, all *saetas* are designed to evoke emotion.

saeta carcelera: any Passional *copla* sung by a prisoner or sung in a gruff or mournful prison house style.

saeta narrativa: a Passional *copla* whose ostensible purpose is to narrate some moment or event of the Passion.

saetero: a singer of *saetas;* if female, *saetera.*

sal/salero: ("salt"); grace; sauciness; pertness.

Santa Caridad: ("Holy Charity"); a Sevillian brotherhood at least four centuries old whose membership was originally limited to bluebloods and whose goal in every age has been penitential service to Christ as He encarnates Himself in the poor and the sick.

Semana Santa: Holy Week. (I have avoided the term "Easter Week" because of its misleading Resurrectional connotations.)

sentencia: synonym of *mandato.*

sino: fate; fortune; destiny.

soldado romano: a man who plays the role of "Roman soldier" in a Holy Week *Estación de Penitencia.*

Soledad: ("Solitude"); shortened form of *Nuestra Señora de la Soledad,* the guise or advocation María assumes after the death of Christ.

sombra: synonym of *fario.*

sudario: ("shroud"); the cloth that girds Christ's loins as He hangs on the cross. Also known as the *paño de pureza,* or cloth of purity.

Umwelt: German term employed by existential and phenomenological psychologists to describe the sphere of natural or biological determinism which the human being-in-the-world must contend with.

vergüenza: pride, shame.

Via Crucis: [Latin] Way of the Cross.

Bibliography

Abascal y Sanz de la Maza, José Rafael de.
  1984 *Brujería y magia (Evasiones del pueblo andaluz)*. Seville: Fundación Blas Infante.
ABC. [Sevillian edition of the national daily newspaper *ABC*.]
Acosta Sánchez, José.
  1979 *Historia y cultura del pueblo andaluz*. Barcelona: Anagrama.
Aguilar Criado, Encarnación.
  1983 *Las hermandades de Castilleja de la Cuesta: Un estudio de antropología cultural*. Seville: Servicio de Publicaciones del Ayuntamiento de Sevilla. [Premio de Ensayo de Etnografía Andaluza, 1981.]
Alcalá Venceslada, Antonio.
  1984 De la solera fina [orig. 1925]. In *Semana Santa en Jaén*, ed. M. López Pérez, pp. 237–241. Córdoba: Publicaciones del Monte de Piedad y Caja de Ahorros de Córdoba.
Alonso del Real, Carlos.
  1971 *Superstición y supersticiones*. Madrid: Espasa-Calpe.
Amezcua, José.
  1973 *Libros de caballerías hispánicos*. Madrid: Ediciones Alcalá.
Aroca Lara, Angel.
  1987 *El Crucificado en la imaginería andaluza*. Córdoba: Publicaciones del Monte de Piedad y Caja de Ahorros de Córdoba.
Bennassar, Bartolomé.
  1985 *Los españoles: Actitudes y mentalidad desde el s. XVI al s. XIX*. San Lorenzo del Escorial (Madrid): Swan. [Orig. 1975.]
Bernal Rodríguez, Manuel, ed.
  1985 *La Andalucía de los libros de viajes del s. XIX (Antología)*. Seville: Editoriales Andaluzas Unidas.
Bernales Ballesteros, Jorge.
  1985 La evolución del paso de misterio. In *Las cofradías de Sevilla*, pp. 51–118. Seville: Servicio de Publicaciones de la Universidad de Sevilla y del Excmo. Ayuntamiento de Sevilla.
Biehler, Robert F.
  1978 *Psychology Applied to Teaching*. 3d ed. Boston: Houghton Mifflin.
Binswanger, Ludwig.
  1958 The Existential Analysis School of Thought. Trans. Ernest Angel. In *Existence*, ed. R. May *et al.*, pp. 191–213. New York: Basic Books.
Blázquez, José María.
  1975 *Diccionario de las religiones prerromanas de Hispania*. Madrid: Istmo.

Bonachera, Trinidad, and María Gracia Piñero.
1985 *Hacia don Juan.* Seville: Servicio de Publicaciones del Excmo. Ayuntamiento de Sevilla.
Brandes, Stanley.
1980 *Metaphors of Masculinity: Sex and Status in Andalusian Folklore.* Philadelphia: University of Pennsylvania Press.
Briones, Rafael.
1985 La Semana Santa de Priego de Córdoba. Funciones antropológicas y dimensión cristiana de un ritual popular. In *La religión en Andalucía: Aproximación a la religiosidad popular,* ed. CETRA, pp. 43–71. Seville: Editoriales Andaluzas Unidas.
Burgos, Antonio.
1982 *Folklore de las cofradías de Sevilla: Acercamiento a una tradición popular.* 3d ed. Seville: Publicaciones de la Universidad de Sevilla.
Calhoun, Cheshire, and Robert C. Solomon, eds.
1984 *What Is an Emotion? Classic Readings in Philosophical Psychology.* New York: Oxford University Press.
Campbell, Joseph.
1968 *Creative Mythology.* Vol. 4 of *The Masks of God.* New York: Penguin Books.
Cansinos Assens, Rafael.
1985 *La copla andaluza.* Granada: Editoriales Andaluzas Unidas. [Orig. 1933.]
Carloni, Alida
1984 La mujer en el corral de vecinos sevillano. In *Antropología cultural de Andalucía,* ed. S. Rodríguez Becerra, pp. 253–266. Seville: Consejería de Cultura de la Junta de Andalucía.
Caro Baroja, Julio.
1957a *Razas, pueblos y linajes.* Madrid: Revista de Occidente.
1957b Semana Santa en Puente Genil. *Revista de Dialectología y Tradiciones Populares (RDTP)* 13:22–49.
1964 Honor y vergüenza: Examen histórico de varios conflictos populares. *RDTP* 20:410–460.
1969 *Ensayo sobre la literatura de cordel.* Madrid: Revista de Occidente.
1974 *Ritos y mitos equívocos.* Madrid: Istmo.
1979 *Ensayos sobre la cultura popular española.* Madrid: Dosbe.
1985 *Las formas complejas de la vida religiosa: Religión, sociedad y carácter en la España de los siglos XVI y XVII.* Madrid: Sarpe.
Carr, Raymond, and Juan Pablo Fusi.
1981 *Spain: Dictatorship to Democracy.* 2d ed. London: George Allen.
Castillo Martos, Manuel.
1988 Aproximación al culto de la Virgen en Sevilla. *ABC,* 17 February 1988, pp. 35–36.
Castón Boyer, Pedro.
1985 La religiosidad tradicional en Andalucía: Una aproximación sociológica. In *La religión en Andalucía,* ed. CETRA, pp. 97–129. Seville: Editoriales Andaluzas Unidas.

Castro, Américo.
1954   *The Structure of Spanish History.* Trans. Edmund L. King. Princeton: Princeton University Press.

Cazabán Laguna, Alfredo.
1984   Saetas de Jaén a Nuestro Padre Jesús y a la Virgen de los Dolores [orig. 1926]. In *Semana Santa en Jaén,* ed. M. López Pérez, pp. 243–244. Córdoba: Publicaciones del Monte de Piedad y Caja de Ahorros de Córdoba.

Christian, William A.
1976   De los santos a María: Panorama de las devociones a santuarios españoles desde el principio de la Edad Media hasta nuestros días. In *Temas de antropología española,* ed. C. Lisón, pp. 49–105. Madrid: Akal.

Comelles, Josep María.
1984   Los caminos del Rocío. In *Antropología cultural de Andalucía,* ed. S. Rodríguez Becerra, pp. 425–445. Seville: Consejería de Cultura de la Junta de Andalucía.

Díaz de la Serna Carrión, Angel, Antonio Salas Delgado, and Juan Mairena Valdayo.
1987   *El Rocío de siempre.* Córdoba: Publicaciones del Monte de Piedad y Caja de Ahorros de Córdoba.

Edmunds, Lowell.
1985   *Oedipus: The Ancient Legend and Its Later Analogues.* Baltimore: The Johns Hopkins University Press.

El Correo de Andalucía (daily newspaper for Andalusian provinces).

Elliott, J. H.
1972   The Decline of Spain. In *Renaissance, Reformation, and Absolutism: 1450–1650,* 2d ed., ed. N. F. Cantor and M. S. Werthman, pp. 202–252. New York: Thomas Y. Crowell.

Epictetus.
1985   Enchiridion. In *Classics of Western Philosophy,* ed. S. M. Cahn, pp. 223–237. Indianapolis: Hackett Publishing Company.

Fell, Joseph P.
1965   *Emotion in the Thought of Sartre.* New York: Columbia University Press.

Fernández Bañuls, Juan Alberto, and José María Pérez Orozco, eds.
1983   *La poesía flamenca lírica en andaluz.* Seville: Servicio de Publicaciones del Ayuntamiento de Sevilla.
1986   *Joyero de coplas flamencas. Antología y estudio.* Seville: Editoriales Andaluzas Unidas.

Flores Arroyuelo, Francisco J.
1985   *El diablo en España.* Madrid: Alianza Editorial.

Foulché-Debosc, R.
1969   *Bibliographie des voyages en Espagne et en Portugal.* Amsterdam: Meridian Publishing Co. [Orig. 1896.]

Frye, Northrop.
1976   *The Secular Scripture: A Study of the Structure of Romance.* Cambridge: Harvard University Press.

García de la Concha, Federico.
1988a La devoción a la Dolorosa en Sevilla: Introducción. *ABC,* 18 March 1988, pp. 45–46.
1988b La devoción a la Dolorosa en Sevilla: Las cofradías y la Dolorosa. *ABC,* 21 March 1988, pp. 35–36.
García Díaz, Sebastián.
1980 *La muerte: Ensayos en clave andaluza.* Seville: Publicaciones de la Universidad de Sevilla.
García Ferrero, Francisco M.
1984 Valor etnográfico de las "Guías de Forasteros": El caso de Sevilla. In *Antropología cultural de Andalucía,* ed. S. Rodríguez Becerra, pp. 267–284. Seville: Consejería de Cultura de la Junta de Andalucía.
Gautier, Théophile.
1985 Sevilla en 1840 [orig. 1840]. In *La Andalucía de los libros de viajes del siglo XIX (Antología),* ed. M. Bernal, pp. 135–166. Seville: Editoriales Andaluzas Unidas.
Gayangos, Pascual de.
1963 *Libros de caballerías.* Vol. 40 of the *Biblioteca de Autores Españoles.* Madrid: Atlas. [Orig. 1857.]
Gilmore, David D.
1987 *Aggression and Community: Paradoxes of Andalusian Culture.* New Haven: Yale University Press.
Gilmore, Margaret M., and David D. Gilmore.
1979 "Machismo": A Psychodynamic Approach (Spain). *Journal of Psychological Anthropology* 2:281–300.
Giménez Caballero, E.
1927 *Los toros, las castañuelas y la Virgen.* Madrid: Editorial Caro Raggio.
Girard, René.
1982 *Le Bouc émissaire.* Paris: Grasset.
Gómez Marín, J. A.
1972 *Bandolerismo, santidad y otros temas españoles.* Madrid: Miguel Castellote, editor.
Gómez Pérez, Agustín.
1984 *La saeta viva.* Córdoba: Vicente Márquez, editor.
Gómez-Tabanera, J. M.
1968 El refranero español. In *El folklore español,* ed. J. M. Gómez-Tabanera, pp. 389–431. Madrid: Instituto Español de Antropología Aplicada.
González Alcantud, Antonio.
1984 Crisis de la Antropología y nacionalismos mediterráneos. In *Antropología cultural de Andalucía,* ed. S. Rodríguez Becerra, pp. 123–150. Seville: Consejería de Cultura de la Junta de Andalucía.
González Casarrubios, Consolación.
1985 *Fiestas populares en Castilla-La Mancha.* Ciudad Real: Servicio de Publicaciones de la Junta de Comunidades de Castilla-La Mancha.
González Cid, María Luisa.
1984 Estructura social, sistema de poder y cofradías en Setenil (Cádiz). In

Antropología cultural de Andalucía, ed. S. Rodríguez Becerra, pp. 373–382. Seville: Consejería de Cultura de la Junta de Andalucía.

González Climent, Anselmo.
1964   *Flamencología*. 2d ed. Prólogo de J. M. de Pemán. Madrid: Escelicer.

González del Piñal, J. M.
1988   Sociología de la religiosidad popular: el barrio de San Bernardo y su hermandad. *Boletín de las Cofradías de Sevilla,* March 1988, pp. 77–81.

González Gómez, Juan Miguel
1985   Sentimiento y simbolismo en las representaciones marianas de la Semana Santa en Sevilla. In *Las cofradías de Sevilla,* pp. 119–152. Seville: Servicio de Publicaciones de la Universidad de Sevilla y del Excmo. Ayuntamiento de Sevilla.

Grambo, Ronald.
1988   Problems of Fatalism: A Blueprint for Further Research. *Folklore* 99:11–29.

Granero, Jesús M.
1981   *Muerte y amor (Don Miguel Mañara)*. Madrid: Imprenta Fareso.

Guichot y Sierra, Alejandro.
1986   *Supersticiones populares andaluzas*. Seville: Editoriales Andaluzas Unidas. [Orig. 1883.]

Gutiérrez Serrano, Federico.
1978   *Semana Santa en Córdoba*. Madrid: Editorial Alpuerto.
1988   San Antonio María Claret, nuestro hermano y maestro. *Boletín de las Cofradías de Sevilla,* March 1988, pp. 111–115.

Handler, Richard, and Jocelyn Linnekin.
1984   Tradition, Genuine or Spurious. *Journal of American Folklore* 97:273–290.

Hare, Augustus John Cuthbert.
1985   Granada [orig. 1873]. In *La Andalucía de los libros de viajes del siglo XIX (Antología),* ed. M. Bernal, pp. 210–226. Seville: Editoriales Andaluzas Unidas.

Harré, Rom, ed.
1986   *The Social Construction of Emotions*. Oxford: Basil Blackwell.

Heran, F.
1979   L'invention de l'Andalousie au XIXe s. dans la littérature de voyage. In *Tourisme et developpement regional en Andalousie,* pp. 5–15. Paris: Boccard.

Izard, Carroll E.
1983   Emotions in Personality and Culture. *Ethos* (Journal of the Society for Psychological Anthropology) 11:305–312.

Jiménez Sampedro, Rafael.
1988   La Casa Real y las cofradías sevillanas. *Boletín de las Cofradías de Sevilla,* March 1988, pp. 14–16.

Krappe, Alexander Haggerty.
1929   *The Science of Folklore*. New York: Barnes & Noble.

La Barre, Weston.
1972   *The Ghost Dance*. New York: Dell.

Larrea Palacín, Arcadio de.
1968   Aspectos de la música popular española. In *El folklore español,* ed. J. M. Gómez-Tabanera, pp. 297–318. Madrid: Instituto Español de Antropología Aplicada.

Levy, Robert I., and Michelle Z. Rosaldo, eds.
1983   Self and Emotion. Special Issue of *Ethos* (Journal of the Society for Psychological Anthropology), vol. ii, no. 3 (Fall 1983).

Llompart, Gabriel.
1968   La religiosidad popular. In *El folklore español,* ed. J. M. Gómez-Tabanera, pp. 217–246. Madrid: Instituto Español de Antropología Aplicada.

López Fernández, Rafael.
1981   *La saeta.* Seville: Grupo Andaluz de Ediciones Repiso-Lorenzo.

López Pérez, Manuel, ed.
1984   *Semana Santa en Jaén.* Córdoba: Publicaciones del Monte de Piedad y Caja de Ahorros de Córdoba.

Lovett, Gabriel H.
1965   *Napoleon and the Birth of Modern Spain.* 2 vol. New York: New York University Press.

Machado y Alvarez, Antonio.
1975   *Colección de cantes flamencos.* Madrid: Demófilo. [Orig. 1881.]
1986   *El folklore andaluz.* Seville: Editoriales Andaluzas Unidas. [Orig. 1881–1882.]

Maldonado, Luis.
1975   *Religiosidad popular.* Madrid: Editorial Cristiandad.

Manfredi, Domingo.
1963   *Geografía del cante jondo.* Madrid: Bullón.

Marco, Joaquín.
1977   *Literatura popular en España en los siglos XVIII y XIX: Una aproximación a los pliegos de cordel.* 2 vol. Madrid: Taurus.

Marín Vizcaíno, Juan José.
1986   *Cofrades y cofradías a través de sus anécdotas.* 2d ed. Seville: Gráficas San Antonio.

Martín Díaz, Emma.
1984   Las echadoras de cartas en la provincia de Cádiz: Una actividad femenina marginal. In *Antropología cultural de Andalucía,* ed. S. Rodríguez Becerra, pp. 319–326. Seville: Consejería de Cultura de la Junta de Andalucía.

Martín Hernández, Francisco.
1981   *Miguel Mañara.* Seville: Publicaciones de la Universidad de Sevilla.

Martínez Ramos, Basilio.
1984   Saetas populares. In *Semana Santa en Jaén,* ed. M. López Pérez, pp. 244–246. Córdoba: Publicaciones del Monte de Piedad y Caja de Ahorros de Córdoba.

Melgar Reina, Luis, and Angel Marín Rújula.
1987   *Saetas, pregones y romances litúrgicos cordobeses.* Córdoba: Publicaciones del Monte de Piedad y Caja de Ahorros de Córdoba.

Mendizábal y García Lavin, Federico de.
1984   Saeta de Nuestro Padre Jesús [orig. 1927]. In *Semana Santa en Jaén,* ed.
        M. López Pérez, pp. 246–250. Córdoba: Publicaciones del Monte de
        Piedad y Caja de Ahorros de Córdoba.
Minkowski, Eugene.
1958   Findings in a Case of Schizophrenic Depression. In *Existence,* ed.
        R. May *et al.,* pp. 127–138. New York: Basic Books.
Mitchell, Timothy.
1988   *Violence and Piety in Spanish Folklore.* Philadelphia: University of Penn-
        sylvania Press.
Molina, Ricardo, and Antonio Mairena.
1979   *Mundo y formas del flamenco.* 2d ed. Seville: Librería Al-Andalus.
Moreno Navarro, Isidoro.
1982   *La Semana Santa en Sevilla: Conformación, mixtificación y significaciones.*
        Seville: Publicaciones de la Universidad de Sevilla.
1984   La antropología cultural en Andalucía: Estado actual y perspectiva de
        futuro. In *Antropología cultural de Andalucía,* ed. S. Rodríguez Be-
        cerra, pp. 93–107. Seville: Consejería de Cultura de la Junta de
        Andalucía.
1985a   *Cofradías y hermandades andaluzas: Estructura, simbolismo e identidad.*
        Seville: Editoriales Andaluzas Unidas.
1985b   Las cofradías sevillanas en la época contemporánea: Una aproximación
        antropológica. In *Las cofradías de Sevilla,* pp. 35–50. Seville: Publica-
        ciones de la Universidad de Sevilla y del Excmo. Ayuntamiento de
        Sevilla.
Nadal, Jordi.
1975   *El fracaso de la Revolución Industrial en España, 1814–1913.* Barcelona:
        Ariel.
Nilsson, Martin P.
1964   *A History of Greek Religion.* 2d ed. Trans. F. J. Fielden. New York:
        W. W. Norton. [Orig. 1925, revised 1952.]
Ortega Sagrista, Rafael.
1984a   El penitente. In *Semana Santa en Jaén,* pp. 193–196.
1984b   La camarera, la mantilla. In *Semana Santa en Jaén,* ed. M. López Pérez,
        pp. 204–208. Córdoba: Publicaciones del Monte de Piedad y Caja de
        Ahorros de Córdoba.
Ortíz Nuevo, José Luis, ed.
1985   *Pensamiento político en el cante flamenco: Antología de textos desde los
        orígenes a 1936.* Seville: Editoriales Andaluzas Unidas.
Palomero Páramo, Jesús Miguel.
1987   *La imaginería procesional sevillana: Misterios, nazarenos y cristos.* 2d ed.
        Seville: Publicaciones del Excmo. Ayuntamiento de Sevilla.
Pascua Sánchez, María José.
1984   *Las actitudes ante la muerte en el Cádiz de la primera mitad del siglo
        XVIII.* Cádiz: Publicaciones de la Excma. Diputación Provincial.
Pérez Gallego, J.
1986   Semana Santa a la española. *El País,* 9 March 1986, pp. 17–18.

Pineda Novo, Daniel.
   1988   Martínez Kleiser y su visión de la Semana Santa sevillana. *Boletín de las Cofradías de Sevilla,* March 1988, pp. 136–146.
Plata, Juan de la.
   1984   *La saeta: La Pasión de Cristo según la canta el pueblo andaluz.* Jeréz de la Frontera: Departamento de Publicaciones de la Cátedra de Flamencología y Estudios Folklóricos Andaluces.
Preston, James J.
   1982   New Perspectives on Mother Worship. In *Mother Worship: Themes and Variations,* ed. J. J. Preston, pp. 325–343. Chapel Hill: University of North Carolina Press.
Provanzal, Danielle.
   1984   Desarrollo, subdesarrollo e identidad cultural: El caso de un pueblo de la Provincia de Almería. In *Antropología cultural de Andalucía,* ed. S. Rodríguez Becerra, pp. 151–166. Seville: Consejería de Cultura de la Junta de Andalucía.
Pulido Bueno, Isidoro.
   1983   La documentación testamentaria en Huelva en el siglo XVII: Una aproximación a su estudio. *Archivo Hispalense* 202:115–140.
Ramírez Rodrigo, María del Prado.
   1985   La cultura popular durante los siglos XVI al XX. In *El arte y la cultura de la provincia de Ciudad Real,* ed. F. Pillet Capdepón, pp. 341–375. Ciudad Real: Excma. Diputación de Ciudad Real.
Reder Gadow, M.
   1983   *Testamentos malagueños del siglo XVIII: Instrumento jurídico y mentalidad social.* Ph.D. dissertation, Facultad de Geografía e Historia, Universidad de Málaga (Spain).
Reina Palazón, Antonio.
   1979   *Pintura costumbrista en Sevilla (1830–1870).* Seville: Publicaciones de la Universidad de Sevilla.
Ringgren, Helmer.
   1967   Islamic Fatalism. In *Fatalistic Beliefs in Religion, Folklore, and Literature,* ed. H. Ringgren, pp. 52–62. Stockholm: Almqvist & Wiksell.
Rivas Alvarez, José Antonio.
   1986   *Miedo y piedad: Testamentos sevillanos del siglo XVIII.* Seville: Publicaciones de la Excma. Diputación Provincial de Sevilla.
Rodríguez Becerra, Salvador.
   1984   Introducción. In *Antropología cultural de Andalucía,* ed. S. Rodríguez Becerra, pp. 15–17. Seville: Consejería de Cultura de la Junta de Andalucía.
Rodríguez Navarro, Eloy.
   1969   *Séneca: Religión sin mitos.* Madrid: Syntagma.
Ropero Nuñez, Miguel.
   1984   *El léxico andaluz de las coplas flamencas.* Seville: Alfar.
Ropp, Theodore.
   1962   *War in the Modern World.* New York: Collier Books.

Rougement, Denis de.
1984   *El amor y Occidente.* 3d ed. Trans. Antoni Vicens. Barcelona: Kairós.
        [Orig. 1938; revised 1956, 1970.]
Ruether, Rosemary Radford.
1974   Misogynism and Virginal Feminism in the Fathers of the Church. In
        Religion and Sexism, ed. R. Radford Ruether, pp. 150–183. New York:
        Simon & Schuster.
Salido Bravo, Antonio.
1984   *Semana Santa de Castro del Río.* Córdoba: Ediciones El Almendro.
Sánchez de Cepeda y Ahumada, Teresa [Santa Teresa de Jesús].
1922   Libro de la vida [orig. 1565]. In *Obras de Santa Teresa de Jesús,* ed. Fr.
        Silverio de Santa Teresa, pp. 1–353. Burgos: Tipografía de "El Monte
        Carmelo."
Sánchez Herrero, José.
1985   Las cofradías sevillanas: Los comienzos. In *Las cofradías de Sevilla,*
        pp. 7–34. Seville: Publicaciones de la Universidad de Sevilla y del Ex-
        cmo. Ayuntamiento de Sevilla.
Santos López, José María de los.
1984   La cultura andaluza, como cultura de la dependencia. In *Antropología
        cultural de Andalucía,* ed. S. Rodríguez Becerra, pp. 109–121. Seville:
        Consejería de Cultura de la Junta de Andalucía.
Santos Torres, José.
1987   *Francisco de Bruna y Diego Corrientes (1776–1781), mito y realidad: His-
        toria y leyenda de El Bandido Generoso y el Señor de Gran Poder.* Seville:
        Salado Industria Gráfica.
Sanz Serrano, María Jesús.
1985   Las artes ornamentales en las cofradías de la Semana Santa sevillana. In
        Las cofradías de Sevilla, pp. 153–183. Seville: Publicaciones de la Univer-
        sidad de Sevilla y del Excmo. Ayuntamiento de Sevilla.
Sartre, Jean-Paul.
1962   *Sketch for a Theory of the Emotions.* Trans. Philip Mairet. London: Me-
        thuen & Co., Ltd. [Orig. 1939.]
Scherer, Klaus, Harald Wallbott, and Angela Summerfield, eds.
1986   *Experiencing Emotion: A Cross-cultural Study.* Cambridge: Cambridge
        University Press.
Scruton, David L., ed.
1986   *Sociophobics: The Anthropology of Fear.* Boulder, Colorado: Westview
        Press.
Seneca.
1946   Letters. In *Latin Literature in Translation,* ed. K. Guinagh and A. P.
        Dorjahn, pp. 588–608. New York: Longmans, Green, and Co.
Siebers, Tobin.
1983   *The Mirror of Medusa.* Berkeley: University of California Press.
Silverio de Santa Teresa.
1922   Al lector. In *Obras de Santa Teresa de Jesús,* ed. Fr. Silverio de Santa
        Teresa, pp. vii–xxxi. Burgos: Tipografía de "El Monte Carmelo."

Solomon, Robert C.
   1984   Emotions and Choice. In *What Is an Emotion? Classic Readings in Philosophical Psychology,* ed. C. Calhoun and R. C. Solomon, pp. 305–326. New York: Oxford University Press.
Spiegelberg, Herbert.
   1972   *Phenomenology in Psychology and Psychiatry: A Historical Introduction.* Evanston: Northwestern University Press.
Strasser, Stephan.
   1977   *Phenomenology of Feeling.* Pittsburgh: Duquesne University Press.
Taylor, Richard.
   1967   Determinism. In *The Encyclopedia of Philosophy,* ed. Paul Edwards, vol. 2, pp. 359–373. New York: Macmillan.
Tele-Sur. [Daily television news program covering Andalusian provinces.]
Tripp, Edward.
   1970   *Crowell's Handbook of Classical Mythology.* New York: Thomas Y. Crowell.
Vega Gutiérrez, José de la.
   1984   El escultor prodigioso. In *Semana Santa en Jaén,* ed. M. López Pérez, pp. 149–150. Córdoba: Publicaciones del Monte de Piedad y Caja de Ahorros de Córdoba.
Zambrano, María.
   1984   La cuestión del estoicismo español. In *Andalucía, sueño y realidad,* ed. D. Romero de Solís, pp. 47–82. Granada: Editoriales Andaluzas Unidas.
Zorrilla, José.
   1988   *Don Juan Tenorio: Drama religioso-fantástico en dos partes,* ed. Aniano Peña. Madrid: Cátedra. [Orig. 1844.]

Index

anti-Semitism, 73, 135–36, 148–49, 151–52, 154, 159. *See also* Judas
armaos. See Roman Soldiers

bandoleros, 74–75, 84–85
baroque, 1, 70, 73, 102, 162
Brandes, Stanley, 14, 18, 37, 86, 186

cante jondo. See flamenco
charity: ideology of, 55, 59–61, 63, 67–68, 82. *See also* Mañara, Miguel
Claret, Saint Antonio María, 167–68
cofradías: history of, 41–42, 50–53, 70–72, 132–33, 165, 168; social psychology of, 92–127; women in, 41, 111–18
coplas, 8–15, 18–19, 78, 82, 128, 136. See also *saetas*
costaleros, 105–10, 162, 169, 171–73
costumbristas, 56, 84–85
Crucificado, Andalusian portrayal of the, 145, 160–64

death: Andalusian attitude toward, 21–25, 27, 50–52, 60–63, 66–67, 164. *See also* penitence; purgatory; testaments
devils, 25–27, 135
Diego Corrientes. See *bandoleros*
Don Juan myth, 56, 65, 133–34

echadoras, 34–36
emotion: and fatalism, 5, 12, 14, 27; and interpretation, 2–4, 91–92; as magical, 15–19, 25, 27–28, 82, 128, 178–80
endemoniadas, 33–34, 36
Epictetus. *See* stoicism
estación ante la cárcel, 76–82

family fixations, 17, 92, 113–27, 149, 156. *See also* María, as Mother figure
fatalism: and fortune-telling, 34–36, 146–47; and gender, 17, 36–39; in Passional narrative, 146–47, 156, 161, 178; and sacraments, 31–32; vocabulary of, 12–13, 19
flagellants, 41

flamenco, 19, 77–78, 87, 89. See also *coplas*
Franciscans, 23, 42–44, 59–60, 166–67
Fray Diego de Cádiz, 43–44, 46, 50
Frye, Northrop, 128–29, 165, 177, 187

Gilmore, David, 4, 14–15, 36–38, 118, 188
González Climent, Anselmo, 13–14, 189
Good Thief, 81–82
Gypsies, 32, 78, 83, 90, 123, 146

hermandades. See cofradías
Hermandad de la Santa Caridad. See Mañara, Miguel

identity symbols in Andalusian culture, 83–91
idolatry, 121, 169–70
imagineros, 139–40, 150, 158, 162–63, 170
Immaculate Conception, 59, 132–34
Inquisition, Spanish, 20

Jews. *See* anti-Semitism
Judas, 148–51

machismo, 36–39, 106, 118, 128
Mañara, Miguel, 6, 18, 21–23, 26–27, 29, 53–69, 75, 133–34
mandato, 138, 140, 146, 157, 160
María: as advocate, 27, 49, 170; as *Mater Dolorosa*, 119, 164–80; as Mother figure, 78–79, 114–16, 121–24, 169–70, 179; as Virgin, 131–32. *See also* Immaculate Conception
maricas, 118–21, 170
Mary Magdalene, 82
Mater Dolorosa. See María, as *Mater Dolorosa*
Mitwelt. See world-design
Moreno, Isidoro, 6, 86–87, 91, 93–94, 103, 106, 116, 118, 125–26, 168, 179, 191

nazarenos, 40, 105, 107, 112
Nuestro Padre Jesús: icons of, 74, 80, 114–16, 122, 125, 142, 144, 152, 169

Palmar de Troya, 30
pasos, 73, 81, 95, 97–98, 102, 105–10, 136, 138, 140–46, 150, 158, 162
passionate fatalism. *See* emotion, and fatalism; fatalism; world-design
patriarchy, 39, 50, 115, 156. *See also* family fixations; *Nuestro Padre Jesús;* penitence
penitence, 21, 23, 25, 40–50, 59, 73, 82, 135
penitentes, 6, 40–41, 105, 159. See also *nazarenos*
penitential brotherhoods. See *cofradías*
penitential charity. *See* charity, ideology of
political aspects of Holy Week, 6, 46, 82, 94, 124–27
proverbs. See *refranes*
purgatory, 49, 52, 61, 66. *See also* testaments

refranes, 8–11, 25
Resurrection, 7, 164–66, 177–78, 180
Roman Soldiers, 104–5, 120, 152, 162, 171
Romance Catholicism, 128–36, 177
romance litúrgico, 154–56
romances de ciego, 135–36

sabias, 33–36
saetas, 2, 7, 43–44, 76–79, 82, 122–23, 125–26, 136–40, 146–54, 162–63, 170–73, 177–80

Sartre, Jean-Paul, 15–19, 25, 193
Santa Caridad. See Mañara, Miguel
Seneca. *See* stoicism
sentencia. See *romance litúrgico*
sociocentrism, 91–92, 99, 101–2, 127, 148, 154
Solomon, Robert, 8, 16–18, 194
Sorrowful Mother. *See* María, as *Mater Dolorosa*
stoicism, 8, 19–20, 22, 24–25
suffrages. *See* testaments
superstition, 28–39

testaments, 23, 27, 51–52, 54–55, 66

Umwelt. See world-design

Veronica, 143, 152, 159–60
Via Crucis, 42–43, 72, 138
Virgin Mary. *See* María, as Virgin
virginity, function of, 38, 131–34

Way of the Cross. See *Via Crucis*
women. See *cofradías,* women in; fatalism and gender
world-design, 5, 14–18, 28, 128, 178. *See also* emotion; family fixations; fatalism

Zeno. *See* stoicism